100 THINGS
ANGELS FANS
SHOULD KNOW & DO
BEFORE THEY DIE

100 THINGS ANGELS FANS SHOULD KNOW & DO BEFORE THEY DIE

Joe Haakenson

TRIUMPH
BOOKS

Library of Congress Cataloging-in-Publication Data

Haakenson, Joe, 1962–
    100 things Angels fans should know & do before they die / Joe Haakenson.
    p. cm.
    Includes bibliographical references.
    ISBN 978-1-60078-776-8
    1. Los Angeles Angels (Baseball team)—History. 2. Los Angeles Angels (Baseball team)—Miscellanea. I. Title. II. Title: One hundred things Angels fans should know & do before they die.
    GV875.A6H33 2013
    796.357'640979496—dc23
                                                                            2012042618
This book is available in quantity at special discounts for your group or organization. For further information, contact:
    Triumph Books LLC
    814 North Franklin Street
    Chicago, Illinois 60610
    (312) 337-0747
    www.triumphbooks.com

Printed in U.S.A.
ISBN: 978-1-60078-776-8
Design by Patricia Frey
Photos courtesy of AP Images unless otherwise indicated

For my parents—my mom, Rose Marie, and my late dad, Ryal, who have always been there for me with love and support. And for my wife, Christina, and children, Braiden and Cade, who remind me that baseball is just a game.

Contents

Foreword

Just recently, I popped in a DVD of the 2002 World Series to inspire my Little League All-Star team before a game. Watching the grainy film, which was obviously created before the advent of the high-definition recordings we are so used to today, the boys and I relived a truly magical experience for all Angels fans. It seems that after 10 years I, too, had become a fan of this great moment in Angels history. In a surreal sense, I was continually reminded through the grainy images that *I really did* play in the 2002 World Series, yet I watched the DVD with the same nervous energy of the 45,000-plus fans attending those games hoping that the Angels would come out on top. I know it sounds crazy, but it's been 10 years since the Series, and after being out of the game for the last six, the big leagues seem like another lifetime for me.

So I guess you can say I've come full circle in my appreciation for the major leagues. Unbelievably, it's been almost 25 years since I first stepped foot in an Angel clubhouse. Of course it was a minor league one, but that didn't matter much as I saw the rows of lockers and each one had an Angels uniform hanging in it. I still remember how bright the color red stood out in contrast against the dark blue tops. And then there were the freshly shined red baseball spikes placed neatly at the foot of each locker, creating a sea of red. Staring at these lockers was like looking at rows of decorated Christmas trees with bright red presents under them. Minor leagues or not, it all seemed the same to me. I was now part of the California Angels. Welcome to professional baseball!

Much like any other family, the Angels became my second family, and that sentiment continues today in retirement. In a lot of ways I was closer to my teammates, coaches, trainers, and front office than I was to my own family. When I reflect on these relationships, it's fun to see how we all "grew up" together and helped bring the Angels their first world championship. Joe Maddon always stands out in my mind for his prophetic mantra in my first year of Instructional League. "You are the guys who will change the face of the organization," he said. "You have to believe you're the foundation for the Angels' first world championship!" Looking into the eyes of young pups like Troy Percival and Garret Anderson, I'm not sure we could envision just how great a ride it would be winning a world championship. But there we were, laying the foundation for the greatness of the organization today.

I played for the Angels from the cradle to the grave, and staying with the Angels for my entire career was important to me. Part of it goes back to the generation I grew up in. It was meaningful for guys like Cal Ripken, Robin Yount, and Don Mattingly to play on the same team throughout their careers, and I wanted to do the same.

While spending my entire career in the Angels' organization is a highlight for me, I feel a little awkward when people call me Mr. Angel. There have been so many great players in the history of the franchise, and to be put at the top somehow does not seem right to me. Besides, there could be no one more deserving of the title than the man who made it all possible, Gene Autry. For eternity, the singing cowboy will be synonymous with the Angels.

Mr. Autry was a great owner and a pleasure to be around. He was a real superstar who had a huge presence whenever he walked into the clubhouse. It was something I appreciated all the more because my dad might have been his biggest fan. One day upon hearing of my dad's admiration, Mr. Autry invited Dad up to his owner's suite to watch the game. My dad rolled back about 40 years in the memory bank and just basked in the presence of his childhood hero. Having Mr. Autry share the inspiration behind the comic books my dad just happened to have with him was the thrill of a lifetime. I will always be grateful to Mr. Autry for that.

When The Walt Disney Co. bought the team from Mr. Autry, no one knew what to expect, but it turned out to be a very exciting time. Being employees, we all got our Silver Passes and could go to Disneyland whenever we wanted. There was talk about a monorail connecting Disneyland to the stadium someday. When I told my kids that Mickey Mouse was my boss, they loved it. We won a World Series under Disney's ownership, so it turned out to be a magical time.

When Arte Moreno took over the franchise in 2003, he possessed the wherewithal to put a competitive team on the field every year and completed the Angels' transformation into a marquee franchise. We went from being a small-market team to a large-market team, playing with the big boys. The Angels have had a great run of success under his tenure with numerous pennants raised in the outfield. But there is still one missing, and that drives Arte to be the best owner in the game today. One of these days I'm confident he, too, will raise that illustrious trophy and realize the dream he had when he first purchased the team.

My time with the Angels has come and gone. Like those great players before me, we are just memories in an aging fan base, trying to pass on our legacy to the next generation. There will always be another season and new players to follow. In the years to come, promising rookies, All-Stars, and maybe even a future Hall of Famer will don the uniform, seeking to write the next chapter for the organization. I will be there like the rest of you, waiting to see what next magical moment awaits us all on this journey as Angels fans.

—Tim Salmon
August 2012

Acknowledgments

I'd like to thank Tom Bast, Adam Motin, and Karen O'Brien at Triumph Books for the opportunity to work on this project and for their help throughout the process. Thanks also go out to Tim Mead and his staff with the Angels, who were always available to answer any questions I had.

Researching 50-plus years of history is a daunting task, but it was much easier thanks to Ross Newhan's book, *The Anaheim Angels: A Complete History*, which provides an inside look with great detail at Angels history from the franchise's inception to the year 2000. Another great source of information came from Rob Goldman's book, *Once They Were Angels*.

I'd also like to thank so many Angels players, coaches, and managers who I've been fortunate enough to interact with since I started as an Angels beat writer in 1989. Starting out as a wide-eyed 26-year-old who spent many a summer night during my high school years hanging out in the bleachers at Dodger Stadium, I didn't know what I was in for. But managers Doug Rader, Buck Rodgers, Marcel Lachemann, Terry Collins, and Mike Scioscia were always pleasant to deal with. Well, almost always, anyway.

Former coach and current Tampa Bay Rays manager Joe Maddon once gave me the shoes off his feet, literally, so I could go into a nightclub in San Francisco that required men to wear black shoes. I only had brown shoes, so Joe loaned me his.

Many Angels players have come and gone through the clubhouse, but a few stand out as my favorites because of who they are as people—Jim Abbott, Chili Davis, David Eckstein, and Tim Salmon.

And a special thanks also goes out to Salmon, who wrote the foreword for this book.

Introduction

They've been called the Los Angeles Angels, the California Angels, the Anaheim Angels, and even the Los Angeles Angels of Anaheim. Although many players, managers, general managers, and even owners have come and gone, they are and will always be the Angels.

Their history is delightful and tragic, memorable and forgettable, and full of some of baseball's most interesting personalities. They were primarily a failure for many years before finally winning a playoff series and ultimately the World Series in 2002, their 42nd year in existence.

Until then, they might have been considered a poor man's Cubs, and they did play their first season at Wrigley Field. Not Wrigley Field Chicago, but Wrigley Field Los Angeles, which has long since turned to rubble.

The Angels are indeed a team that for so long was difficult to love. They were endearing because so many players were colorful characters, starting with Bo Belinsky who put the Angels on the map more for his Hollywood party lifestyle than for his pitching.

Nowadays, Angels fans are everywhere. It's much easier to love a winner. The Angels reached the playoffs in only three of their first 41 seasons. But starting with the 2002 World Series crown, the Angels went to the playoffs six times in eight seasons through 2009. Manager Mike Scioscia left the rival Dodgers organization to manage the Angels to their recent successes, which seems fitting.

It was Dodgers owner Walter O'Malley who "graciously" accepted the Angels to Southern California only to make life difficult for Angels owner Gene Autry behind the scenes when the two shared Dodger Stadium from 1962–65.

Autry was eager to branch out and break away from the Dodgers' grip in Southern California, and he found growth and prosperity in Orange County. Angels fans finally have a history they can reflect on with pride—and maybe even chuckle at some of the failures.

As a beat writer covering the team from 1989–2005, I had the chance to meet Gene Autry, Michael Eisner, and Arte Moreno. I was a firsthand witness to the seemingly never-ending struggles of the 1990s, and I will never forget that humming sound created by the ThunderStix during the 2002 playoffs and World Series.

This book is a look back at the good, bad, and ugly—all of it uniquely Angels.

1 Won for the Cowboy

It was a mantra that was rooted in admiration and devotion for their owner, but one that in all likelihood prevented them from achieving it.

"Win one for the Cowboy."

Gene Autry was the beloved original owner of the Angels, and those in the organization wanted nothing more than to get the Singing Cowboy what he so desperately desired—a World Series title.

From the time Autry purchased the American League's expansion franchise in 1961 for $2.1 million until his death in 1998, a seemingly endless parade of general managers, managers, and players came and went, ultimately failing to get the entertainment legend to the top of the baseball world.

Autry paid millions of dollars to players with Hall of Fame credentials, such as Rod Carew, Reggie Jackson, Frank Robinson, Nolan Ryan, and Don Sutton. Autry gave his general managers the freedom to make the deals they felt would put the team at the top. But those decisions often came at the expense of building a strong future, mortgaging the farm system for a big name with diminishing skills.

Ultimately, "Win one for the Cowboy," became "Win one for the Cowboy, and hurry up." However, according to Autry's wife, Jackie, it was a philosophy that was perpetuated not by Autry himself, but by those in the organization who felt more and more pressure to win immediately as Autry got up there in years.

"To my knowledge, Gene never once said, 'Look guys, I'm not going to be around much longer, we've got to get it done this year,'" Jackie Autry said in Ross Newhan's *The Anaheim Angels: A Complete History.* "Gene wanted to win for the fans and the people who worked for him in the organization, but as he aged and his health began to fail, there were times I got a sense of urgency and even panic from our baseball people that if we don't do it this year, he may not be around next year, and that wasn't beneficial to the organization.

"We started skewing in wrong directions. We simply mortgaged the future at times. We probably could staff two major league teams with the kids we lost from our farm system."

As fate would have it, the Angels finally won that elusive World Series, beating the San Francisco Giants in Game 7 of the World Series on October 27, 2002, just four years, three weeks, and four days after Autry died at age 91.

And though Autry was not around to personally witness it, his legacy was felt strongly within the organization. It reached all the way into the clubhouse where Tim Salmon, the club's right fielder who had also experienced the disappointing losses and crushing failures with the team, had been thinking about it as the Angels got closer and closer to a championship.

"What if we really win it all?" Salmon remembered thinking. "We've got to find a way to get Gene Autry on the field any way we can. What would be reflective of that idea? It was his hat."

A few days before Game 7, Salmon asked Jackie Autry for one of Gene's cowboy hats—a pristine-looking white Stetson—and hid it in the Angels clubhouse. Moments after the final out of Game 7, Salmon raced into the clubhouse and retrieved the Stetson, then he took it onto the field, holding it aloft as he and his teammates danced and skipped across the Edison Field outfield in celebration.

In their 42nd season, they did it. The Angels won one for the Cowboy.

World Series 2002, Game 6— Spiezio Lifts a Franchise

It wasn't one of those no-doubt-about-it type of home runs, such a mammoth blast that the ball seems to disappear in an instant. Scott Spiezio's home run was merely a high fly ball hit in exactly the right spot at the right time—just inside the right-field foul pole and only a couple of rows deep. Although some might say it was long overdue.

Spiezio's three-run homer in the bottom of the seventh inning in Game 6 of the 2002 World Series not only started a rally that led to the Angels' Game 6 victory but also carried over to the series-clinching Game 7 win over the San Francisco Giants.

"I didn't know it was gone when I hit," Spiezio said. "I was praying. I was saying, 'God, please just get over the fence.' It seemed like it took forever."

The same could be said about the Angels, who, in their 42nd season, after years of heartbreak, disappointment, failure, and even tragedy, finally won the World Series. Spiezio was in the middle of it all after taking over first base from Mo Vaughn a year earlier.

The Angels trailed in the series 3–2 and appeared destined for a Game 6 loss, trailing 5–0 to the Giants entering the bottom of the seventh. Giants starting pitcher Russ Ortiz had shut out the Angels on just two hits through six innings, and he opened the seventh by getting Garret Anderson on a ground-out. But the Angels got the rally started on consecutive singles by Troy Glaus and Brad Fullmer, bringing up Spiezio.

Giants manager Dusty Baker took Ortiz out of the game but gave the ball to Ortiz to take with him to the dugout as a keepsake—bad move. Felix Rodriguez replaced Ortiz, and Spiezio worked the count full before golfing a low-and-inside fastball—clocked at

Scott Spiezio watches the flight of his three-run home run against the San Francisco Giants in the seventh inning of Game 6 of the World Series in Anaheim, California, on Saturday, October 26, 2002. (AP Photo/Kevork Djansezian)

95 mph—into the right-field seats just beyond the reach of Giants right fielder Reggie Sanders.

The Angels still trailed 5–3 going to the eighth but put together another rally. Darin Erstad hit a solo homer, and Glaus hit a two-run double to give the Angels a 6–5 lead. But when fans reflect on Game 6, it is Spiezio's home run that first comes to mind.

"Yeah, I guess it's the biggest at-bat I've had in my life," Spiezio said, "and the biggest hit."

It was such a peak moment that maybe it was natural for Spiezio's career to spiral downward from there. He played one more season with the Angels and put up decent numbers, hitting

.265 with 16 homers and 83 RBIs in 158 games in 2003. He turned that into a three-year, $9 million free-agent contract with the Mariners but was a bust and was released by the club before his contract was up.

He later hooked up with the Cardinals and briefly revitalized his career, playing in 119 regular season games for the 2006 World Series champs, even getting a few more World Series at-bats but going 0-for-4 with a walk in the Series victory over the Tigers.

Ultimately, the Cardinals released Spiezio after he was arrested on charges of drunk driving and assault. His baseball career eventually ended after playing for the Newark Bears of the independent Atlantic League in 2010 after a stint with the Orange County Flyers of the independent Golden Baseball League, a meager finish for the player who hit the biggest home run in Angels history.

Game 7

For those who experienced the Angels' run through the 2002 playoffs, it was an emotional blur. After 41 years of futility, the Angels reached the brink of winning the World Series, and it was hard to believe.

The Angels beat the Yankees and Twins in the playoffs then rallied with a dramatic Game 6 win in the World Series to force Game 7 against the San Francisco Giants.

The first six games of the Series featured impressive offense, but Game 7 was all about pitching. The Angels used four pitchers in the decisive game, and three of them weren't on the major league roster when the season began six months earlier.

Only closer Troy Percival, who pitched the ninth to finish the 4–1 victory, wasn't a rookie. Brendan Donnelly, a 31-year-old rookie who had toiled in the minors for years and also pitched as a replacement player during the player's strike in 1994, blanked the Giants in the sixth and seventh innings. Francisco Rodriguez, just 20 years old and not called up to the big club until September, threw a scoreless eighth.

The Angels' starting pitcher for Game 7 was rookie John Lackey, and his appearance was the result of a bold move by manager Mike Scioscia that might have won the game for the Angels. Ramon Ortiz was on schedule to make the start on a normal four days of rest. But Ortiz, despite a live arm, was inconsistent and jittery under the spotlight. Scioscia turned to Lackey, a tall Texan who played quarterback in high school in front of big crowds, and Lackey responded by allowing only one run in five innings, becoming the first rookie to win Game 7 of the World Series in 93 years.

Conversely, Dusty Baker opted against starting Kirk Rueter on three days of rest despite the Angels' trouble with soft-throwing lefties. Rueter had given up three runs in six innings of Game 4, a 4–3 Giants win.

Baker instead went with Livan Hernandez on his regular four days rest, even though the Angels hammered Hernandez for six runs in 3⅔ innings of a 10–4 victory in Game 3.

Still, the Angels found themselves in a familiar spot early, falling behind and needing a rally. The Giants got singles by Benito Santiago and J.T. Snow followed by a sacrifice fly from Reggie Sanders for a 1–0 lead in the second inning.

The Angels put together a two-out rally in the bottom of the inning when Game 6 hero Scott Spiezio walked and then scored on a double by Bengie Molina, tying the game at 1–1.

The Angels went ahead for good in the third inning, getting the rally started on consecutive singles by David Eckstein and

Darin Erstad. Tim Salmon was hit by a pitch, bringing up Garret Anderson.

Anderson left the Angels after the 2008 season as the club's all-time leader in extra-base hits, but in the World Series to that point, he had none. When he stepped into the box in the third inning of Game 7, all of his eight hits in the Series had been singles. But that changed in a dramatic way when he ripped a fastball from Hernandez into the right-field corner for a three-run double and 4–1 lead.

"[Hernandez] didn't want to walk me because he didn't have anywhere to put me," Anderson said. "It was still early in the game, and he needed to throw strikes."

Lackey and the Angels' bullpen—so good all season—took it from there with Donnelly to Rodriguez to Percival. Throughout the Series, Percival had to battle more than Barry Bonds and the Giants hitters. The night before Game 7, Percival said he didn't sleep "because I had death threats."

It turns out he started receiving those threats after hitting Alfonso Soriano with a pitch in the playoff series against the Yankees. "I carried a gun with me to the park," Percival said. "It was not a very comforting time, but I had a job to do."

After retiring Kenny Lofton on a fly to Erstad in center field, Percival, his Angels teammates, and all the long-suffering Angels fans could rejoice.

"What stands out more than anything about the whole play-offs and World Series was that I saw the fans and the game from a whole different perspective than I'd ever seen in Anaheim before," said Tim Salmon, who suffered through many disappointments with the club ever since breaking into the majors as the American League Rookie of the Year in 1993. "The fans were electric, the color, the excitement, the true sense of home-field advantage in every sense was evident."

1979—Yes We Can!

The credit for the Angels winning their first division title in 1979 is widespread.

Jim Fregosi was in his first full season as the club's manager after taking the job during the 1978 season, and he brought with him a no-nonsense attitude earning the respect of the players. Don Baylor settled his differences with the club, rescinded a trade demand, and ended up winning the franchise's first MVP award. General manager Buzzie Bavasi made astute moves, trading for Rod Carew and "Disco" Dan Ford and refusing to trade Carney Lansford. But if there was a singular moment that pushed the Angels over the top for the first time, credit might be given to the Cowboy himself, owner Gene Autry.

In mid-September, the Angels were in Kansas City for a four-game series with the Royals. The Angels had lost two of the first three games of the series, with the second-place Royals cutting the Angels' American League West lead to two games. With one game to play in the series, a Royals victory would reduce their deficit to one game and put the pressure on the Angels. But Autry had other ideas.

Autry was in the radio business, so it was easy for him to secure previously aired tape from radio shows. He was able to get a tape from a Palm Springs radio station that aired Royals owner Ewing Kauffman saying he didn't care who won the division…as long as it wasn't the Angels.

Kauffman didn't want to see the Angels win, knowing that Autry had been active in the free-agent market since free agency had been granted to players three years earlier. Ironically, Autry was against the idea of free agency, knowing that players' salaries would escalate.

But Autry bought into it anyway, knowing he had to in order to compete.

Autry sent the tape to Fregosi in Kansas City and instructed him to play it for the players before that fourth game of the series. The Angels won that game 11–6, increased their division lead to three games, and ultimately clinched the title against the Royals on September 25 at Anaheim Stadium.

"This is a dream come true," said Angels second baseman Bobby Grich, who grew up in nearby Long Beach and first joined the Angels as a free agent in 1977. "I've been an Angels fan since I was a kid. I used to come out to this park when Fregosi and [Bobby] Knoop were playing. I'd sit in the stands and say, 'I'd like to be out there some day.' Now here I am. It's unbelievable."

It really wasn't all that unbelievable considering how the Angels went into the 1979 season. It started with Fregosi leaving the Pittsburgh Pirates as a player and accepting the Angels' managerial job after the firing of Dave Garcia in June. The difference was immediate.

"When I got here, pitchers did what they wanted to do, regulars did what they wanted to do," Baylor said. "There was no control in the organization. In doubleheaders, pitchers would leave the park once they were taken out of the game. The first time it happened, [Nolan] Ryan said, 'That's the way we do it. That's part of it.' Jimmy said, 'No, that's not part of it. That's not the way we do it.' He stopped it right there."

Baylor took Fregosi's cue and was a leader on the field and in the clubhouse. He hit 36 homers, stole 22 bases, drove in 139 runs, and batted .296 on his way to the MVP award.

"Donny carried the whole team on his back," Carew said. "He came through with the big clutch hits and home runs all year. He was the straw that stirred the drink."

Dave Frost and Nolan Ryan each won 16 games, and Jim Barr won 10. Frank Tanana was hurt for much of the year, but he pitched a complete game in the division-clinching win. But the "Yes We Can" mantra came from the confidence in the offense, which pounded the ball all season.

Besides the contributions from Baylor, Brian Downing hit .326 and drove in 75, Carew hit .318, Grich hit 30 homers with 101 RBIs and batted .294, and Ford hit .290 and drove in 101 runs. Willie Aikens (21 homers, 81 RBIs, .280) and Lansford (19 homers, 75 RBIs, .287) also provided punch to a lineup that averaged 5.3 runs per game.

"We just pummeled everyone," Baylor said. "Every day we went to the park, we had it in our minds that we were going to win."

As ecstatic as the Angels were to win the division, disappointment fell upon the organization once again when they were eliminated 3–1 in the American League Championship Series to the Baltimore Orioles. It started badly even before the playoffs during a party celebrating the club's division-clinching victory. Barr was in a bar and saw a fan with a plastic toilet seat that said "Royal Flush." Barr punched it and broke a finger on his pitching hand.

The Angels lost the first two games in Baltimore, and on the flight home broadcaster Don Drysdale, the former Dodgers pitcher, accused Barr of malingering. The two nearly came to blows before being separated, and Drysdale later apologized.

The Angels rallied to win Game 3 4–3, but the Orioles finished it with an 8–0 win in Game 4 on a shutout by Orioles pitcher Scott McGregor.

5 Big "A" Stands for Albert

The Angels have acquired their share of big-name superstars over the years. Reggie Jackson, Rod Carew, Frank Robinson, Don Sutton, and Nolan Ryan all made stops in Anaheim on their way to the Hall of Fame.

It can be argued that only Ryan played in an Angels uniform while in his prime, throwing four of his record seven no-hitters with the club. But now Ryan will have company. The Angels shocked the baseball world in the winter of 2011–12 when they signed Albert Pujols to the second-largest contract in major league history, smack dab in the middle of what is surely becoming a Hall of Fame career.

Only Alex Rodriguez has ever signed a major league contract worth more than the 10-year, $240 million contract the Angels gave Pujols, the former Cardinals slugger who won three National League MVP awards (he was second four other times) in his 11 seasons in St. Louis.

Rodriguez signed a 10-year deal with Texas for $252 million, and a 10-year $275 million deal with the New York Yankees.

Slugging Percentage

Top career slugging percentage in major league history (minimum of 3,000 plate appearances, through 2011):

1. Babe Ruth (.6897)
2. Ted Williams (.6338)
3. Lou Gehrig (.6324)
4. Albert Pujols (.6168)
5. Jimmie Foxx (.6093)

First baseman Albert Pujols jokes with first base umpire Manny Gonzalez while playing the Colorado Rockies in the eighth inning of the Angels' 11–5 victory in Denver on Saturday, June 9, 2012. Pujols led the Angels to the win with a two-run home run and four RBIs in the game. (AP Photo/David Zalubowski)

The signing of Pujols was not only shocking to so many after the fact, but the Angels' initial interest came as a surprise to Pujols and his agent, Dan Lozano. Lozano seemed to have narrowed the potential suitors to the Cardinals and Marlins when he got a phone call from Angels general manager Jerry Dipoto during the Winter Meetings in Dallas in the first week of December 2011.

Dipoto called Lozano and asked him if he had time to talk the following day.

"Sure," Lozano said. "About what?"

"About No. 5," Dipoto responded.

"I got a big smile on my face," Lozano remembered, "and I said, 'Absolutely.'"

The smiles spread from there, from the Angels' front office to the team's players and to their thousands of fans. And, of course, that included their owner, Arte Moreno.

"For me," Moreno said, "it's like a dream come true."

Moreno played a big and potentially pivotal role in landing Pujols, following up Dipoto and Lozano's initial conversation with a number of phone calls to Pujols and his wife, Deidre.

"What he made me feel in those phone calls I had with him was how bad he wanted me," Pujols said. "I'm like, 'How about this guy? I don't even know him.' And when I made that decision, he told me that I was his partner, and that means a lot. I'm going to spend my 10 years here and try to bring what I have learned in the city of St. Louis for 11 years."

Lozano echoed Pujols' sentiments regarding Moreno.

"I think he was just able to touch a part in Albert's heart that not a lot of other people were able to get to," Lozano said.

Pujols came to the Angels at age 32 with offensive numbers that would be Hall of Fame worthy if he never batted again—.328 batting average, 445 home runs, 1,329 RBIs, .617 slugging percentage, and a .420 on-base percentage.

Significant Free Agents

The signing of Albert Pujols to a 10-year, $240 million contract was the most notable free-agent signing in Angels history. There have been others that were not only significant but successful. Here are five notable free-agent signings prior to Pujols:

1. **Vladimir Guerrero (2004–09)**—The Angels won the American League Western Division in five of the six years Guerrero was with the club, and it was no coincidence. He was the American League MVP in 2004 and the centerpiece of the lineup for his stay in Anaheim, during which he averaged 29 homers and 103 RBIs per season while batting .319.

2. **Bobby Grich (1977–86)**—Grich is one of only two Angels (Brian Downing) to play on each of the first three American League Western Division championship clubs (1979, '82, '86). He ranks in the top 10 in club history in home runs, RBIs, runs scored, and extra-base hits.

3. **Don Baylor (1977–82)**—In 1979 Baylor was the first and only Angel to win the MVP award before Guerrero did it 25 years later. He was a leader on and off the field for the club's first two division titles in 1979 and 1982. He ranks among the top 10 in club history in homers and RBIs.

4. **Reggie Jackson (1982–86)**—Jackson played on two division winners (1982, '86) and hit his 500th career homer in an Angels uniform on September 17, 1984, the 17th anniversary of his first career homer. By the time Jackson was inducted into the Baseball Hall of Fame in 1993, Yankees owner George Steinbrenner said letting Jackson leave the Yankees to sign with the Angels was his biggest mistake as an owner.

5. **Bartolo Colon (2004–07)**—Colon's stay was short, but his impact was profound in his first two years with the team. He won 18 games in 2004 and followed that up in 2005 by winning the Cy Young Award, the second in Angels history (Dean Chance, 1964), going 21–8 with a 3.48 ERA in leading the Angels to the American League Championship Series.

But what impressed so many of Pujols' new teammates in their first spring training together was more than the numbers. It was his work ethic. For fun, some Angels tried to break Pujols' concentration in the batting cage, to no avail.

"We scream at him, do different things like that, and he just keeps focusing," Angels outfielder Torii Hunter said. "When he's done, he'll say something funny, but other than that, he's very much locked in. He doesn't play around in the cage. That's work time. That's why he's a true professional."

Pujols, though, was just one of the guys when, in his first team meeting with the club, his cell phone rang and he was fined.

But he could afford it.

6 Radio Days, Major League Stage— Gene Autry Owns the Angels

Gene Autry loved baseball.

Owning a major league baseball team, though, was never really the goal. He had dreams of being a major league player, was a childhood friend of Dizzy Dean, and was even offered a minor league contract—for $100 a month—by the St. Louis Cardinals.

A slick-fielding, no-hit shortstop playing for an American Legion team in his hometown of Tioga, Texas, Autry decided he was better off keeping his job as a railroad telegrapher than trying to become a big leaguer. The choice was a good one, as a chance meeting with Will Rogers led to Autry pursuing a career in music and ultimately a career in Hollywood that was so successful that Autry became a business mogul in broadcasting.

Autry started Golden West Broadcasting and owned dozens and radio stations up and down the west coast. And when the

Dodgers moved west from Brooklyn in 1958, Autry landed the radio broadcast rights for his Los Angeles station KMPC.

By 1960, however, Dodgers owner Walter O'Malley decided to change stations, dropping KMPC for the more powerful KFI. Turns out O'Malley said he couldn't always pick up the Dodgers' road games on KMPC when he was in his retreat home in the San Gabriel Mountains above Los Angeles.

Autry couldn't believe he was losing the rights to broadcast the Dodgers games. "I was shocked," Autry said. "Bob Reynolds, my partner, and Stan Spero, my general manager at KMPC, had personally negotiated with O'Malley and believed they had his word on a contract renewal.

Former President Richard Nixon shares some good times with California Angels player Reggie Jackson (right) and club owner Gene Autry in the Angels' locker room on Monday night, April 3, 1984, at Anaheim Stadium.
(AP Photo/Doug Pizac)

Cowboy Code

In the 1940s and '50s Gene Autry had hit radio shows like *Gene Autry's Melody Ranch* and one featuring his horse, *The Adventures of Champion*.

With so many young listeners aspiring to emulate him, Autry came up with the Cowboy Code, or Cowboy Commandments. Under this code, a cowboy must:

—Never shoot first, hit a smaller man, or take unfair advantage.

—Never go back on his word or a trust confided in him.

—Always tell the truth.

—Be gentle with children, the elderly, and animals.

—Not advocate or possess racially or religiously intolerant ideas.

—Help people in distress.

—Be a good worker.

—Keep himself clean in thought, speech, action, and personal habits.

—Respect women, parents, and his nation's laws.

—Be a patriot.

"We had spent all kinds of money supporting his fight to build [Dodger Stadium] in Chavez Ravine. It was hard to believe. The ironic thing is that the Dodgers ultimately ended up on a station whose nighttime power is so weak you have trouble picking up the games even in Orange County. I guess those things have a way of evening up."

Autry, though, was in luck. After the 1960 season, Major League Baseball decided to expand, adding teams in Washington D.C. and Los Angeles. Autry immediately worked to secure the broadcast rights to Los Angeles' newest franchise.

Autry met with the proposed new ownership group that included Hall of Famer Hank Greenberg and Bill Veeck and secured the rights if that ownership group was approved. But it was not, thanks in part because of O'Malley's reluctance to share his gold mine, particularly with a group that included a noted showman like Veeck.

Autry and his business partners then decided to try to buy the franchise themselves, if for no other reason than to secure the broadcast rights. Autry had a good relationship with Joe Cronin, the president of the American League, thanks to Autry's graciousness to Cronin's sons years earlier. When the Gene Autry Rodeo made a stop in Boston Garden back when Cronin was the manager of the Red Sox, Autry agreed to meet Cronin's sons and autographed cowboy hats for them.

So when Autry expressed interest in the new franchise, Cronin encouraged Autry to apply. "Anybody who loves kids that much has to be good for baseball," Cronin told the league's owners.

The biggest potential obstacle—O'Malley—was on board, just as long as Autry agreed to pay $350,000 to O'Malley in indemnification. Autry agreed and then paid $2.1 million for entry fees into the league. Gene Autry was now a major league owner, and in 1961 the Los Angeles Angels were born.

7 The Ryan Express

It was May 1972 and Nolan Ryan was a month into his first season with the Angels. The Mets had given up on him after parts of five seasons in New York, trading him to the Angels for popular shortstop Jim Fregosi.

Ryan had thrown a shutout in his first start with the Angels but lost his next two starts. The Angels had taken a chance on the hard-throwing Texan but felt they needed to scrap some of his bad habits and start from scratch.

Pitching coach Tom Morgan worked diligently with Ryan, and conditioning coach Jimmie Reese made sure Ryan didn't take any shortcuts in workouts. Catcher Jeff Torborg was influential, as well.

But what might have been as significant as anything was a discovery Ryan made at Anaheim Stadium in May '72. In a storage area in the bowels of the stadium trainer Freddie Frederico had a Universal weight machine, and one day Ryan found it.

Ryan began using the machine, which had four stations—bench press, military press, lat pulldown, and leg press. Ryan worked out in secret because in those days weight training was frowned upon. It was believed it made muscles tight, and that would be especially bad for a pitcher. But Ryan found it helped him with his stamina and flexibility.

"In those days, they didn't want pitchers lifting, so I had to do it on the quiet side," Ryan said. "I felt like there had to be other things you could do to strengthen yourself, that's why I started doing it.

"With the weights, we were a little before our time. It was new back then, and when we look back we can see the impact it has had on the game. For me, that weight room in Anaheim established a foundation that I worked off of the rest of my career."

Indeed.

Ryan wound up pitching a remarkable 27 seasons in the majors, all the way up to age 46. He threw a record seven no-hitters, including No. 7 at the age of 44. His 5,714 strikeouts are by far the most in big-league history.

Ryan pitched eight seasons for the Angels from 1972–79, which included the best seasons of his career. It was with the Angels that he threw four of his no-hitters, and he had four seasons in which he won 19 games or more, never matching that total during his time with the Mets, Astros, or Rangers.

For as much angst as was caused in Anaheim when the club traded away Fregosi to get Ryan, even more came about when the Angels let Ryan go. The Angels won their first division title in 1979 and Ryan was a big part of it, going 16–14.

After negotiations failed and Ryan signed a free-agent contract with the Astros, Angels general manager Buzzie Bavasi uttered those words that would haunt him for years—"All I have to do is find two pitchers capable of going 8–7 each," Bavasi said, referring to Ryan's 16–14 record in '79.

But the roots of Ryan's departure were planted even before the 1979 season began. Knowing his contract was expiring after the '79 season, Ryan asked his agent to reach out to the Angels after the 1978 season. Ryan did not want to be distracted with contract negotiations during the season.

Ryan's agent, Richard Moss, sent Bavasi a letter asking for a four-year contract at $550,000 per year. Bavasi then went to owner Gene Autry, but Autry was hesitant. Ryan was bothered by arm issues in 1978 and went 10–13, so Autry thought it would be better to wait and see how Ryan performed in '79.

"The Angels don't owe me anything, but I do feel that I've given them everything I've got and that I have made contributions at the gate and on the field," a disappointed Ryan said at the time. "I've been loyal, and I would expect the same from them. Buzzie has said he might be willing to look at the situation somewhere around the All-Star break, but that's unsatisfactory. I don't expect an offer, and I don't expect my attitude to change."

After the season, Ryan became the majors' first million-dollar-a-year pitcher, signing with the Astros for four years at $1.1 million per season. And in playing in Houston, he was just a half-hour from his hometown of Alvin, Texas.

Moss did give the Angels a chance, submitting a proposal for $1 million a year. Moss said it was a negotiating starting point, and he and Ryan waited for a counter-proposal that never came.

Bavasi, formerly the GM of the Dodgers, later admitted he was old-school and simply had trouble with the exploding salaries in the majors at the time.

"I think it's been hard for any old-timer to justify the present-day salary scale," Bavasi said. "I just can't see anybody 60 times better than Jackie Robinson. Or name a pitcher 30 times better than Sandy Koufax.... Remember that Ryan was basically a .500 pitcher his last two years with us. There's no doubt that he's now a Hall of Famer, but I had to look at wins and losses, whether we were winning pennants with a pitcher who wanted $1 million, and it wasn't happening."

Years later, Ryan expressed mixed feelings about his time with the Angels.

"I used to hear a lot of comments about being only a .500 pitcher, but it wasn't as if those Angels teams were only one player away," he said. "You could have added Babe Ruth and it wouldn't have made that much difference.

"On the other hand, pitching for those Angel teams made me a more focused and better pitcher since I didn't have the luxury of making a mistake. I consider those years the foundation of my career."

1986—No Series for You

A World Series victory can do a lot for a troubled franchise, and the Angels' 2002 championship is a perfect example. The Angels had reached the playoffs only three times in their first 41 seasons, but the 2002 World Series appearance started a stretch in which the Angels reached the playoffs in six of eight seasons.

But not even that first World Series victory has completely taken the sting out of the Angels' playoff loss in 1986, a loss that seemed to send the franchise into a tailspin that lasted 16 years.

The Angels had one of their best teams in franchise history with big names like Reggie Jackson, Doug DeCinces, Bobby Grich, Bob Boone, Brian Downing, and the emergence of Wally Joyner. On the mound, pitchers Mike Witt, Kirk McCaskill, and Don Sutton each won 15 games or more.

Manager Gene Mauch guided the club to the American League Western Division title, and it took a 3–1 lead over the Boston Red Sox into Game 5 of the American League Championship Series at Anaheim Stadium.

Game 5. It still brings chills to Angels fans who are unfortunate enough to remember.

As Jackson and Mauch stood arm-in-arm near the top step of the Angels dugout, the Angels one strike away from finally getting owner Gene Autry to the World Series, Dave Henderson broke their hearts.

Henderson's two-run home run in the top of the ninth inning off Angels reliever Donnie Moore gave the Red Sox a 6–5 lead, but it did not win the game. It will always be known as the signature moment of that game, but there was so much more to that Game 5 loss.

The Angels took a 5–2 lead into the top of the ninth inning, still riding the right arm of Witt, who had won 18 games that season. Bill Buckner, who would go on to experience his own level of infamy in the World Series against the Mets, singled off Witt to begin the inning.

Witt then struck out Jim Rice for the first out, but Don Baylor followed with a two-run homer to make it 5–4. Witt responded by getting Dwight Evans on a pop out for the second out.

Then Mauch, in a move second-guessed for years, replaced Witt with lefty Gary Lucas to face the left-handed-hitting Rich Gedman. Gedman had a single, double, and home run against Witt in the game and was 0-for-2 against Lucas that season, so Mauch "played the percentages."

But Lucas, who had not hit a batter with a pitch all year, hit Gedman with his first pitch. Then Mauch went to Moore out of the bullpen, and on a 2–2 pitch, Henderson hit Moore's hanging split-finger pitch over the fence for a 6–5 Red Sox lead.

The Angels then tied the game in the bottom of the ninth on Rob Wilfong's RBI single. They had the bases loaded with one out when DeCinces, who drove in 96 runs during the regular season, swung at the first pitch from Steve Crawford and flied out to shallow right field, the ball not going deep enough to get Wilfong home.

Grich lined out for the final out of the ninth, Henderson drove in the game-winning run with a sacrifice fly in the top of the 11th, the Angels were blown out in Games 6 and 7 in Boston, and the Angels went quietly into the night. The Game 5 loss was simply too much to overcome.

"I remember sitting in a hotel room in Anaheim after that fifth game, and I asked my husband [owner Gene Autry] if he really wanted to go back to Boston and he said no," Jackie Autry said. "If we felt that way, can you imagine how the players felt?

"I mean, we had come off such a high in the Saturday [Game 4] game. We had the momentum. It was a shame. I don't blame Donnie Moore. I don't blame Gene Mauch, and I don't remember any circumstances where my husband second-guessed [Mauch]. I blame Doug DeCinces. We had the bases loaded. The kid [Crawford] was obviously petrified, and [DeCinces] swung at the first pitch. God."

9 The Rock—Mike Scioscia

Mike Scioscia became well-known for his ability to block.

As a catcher who played for the Dodgers, Scioscia never failed to stand his ground in protecting the plate despite being vulnerable to vicious collisions. But the blocking he really wanted to do was as an offensive lineman, dreaming he would play for legendary coach Joe Paterno at Penn State.

It didn't happen.

"A recruiter said I was too small and too slow for guys at that level," Scioscia said.

Fortunately for Scioscia, he had options. He was a good enough athlete to be a three-sport star at Springfield High School while growing up in Morton, Pennsylvania, playing football, baseball, and basketball.

Baseball was his best sport. Scioscia was named the Delaware County player of the year in both 1975 and '76, and he was offered a full-ride scholarship to go to Clemson. He also received a scholarship offer to play football and baseball at the University of Delaware, and he was drafted in the first round of the 1976 major league draft by the Dodgers with the 19th pick overall.

"My mom [Florence] taught school for 30 years, so she supported going to Clemson," Scioscia remembered. "My dad [Fred] said it might be my only opportunity to play pro ball. They were split, and so it was up to me."

Scioscia was still undecided but was leaning toward going to Clemson when everything changed one day in July 1976, one month after the draft. Scioscia, a mere 17 years old, was at home when the phone rang.

Mike Scioscia argues with home-plate umpire Lance Barrett during the first inning of a game against the Chicago White Sox in Chicago on Friday, August 3, 2012. (AP Photo/Nam Y. Huh)

"I was two weeks away from going [to Clemson]," Scioscia recalled. "The Dodgers were in town to play the Phillies, and I got a call from Tom Lasorda. He was the third-base coach at the time, and he invited me to work out at the stadium before one of the games. He said someone would be at my home in an hour to pick me up. I grabbed my spikes and glove and left a note for my parents telling them where I was. I could just imagine my mom reading that note."

The next day, Scioscia was on a plane to Bellingham, Washington, to begin his professional baseball career. He went on to play 13 seasons in the majors from 1980–92, all with the Dodgers. He was a two-time All-Star and played in two World Series. He also caught Fernando Valenzuela during "Fernandomania" and Orel Hershiser during Hershiser's remarkable 59 consecutive scoreless-innings streak.

After his playing career ended, Scioscia transitioned into a coaching role with the Dodgers, first serving as the organization's minor league catching coordinator in 1995 and '96. He was manager Bill Russell's bench coach in 1997 and '98, but things changed dramatically when the O'Malley family sold the team to Rupert Murdoch's Fox Group.

Russell and general manager Fred Claire were fired, and Kevin Malone was hired as the team's new GM. Malone hired Davey Johnson as the club's new manager for the 1999 season, and Scioscia managed the Triple A Albuquerque Dukes.

After the season, Scioscia requested a meeting with Malone.

"That's when I knew I needed to take steps in order to become a major league manager," Scioscia said. "I was wondering where the organization was going, if they could give me an idea. [Malone] said there were so many things in transition that they weren't clear. I thought the best thing for me was to get out early and give myself the opportunity to look for some spots."

Scioscia had been loyal to the Dodgers, previously turning down opportunities to interview for managerial openings with

Tampa Bay and the Chicago White Sox. But now, Scioscia was looking for an opportunity, and it so happened that there was one just down the freeway.

The Angels were a mess in 1999, resulting in the resignation of both manager Terry Collins and GM Bill Bavasi. Former Yankee Bob Watson appeared to be the frontrunner to become the new Angels' GM, and he would certainly hire one of his former Yankee teammates—like Willie Randolph or Chris Chambliss—to be his manager.

But Angels president Tony Tavares surprised many with his hiring of the understated financial wizard Bill Stoneman, who had been with the Montreal Expos. By the time Stoneman was hired, managerial candidates like Phil Garner and Don Baylor had already signed on with other teams, so Scioscia got an interview with an assist from Claire, the former Dodgers GM who thought highly of Scioscia.

"Bill Stoneman called me before he hired Mike," Claire said. "We talked for 45 minutes to an hour, and I told Bill, 'If you hire Mike it will be a great decision for your organization. He will be a successful manager. He was respected as a player and coach, he's well prepared, and he's dedicated. He does everything he possibly can.'"

Scioscia was hired before the start of the 2000 season, and three years into his managerial career, the Angels won the World Series. Success continued throughout the decade, the Angels reached the playoffs in six of his first eight seasons at the helm, and Scioscia won American League Manager of the Year honors in both 2002 and 2009.

In 2009, Scioscia, already the franchise's winningest manager, was given a 10-year contract extension, keeping him in the Angels' dugout through the 2018 season.

10 The Angels Win a Playoff Series, Finally!

Angels fans have mixed feelings about 1979, '82, and '86. After all, the Angels won the AL West those seasons and reached the playoffs. But the excitement was tempered in each of those seasons with playoff losses.

And not just any playoff losses. Of course, the "one strike away" loss to the Red Sox in '86 hurts the most, but the Angels were one game away in '82 and couldn't break through.

The 2002 season is remembered for the dramatic seven-game World Series victory over the San Francisco Giants, but the Angels first had to snap out of their playoff funk against the mighty New York Yankees in the American League Division Series.

If reaching the playoffs was a long shot, certainly the idea of beating the Yankees was even more of a stretch. The Yankees won 103 games in 2002 in winning the AL East and had gone to the World Series the previous three consecutive seasons and four of the previous five.

Although they did win 99 games that season, the Angels were the wild card entry into the playoffs, and not many people outside those who had seen the Angels daily gave them much of a chance to beat the mighty Yankees.

The Angels insisted they weren't affected by history or perception.

"The pressure's off now," Angels center fielder Darin Erstad said before the start of the series. "Now the fun begins."

Experience? The Angels had only one player—pitcher Kevin Appier—with any playoff experience.

"Experience always helps," Angels closer Troy Percival said. "What can you do? It's still baseball. The bases are still 90' apart.

The mound is still 60' 6" from home plate. We have a good team, and we're not scared to go up against anybody."

In Game 1 at Yankee Stadium, the Angels took a 5–4 lead into the eighth inning. Reliever Ben Weber replaced starter Jarrod Wasburn to start the inning and retired the first two batters before walking Alfonso Soriano and Derek Jeter.

With the potential tying run in scoring position, Angels manager Mike Scioscia decided against going to Percival, instead opting for the lefty Scott Schoeneweis to face the left-handed-hitting Jason Giambi.

Giambi singled and drove in the tying run, and Scioscia then brought in Brendan Donnelly, who yielded a game-breaking three-run homer to Bernie Williams.

The Yankees won Game 1 8–5, and Scioscia stood his ground and defended his decision afterward. "I didn't mind Schoeny against Giambi, he's done a good job the times he's faced Jason," Scioscia said. "He made a good pitch. Jason's strong. He didn't get all of it, but he got enough of it."

In Game 2, the Angels' offense came alive with 17 hits. Tim Salmon and Scott Spiezio homered for the Angels but they still trailed 5–4 going into the eighth. Leading off the eighth inning, Garret Anderson homered to tie the game, and Troy Glaus followed with a homer to put the Angels up 6–5. They added another run in the inning and took a 7–5 lead into the bottom of the eighth.

The Yankees mounted an eighth-inning rally, just like in Game 1, putting two on with two out. But this time Scioscia summoned Percival out of the bullpen.

Percival made things interesting, hitting Soriano with a pitch to load the bases. But he got Derek Jeter looking at strike three to end the threat.

Percival gave up a run in the ninth, but the Angels held on for an 8–6 win and tied the series at one game each. "I thought the elements were right to use Percy," Scioscia explained. "Last night pointed us in a different direction."

In Game 3, the Angels' offense and bullpen rescued a poor performance by starting pitcher Ramon Ortiz, who appeared jittery under the bright lights of the big stage.

The Yankees took a 6–1 lead, but the Angels' offense put constant pressure on the Yankees pitchers. Tim Salmon's two-run double in the third made it 6–3. Adam Kennedy had a solo homer in the fourth and a sacrifice fly in the sixth to make it 6–5.

Scott Spiezio's two-out single in the seventh drove in Anderson to tie the game at 6–6. In the eighth, Erstad broke the tie with an RBI double, and Salmon hit a two-run homer to put the Angels up 9–6, and that's how it ended.

"You just keep playing offense when you get down like that," said Angels shortstop David Eckstein. "In the dugout we were saying, 'Let's just score one run an inning.' That was our goal. We approached the game offensively like we have all year."

The bullpen was also clutch in relief of Ortiz, who lasted less than three innings. John Lackey, Schoeneweis, Francisco Rodriguez, and Percival combined to shut out the Yankees on one hit over the final six innings, and the Angels were up in the series 2–1.

One game away. Again.

In Game 4, the Angels did their best to remove the chance for any late-inning dramatics from the Yankees. It came in an eight-run fifth inning that turned a 2–1 deficit into a 9–2 lead. The team had 10 hits in the fifth inning alone and held on for a 9–5 win and the first playoff series victory in club history.

"Nobody gave us a chance against the Yankees," Salmon said. "They are a great club. Maybe we caught them on a bad week or something, I don't know. But we went toe-to-toe with them, and we answered the bell every time we had to."

11 World Series 2002—Game 1

Many long-suffering fans consider October 19, 2002, the date that hell froze over. Through so many ups and downs and more tragedy than triumph, the Angels did what many thought would never happen—make it to the World Series. But while fans and followers of the club were celebrating, the 2002 Angels said they had to approach it like any other game. After all, that's how they managed to get to the World Series in the first place.

"There's no such thing as stepping up your game in the World Series," Angels manager Mike Scioscia said. "It's executing the same way you did all year long to get to this level. Our guys are in their element when they're playing their style of game, and that's what you want them to bring."

So much talk going into the Series was about Giants slugger Barry Bonds, and deservedly so. But Game 1 showed there was more to the Giants than Bonds.

Bonds, of course, did what he does—he homered in his first career World Series at-bat—but it was Reggie Sanders and J.T. Snow who led the Giants to a 4–3 victory in Game 1. Sanders hit a home run in the second inning, and he singled with two outs in the sixth. Snow followed Sanders' sixth-inning single with a two-run home run.

Troy Glaus hit two home runs for the Angels off Giants starter Jason Schmidt, but both home runs came with the bases empty. Adam Kennedy had an RBI single for the third Angels run, but they missed other scoring opportunities.

"We had two situations with runners on third base [and one out] and didn't get the job done," Angels hitting coach Mickey Hatcher said. "I know those two guys [Darin Erstad and Tim

Angels 2002 Roster

The following players were on the Angels' active major league roster at one time or another during their 2002 World Series championship season:

Alfredo Amezaga, Garret Anderson, Kevin Appier, Clay Bellinger, Mickey Callaway, Dennis Cook, Jeff DaVanon, Brendan Donnelly, David Eckstein, Darin Erstad, Jorge Fabregas, Sal Fasano, Chone Figgins, Brad Fullmer, Benji Gil, Troy Glaus, Adam Kennedy, John Lackey, Al Levine, Mark Lukasiewicz, Bengie Molina, Jose Molina, Jose Nieves, Alex Ochoa, Ramon Ortiz, Orlando Palmeiro, Troy Percival, Lou Pote, Julio Ramirez, Francisco Rodriguez, Tim Salmon, Scott Schoeneweis, Aaron Sele, Scot Shields, Scott Spiezio, Donne Wall, Jarrod Washburn, Ben Weber, Matt Wise, and Shawn Wooten.

Salmon] who had the opportunities are not very happy about it right now. They're going to come out [in Game 2] and be pissed off. You better watch out."

The Game 1 loss for the Angels was their first at home during the 2002 postseason after having won their first five. But the Game 1 loss was nothing new—they also lost the playoff openers to the Yankees and Twins that year before rallying to win each series.

"I'm not going to say we have them right where we want them, but we've been here before," Angels designated hitter Brad Fullmer said. "So we're not going to panic. We're not overly concerned. Certainly you don't want to lose the first game, but we've shown we can bounce back."

Jarrod Washburn, who won a career-best 18 games in 2002, was the Angels' Game 1 starter. He gave up only six hits in 5⅔ innings, but three of those hits were home runs (Bonds, Sanders, and Snow).

The Angels out-hit the Giants 9–6 but failed to get hits in big situations. They were 1-for-8 with runners in scoring position.

"We saw some positive things tonight, it's just the score wasn't where we want it to be," Scioscia said. "If we play with that aggressiveness offensively, I think our offense will be where we want it to be."

12 Watch the Angels Beat the Dodgers in the World Series

It's been said the Angels have played in the shadow of the Dodgers ever since they came into the league in 1961. And while much has changed since the Angels had to pay for the window cleaning in their windowless offices at Dodger Stadium, the battle rages on.

While there will forever be a battle for TV ratings, sponsors, and attendance, the only true way to settle the score—once and for all—would be in a Freeway World Series.

Although the Angels have been the more successful team on the field since the turn of the century, Dodgers fans seem to continue to hold an air of superiority that irks Angels fans. For any Angels fan, no World Series victory would be sweeter than one that included the Dodgers on the losing end.

"I got the sense they looked down on us," said Tim Salmon, the Angels' all-time home run leader who played much of his career in the 1990s when the Dodgers had players like Mike Piazza, Eric Karros, Raul Mondesi, and Hideo Nomo, all Rookie of the Year Award recipients like Salmon. "They had good teams, and their big names made us feel like a JV team.... But I don't sense that feeling anymore."

The divide between the two teams was significantly blurred in 2000 when the Angels hired Mike Scioscia to manage the club. Scioscia was a tried-and-true Dodger, part of the 1988 World Series championship team, and he was paying his dues in the minor league system to one day become the club's manager.

Fred Claire, the Dodgers GM from 1987–98, seemed to favor Sciosica as well, but when the O'Malley family sold the franchise to News Corp.'s Fox Entertainment Group in 1998, Claire was out. And in essence, so was Scioscia.

Freeway Series

The annual Freeway Series was nothing more than an exhibition until 1997 when interleague play was implemented. Here's how the Angels and Dodgers have fared against each other from 1997–2012.

1997—Dodgers 4 wins; Angels 0 wins
1998—Angels 3, Dodgers 1
1999—Dodgers 4, Angels 2
2000—Angels 4, Dodgers 2
2001—Angels 4, Dodgers 2
2002—Angels 3, Dodgers 3
2003—Angels 4, Dodgers 2
2004—Angels 3, Dodgers 3
2005—Angels 5, Dodgers 1
2006—Dodgers 4, Angels 2
2007—Angels 5, Dodgers 1
2008—Angels 3, Dodgers 3
2009—Angels 3, Dodgers 3
2010—Angels 5, Dodgers 1
2011—Angels 4, Dodgers 2
2012—Angels 4, Dodgers 2

Total—Angels 54 wins, Dodgers 38 wins

Seeing the writing on the wall, Scioscia left the Dodgers and soon was swooped up by the Angels. Angels general manager Bill Stoneman called Claire to ask about Scioscia, and Claire told him it would be a great hire. Not only was Scioscia hired, but he brought former Dodgers with him—hitting coach Mickey Hatcher, first base coach Alfredo Griffin, and third base coach Ron Roenicke.

In Scioscia's third season as the Angels manager, they won the World Series. Scioscia was free to gloat, to rub it in the Dodgers' faces, but he didn't. He wouldn't even call it a rivalry.

If the Dodgers hated any team, they hated the Giants, not the Angels.

"Rivalries are going to exist more so within your division," Scioscia said. "Those are the teams you're trying to get past to win a pennant. It's not like the Yankees and the Mets or the Giants and the A's, because those teams have played each other in the World Series. We haven't had those games with the Dodgers yet."

Yet.

But they have played in the regular season since the inception of interleague play. Before then, the Freeway Series was nothing more than the final few games of spring training. Only it didn't seem that way, not when Anaheim Stadium often held more than 60,000 fans for a game against the Dodgers.

Now the two teams play games that matter, even though it's not the World Series. Since interleague play began in 1997, the Angels have essentially dominated the series, going 54–38 for a .587 winning percentage through the 2012 season.

The closest the two teams got to playing each other in the World Series came in 2009 when both clubs reached their respective league championship series. However, both teams lost—the Dodgers to the Phillies and the Angels to the Yankees.

Getting to the World Series of course is no easy task and is always something for Angels fans to be excited about. But beating the Dodgers in the Fall Classic? Priceless.

13 Donnie Moore and "The Pitch"

Ralph Branca gave up the Shot Heard 'Round the World when Bobby Thomson's 1951 home run lifted the New York Giants over the Brooklyn Dodgers to the National League pennant. Branca seemed to handle it relatively well, keeping a sense of humor and maintaining a sense of perspective.

For the Angels' Donnie Moore, giving up a dramatic home run became too much to overcome. Moore had a 2–2 count on Dave

Henderson in Game 5 of the 1986 playoffs in the top of the ninth inning. The Angels were one strike away from beating the Boston Red Sox in the American League Championship Series and qualifying for their first World Series in club history.

Moore threw the pitch, a forkball, and Henderson connected, hitting a two-run home run over the head of exasperated left fielder Brian Downing and over the fence for a 6–5 lead.

The Angels tied the game in the bottom of the ninth but couldn't get a second run across that would have won the game, Doug DeCinces popping out to shallow right field and Bobby Grich lining out.

The Red Sox ultimately scored the winning run of the game in the 11th inning, coming on Henderson's sacrifice fly off Moore, who had been battling a sore shoulder most of the season. Despite all the twists and turns in the game, the spotlight was on Henderson's homer in the ninth that would be remembered in infamy.

"He was fouling off fastballs," Moore said after the game when asked about his decision to throw a forkball. "I should have stayed with fastballs. I'm a human being, and I didn't do the job."

After reflecting on the pitch over the off-season, Moore still sounded like someone trying to convince himself that there was no reason to be hard on himself. "I've thought about it a couple times," Moore said during spring training of 1987. "But I haven't let it dominate me or anything. I had never thrown that big of a home run before. And you know what? When I look back on the tape, it wasn't that bad of a pitch. It was a low and outside off-speed pitch. In retrospect, I just think it was a bad selection. He is a breaking-ball hitter. I should have thrown him something hard.

"Some of the stuff that's happened since has been tough. But you've got to forget about it. I know I have. I made one bad pitch. It didn't cost us the pennant. It cost us a game."

Moore first broke into the majors in 1975 with the Chicago Cubs, and he went to the Cardinals, Brewers, and Braves before joining the Angels in 1985. He had the best season of his career with the Angels that year, going 8–8 with a 1.92 ERA and 31 saves in 1985.

He followed that up with a solid year in 1986, going 4–5 with a 2.97 ERA and 21 saves despite that nagging shoulder injury.

He played two more seasons with the Angels, who released him late in the 1988 season at age 34. He tried to resume his career in 1989, signing a minor league deal with the Kansas City Royals, but he was released by the club in June.

Only a month later, on July 18, 1989, at his home in Anaheim Hills, Moore shot and wounded his wife, Tonya, then shot and killed himself.

"Ever since he gave up the home run, he was never himself again," said David Pinter, Moore's agent. "He blamed himself for the Angels not going to the World Series. He constantly talked about the Henderson home run. I tried to get him to go to a psychiatrist but he said, 'I don't need it, I'll get over it.' But as many times as I tried to tell him that one pitch doesn't make a season, he couldn't get over it. That one pitch killed him."

In an interview with *GQ* magazine, Tonya Moore placed some of the blame on the fans.

"I'll never forgive the fans for what they did to my husband. Never, ever," she said.

14 World Series 2002—Game 2

Game 1 of the 2002 World Series was the Angels' debut in the Fall Classic. But Game 2—on October 20, 2002—marked the Angels' first-ever victory in a World Series game.

Game 2 was the kind of game that might be more common in the schoolyard, when you might use cardboard for bases, use "invisible" base runners, and expect one defensive player to cover the entire outfield.

The Angels and San Francisco Giants combined for 28 hits in Game 2, including a 485' blast by Barry Bonds. But no hit was bigger than Tim Salmon's two-run homer off Giants reliever Felix Rodriguez in the bottom of the eighth inning.

It was Salmon's second homer of the game, and it snapped a 9–9 tie in an eventual 11–10 victory by the Angels in a game the Angels desperately needed because it tied the Series at one game apiece.

The Angels scored five in the first inning, but the Giants rallied and led 9–7 in the fifth inning. The Angels had tied the game at 9 by the time they came to bat in the bottom of the eighth. With one out, David Eckstein singled. Darin Erstad followed and fouled off several pitches before he finally flied out for the second out of the inning, bringing up Salmon.

"When Ersty was battling, I really felt like there was a chance he was going to get on base, either a walk or something," Salmon said. "I was thinking I was going to have a guy in scoring position, and I had to get ready for that. But when he made an out with a guy on first, it changed my thinking. If anything, maybe it helped me relax. I don't hit home runs when I go up there trying to hit them."

While Salmon came up big for the Angels at the plate, 20-year-old Francisco Rodriguez was equally big on the mound. The Giants had nine runs and 11 hits through five innings, shelling Angels starter Kevin Appier for five runs in just two innings.

John Lackey, who would start Game 7 a week later, also struggled, giving up two runs in 2⅓ innings. Ben Weber was no better, allowing two runs and four hits while recording only two outs.

But Rodriguez came in to start the sixth and turned around the game. Rodriguez pitched three innings—the sixth, seventh, and eighth—and retired all nine batters he faced, needing just 26 pitches, 22 of which were strikes. He faced Bonds once, getting him on a ground-out to first, and allowed only one batter to even hit the ball out of the infield. Even that was a fly out to shallow center field by David Bell.

"That was incredible," Angels manager Mike Scioscia said. "For him to step up, give us three innings, and do it under 30 pitches was incredible. That was the game right there."

Well, almost.

After Salmon's home run in the bottom of the eighth gave the Angels a lead, Scioscia turned to closer Troy Percival to pitch the ninth. Bonds was due up third in the inning, so keeping the first two batters off the bases was of paramount importance.

Percival got Rich Aurilia and Jeff Kent on fly balls to left field, bringing up Bonds with no chance to tie the game.

"I threw my first pitch as hard as I could right down the middle," Percival said. "I think I supplied all the power there. That's what I'm going with anyway. I told myself if I get the first two guys, it doesn't matter how far he hits it. Then I'd get the next guy."

He did as Benito Santiago popped out to second base to end the game.

15 Hall of Famer Rod Carew

Rod Carew's tenure with the Angels came in two phases—player and coach. The fact that he was either was the stuff of folklore.

He grew up in Panama's Canal Zone, suffering at the hand of an abusive father and dreaming of a chance to play in the big leagues. He listened to Armed Forces Radio, which broadcast major league games and gave him a goal to aim for.

Rod Carew hits his 2,997th career base hit during the first inning of a game at Anaheim Stadium on August 3, 1985. (AP Photo/Rod Boren)

"We were poor but not impoverished," Carew said. "There were times my dad would bring food home and he'd put his name on it and you couldn't touch it. But we never starved. If I was really hungry, I could go into the woods and get mangos and coconuts to eat."

Eventually, Carew's mother moved Carew and his siblings to the concrete jungle, New York City, where Carew ultimately got noticed playing in a city league. The Minnesota Twins, in New York to play the Yankees, offered him a tryout.

It didn't take long for the Twins to see what they wanted to see. "Get him out of here!" Twins manager Sam Mele said. "I don't want the Yankees seeing him."

The Twins signed Carew, sent him to the minor leagues, and three years later in 1967 he was the Rookie of the Year. In 1969, he hit .332 and won the first of his seven American League batting titles.

Carew was an artist with the bat, spraying line drives all over the field. He was also a great bunter and base stealer. In 1969 he stole home six times, tying Ty Cobb's single-season record.

Carew was on his way to another batting title in 1970, hitting .376 in June, when an injury sidelined him until September, where he went 0-for-5, dropping him to .336. Despite his success, Carew was always tinkering with his stance, and in 1972, he made a significant adjustment because of one person.

That year, Carew got his first look at Nolan Ryan, who had been traded from the Mets in the National League to the Angels in the American League. Carew had always been able to catch up with a fastball, but Ryan's was different.

"When I came to the big leagues, I would hold my hands straight up and hit anybody," Carew said. "But I couldn't hit Nolan because he'd overpower me upstairs. So I started crouching and noticed I would see the difference in his fastball when I was down better than when I stood straight up. From then on I was able to handle his fastball a little bit better."

And everybody else's fastball, as well.

Carew won four consecutive batting titles from 1972–75 and then two more in 1977 and '78. He was named the American League MVP in '77 when he led the league in hits (239), runs (128), triples (16), batting average (.388), and on-base percentage (.449). He also drove in a career-best 100 runs that year.

Carew flirted with .400 in 1977 as he fell eight hits short of becoming the first player since Ted Williams in 1941 to reach the magical mark. He was hitting better than .400 as late as July 10 and never fell below .374 the rest of the season.

Despite the batting title in '78, the Twins knew Carew was eligible to become a free agent after the 1979 season and also knew they wouldn't be able to afford him. The Twins started shopping Carew and nearly traded him to the Yankees or Giants, but Carew preferred the Angels, and that's where he went.

Carew made an impact even before taking the field, as season-ticket sales nearly doubled. And by the end of Carew's first season in Anaheim, the club set an attendance record, drawing more than 2.5 million fans in 1979.

Of course, it was more than Carew in '79, as the Angels won their first American League West division title. He played seven seasons with the Angels, hitting better than .300 five times and hitting .314 overall with the club. In 1985 he reached the magical 3,000-hit mark, finished with 3,053 hits, and retired, giving way to Wally Joyner at first base.

"When you get in the class with Ty Cobb and Rogers Hornsby and Pete Rose, it means a lot," Carew said after reaching 3,000. "This is something I thought I'd never accomplish, but I've been around for 19 years, and if you stay around for 19 years, good things happen to you."

Longest Hitting Streaks in Angels History
28—Garret Anderson (1998)
25—Rod Carew (1982)
23—Anderson (2008), Jim Edmonds (1995)
22—Sandy Alomar (1970)
21—Darin Erstad (2005), Robb Quinlan (2004), Randy Velarde (1996), Bobby Grich (1981)
20—Kendrys Morales (2009), Vladimir Guerrero (2006), Tim Salmon (2003), Grich (1979)

Carew returned to the Angels as the hitting coach in 1992 and stayed there through 1999. When Mike Scioscia was hired as manager for the 2000 season, he chose Mickey Hatcher to be his hitting coach.

Carew was instrumental in the development of a number of Angels hitters, none more so than Garret Anderson, who has become the franchise's all-time hits leader.

"Each year we would work on something new," Carew said. "One year it might be elevating the ball into the gaps, another it might be going the other way. Because I was honest and shot straight with him, he trusted me and took to heart the things I was trying to teach him. Garret plays the game identical to the way I did, so it made my job easier."

Carew is a hero in his home country of Panama, where he has retained his citizenship.

"Every time I go back and walk the streets, the kids know who I am," he said. "They know what I've done and can recite all my accomplishments for all the years I played in the big leagues. I kept my citizenship there because I wanted kids to have someone to look up to and say, 'If Rod Carew can make it, any of us can.'"

16 Watch a Gene Autry Movie

Gene Autry is the only performer ever to be awarded stars on the Hollywood Walk of Fame in five categories (film, television, music, radio, and live performance). He was a telegrapher for the St. Louis–San Francisco Railway after leaving high school in 1925 and often brought along his guitar so he could pass the time while working the late shift.

Gene Autry Movies

Before becoming an owner of a Major League Baseball team, Gene Autry appeared in 94 films from 1934 to 1959.

In Old Santa Fe (1934)	The Old Barn Dance (1938)
Mystery Mountain (1934)	Gold Mine in the Sky (1938)
The Phantom Empire (1935)	Man from Music Mountain (1938)
Tumbling Tumbleweeds (1935)	Prairie Moon (1938)
Melody Trail (1935)	Rhythm of the Saddle (1938)
The Sagebrush Troubadour (1935)	Western Jamboree (1938)
The Singing Vagabond (1935)	Home on the Prairie (1939)
Red River Valley (1936)	Mexicali Rose (1939)
Comin' Round the Mountain (1936)	Blue Montana Skies (1939)
The Singing Cowboy (1936)	Mountain Rhythm (1939)
Guns and Guitars (1936)	Colorado Sunset (1939)
Ride Ranger Ride (1936)	In Old Monterey (1939)
Oh, Susanna! (1936)	Rovin' Tumbleweeds (1939)
The Big Show (1936)	South of the Border (1939)
The Old Corral (1936)	Rancho Grande (1940)
Round-Up Time in Texas (1937)	Shooting High (1940)
Git Along Little Dogies (1937)	Gaucho Serenade (1940)
Rootin' Tootin' Rhythm (1937)	Carolina Moon (1940)
Yodelin' Kid from Pine Ridge (1937)	Ride, Tenderfoot, Ride (1940)
Public Cowboy No. 1 (1937)	Melody Ranch (1940)
Boots and Saddles (1937)	Ridin' on a Rainbow (1941)
Springtime in the Rockies (1937)	Back in the Saddle (1941)

One night while singing and strumming his guitar, Autry had a chance meeting with Will Rogers, who encouraged Autry to pursue a career in music. As soon as he saved up enough money, Autry was off to New York, and a legendary entertainment career was born.

Autry's roots were in music, but he benefited from the onset of the electronic age and eventually turned to radio and then naturally to television and film. Autry made his film debut in 1934 in *In Old Santa Fe*, as part of a singing cowboy quartet. In 1935 he landed the lead role in the 12-part serial *The Phantom Empire*.

44

The Singing Hill (1941)	Mule Train (1950)
Sunset in Wyoming (1941)	Cow Town (1950)
Under Fiesta Stars (1941)	Hoedown (1950)
Down Mexico Way (1941)	Beyond the Purple Hills (1950)
Sierra Sue (1941)	Indian Territory (1950)
Cowboy Serenade (1942)	The Blazing Sun (1950)
Heart of the Rio Grande (1942)	Gene Autry and the Mounties (1951)
Home in Wyomin' (1942)	Texans Never Cry (1951)
Stardust on the Sage (1942)	Whirlwind (1951)
Call of the Canyon (1942)	Silver Canyon (1951)
Bells of Capistrano (1942)	The Hills of Utah (1951)
Sioux City Sue (1946)	Valley of Fire (1951)
Trail to San Antone (1947)	The Old West (1952)
Twilight on the Rio Grande (1947)	Night Stage to Galveston (1952)
Saddle Pals (1947)	Apache Country (1952)
Robin Hood of Texas (1947)	Barbed Wire (1952)
The Last Round-Up (1947)	Wagon Team (1952)
The Strawberry Roan (1948)	Blue Canadian Rockies (1952)
Loaded Pistols (1948)	Winning of the West (1953)
The Big Sombrero (1949)	On Top of Old Smoky (1953)
Riders of the Whistling Pines (1949)	Goldtown Ghost Riders (1953)
Rim of the Canyon (1949)	Pack Train (1953)
The Cowboy and the Indians (1949)	Saginaw Trail (1953)
Riders in the Sky (1949)	Last of the Pony Riders (1953)
Sons of New Mexico (1949)	Alias Jesse James (1959)

In all, Autry appeared in 94 films from 1934–59, and he also starred in 91 episodes of *The Gene Autry Show* television series. He made his final on-screen appearance as an actor in the 1985 TV movie *All-American Cowboy*.

Autry's movies always featured Autry as the good guy trying to do the right thing, overcoming adversity, and ultimately saving the day. He played his guitar and sang, and he always had his trusty horse, Champion.

His movies had a pure and simple message, a sharp contrast to the more violent westerns that were made in subsequent years. "I could never have played scenes like where the Sundance Kid kicks the guy in the nuts [in *Butch Cassidy and the Sundance Kid*] or anything like Clint Eastwood does," Autry said. "I couldn't shoot a man in the back. I couldn't take a drink at a bar. They would have run me out of town."

Just as his film career was taking off, Autry took off overseas and served in the military during World War II. He was a C–47 Skytrain pilot in the U.S. Air Force, holding the rank of Flight Officer in the Air Transport Command, and he flew missions over the Himalayas between Burma and China.

Autry always knew the difference between real heroes and those he played on film.

"I think the he-men in the movies belong in the Army, Marine, Navy, or Air Corps," Autry said in 1942. "All of these he-men in the movies realize that right now is the time to get into the service. Every movie cowboy ought to devote time to the Army winning, or to helping win, until the war is over—the same as any other American citizen. The Army needs all the young men it can get, and if I can set a good example for the young men, I'll be mighty proud."

17 ALCS 2002—They Win, They're In!

After disposing of the storied and powerful New York Yankees in the American League Division Series, the Angels still had one obstacle standing in the way of their first World Series in franchise history. While the Yankees boasted a classic history and played in hallowed Yankee Stadium, the Angels' opponent in the American League Championship Series could not have been more different.

The Minnesota Twins had been threatened with contraction and played their games indoors in the ugly Metrodome on artificial turf with a blow-up roof. But they still presented a significant challenge to the Angels because of their pitching.

And in Game 1, the Twins did something the Yankees could not—shut down the explosive Angels offense. Twins starter Joe Mays gave up just one unearned run and four hits in eight innings. He retired the final 13 batters he faced and handed over the ball to closer Eddie Guardado, who pitched a scoreless ninth to finish off a 2–1 victory.

The Angels had faced Roger Clemens, Andy Pettitte, Mike Mussina, and David Wells in the series against the Yankees, but it was the lesser-known Mays who shut down the Angels.

"It doesn't matter what the names are, it matters where you throw the ball," Angels first baseman Scott Spiezio said. "He didn't give us pitches to hit. There was very little in the zone where you could be aggressive. It seems like we took the same approach up there, but you can only do what the pitcher gives you."

In Game 2, the Angels quickly made it clear the offense would not remain stuck in the mud. Darin Erstad, the second batter of the game, hit a two-strike pitch from Twins pitcher Rick Reed over the fence in center field for a 1–0 lead. The Angels scored three runs in the second inning, then in the sixth, Brad Fullmer's two-run homer put the Angels ahead comfortably at 6–0.

Angels starting pitcher Ramon Ortiz, shaky in his first playoff start against the Yankees, shut out the Twins through five innings, but gave up three runs in the sixth and couldn't make it out of the inning.

Once again, the Angels bullpen came to the rescue as Brendan Donnelly, Francisco Rodriguez, and Troy Percival shut down the Twins for the final 3⅔ innings to close it out and tie the series at one game apiece.

"I hope I never see that guy again," the Twins' Doug Mientkiewicz said of Rodriguez, the 20-year-old phenom called up from the minors only a month earlier in September. "That stuff should be in another league. That's some of the best stuff I've ever seen."

In Game 3, the Angels' Jarrod Washburn and the Twins' Eric Milton locked horns in a pitcher's duel. Garret Anderson homered in the second inning to give the Angels an early 1–0 lead, and it held up until Washburn surrendered a two-out RBI double to Jacque Jones in the seventh.

In the bottom of the eighth with Milton out of the game, the Angels got all the offense they needed when Troy Glaus homered off J.C. Romero to put the Angels up 2–1. Percival again closed it out with a scoreless ninth but not without some big help from the defense. Alex Ochoa, in right field as a defensive replacement for Salmon, made a diving catch on a drive hit by Mientkiewicz leading off the inning. And Anderson's sliding catch on A.J. Pierzynski's blooper was the final out of the game.

The Angels had a 2–1 win and a 2–1 series lead.

"I don't know how to describe that," Twins manager Ron Gardenhire said. "That was a great baseball game. I mean, you really feel proud to be a part of something like that. We pitched very good. They pitched very good. They made some great plays at the end. Does it get any better than that?"

Apparently, yes, it does. At least for the Angels.

In Game 4, the baseball world got a taste of things to come as rookie John Lackey pitched the game of his life, holding the Twins scoreless on three hits through seven innings.

Twins starter Brad Radke held the Angels scoreless through six, but the Angels scored twice in the seventh and then broke through for five runs in the eighth against the Twins bullpen to put the game away in an eventual 7–1 win.

"It's all blurry to me, or dreamlike," Salmon said. "The last couple of weeks have been so exciting; there's been so much energy.

And we're experiencing everything for the first time. I've been in the league 10 years, and I feel like a rookie."

Taking a 3–1 series lead was nice, but by no means were the Angels comfortable. After all, the victory came on the 16th anniversary of Game 5 of the 1986 ALCS and Dave Henderson's series-changing home run off Donnie Moore.

"Somehow we've got to take [Game 5] like all the other games we've played," Angels shortstop David Eckstein said. "If there's too much emotion, you can't keep your focus. But the reason we're in this situation is because we've been able to deal with situations like this all year. It seems like we've been playing playoff games since the All-Star break."

One more win and they were in. But that last victory to reach the World Series had been in front of them before. The Angels took nothing for granted and left no doubt. A 10-run seventh inning in Game 5, highlighted by Adam Kennedy's third home run of the game, lifted the Angels to a 13–5 series-clinching victory.

The Angels had previously played six games with a chance to advance to the World Series but lost all six—three to Milwaukee in 1982 and three to Boston in 1986. But No. 7 was their lucky number.

The Angels were in the World Series.

18 No Fish Tale—Tim Salmon

No Angel has hit more home runs than Tim Salmon.

And no Angel has struck out more than Tim Salmon.

Salmon's Major League Baseball career lasted 14 seasons—all 14 in an Angels uniform—and was full of ups and downs, very much reflective of the Angels organization itself.

Tim Salmon rounds the bases after hitting a solo home run against the Texas Rangers during the second inning of a game on Saturday, August 5, 2006, in Anaheim, California. (AP Photo/Jeff Lewis)

Salmon was the American League Rookie of the Year in 1993, but he never made an All-Star team. His 299 home runs are the most in franchise history, as are his 1,360 strikeouts. He was a big part of some bad 1990s teams and other 1990s teams that were good but collapsed in the end. He was also a big part of the 2002 World Series championship team.

But before finally nabbing that trophy and holding it aloft to the appreciative crowd after the Game 7 victory over the San Francisco Giants, however, Salmon nearly became an ex-Angel like so many others before and after him.

Salmon went to spring training in 2001 knowing his contract was due to expire after the season, making him a free agent. He had grown up in the Phoenix area, was raising his family there, and was seriously considering signing with the Arizona Diamondbacks. That is, if the Angels didn't trade him there first.

But in March 2001, before any of that could happen, Salmon signed a four-year contract with the Angels that would make him an Angel for good. The key moment came a month earlier when Salmon was in Orange County for his charity golf tournament. He decided to stop by the Angels' offices and chat with general manager Bill Stoneman. Salmon didn't know Stoneman well, as Stoneman had become the club's GM only one year earlier.

Salmon had concerns that Stoneman's reputation as being fiscally frugal would result in a rebuilding mode and forsake winning in the immediate future. "The real turning point was meeting with Bill and discussing the issues," Salmon said. "It was nice to see a philosophy and a game plan, and being let in on that vision."

Stoneman made the most of his chance meeting with Salmon.

"I considered it an opportunity to talk and to share some of my own views, and he shared his," Stoneman said. "I'm not the sort of person who's open with what I'm going to do tomorrow, and sometimes that gets in the way of what I want to accomplish.... I guess what I said to him was what he wanted to hear."

Salmon's contract was four years and $40 million, not chump change by any means, but had he tested the free-agent market, he stood to make more.

"The way the market's shaping up, it would probably put him at $12-13 million per year," Ted Updike, Salmon's agent, said at the time. "His decision to stay has effectively cost him $6-10 million or more. His goal has never been to get top dollar. He wants to play the game and be compensated fairly in the industry he's in.... We didn't approach it saying, 'There are our demands.' Our approach was, 'Where do we fit in?' I wish there were more Tim Salmon–type stories in the sports pages. To find stories like this, you have to go to *Readers Digest*."

Salmon retired after the 2006 season, but he is still around, working as part of the television broadcast team with the club.

"I always felt if you had a chance to stay in the same place your whole career, it would be something special," Salmon said. "It's like in college where you have an alma mater. It's something you're behind. That's what I have with the Angels. I really feel it's a part of my family. I look around and see coaches I saw when I was in A-ball, scuffling. It's nice to have those long-lasting relationships."

19 Heart of a Hero—Jim Abbott

He pitched in the major leagues for 10 seasons, winning 87 and losing 108. He won as many as 18 games one season, but he also lost 18 another season. A quick glance at his bubble-gum card seems to reveal nothing more than a guy who was a decent pitcher but was nothing special.

That couldn't be further from the truth.

Jim Abbott was a true hero in a game in which the term is used far too often. And he wasn't a hero simply because he pitched in the major leagues despite being born without a right hand.

It was how Abbott handled himself as a kid who was often teased, and how Abbott handled himself as a professional athlete

Rookie pitcher Jim Abbott delivers a pitch against the Boston Red Sox on his way to a four-hit shutout in Boston on August 31, 1989. Abbott helped his team to a 4–0 victory and ended a nine-game winning streak by the Red Sox. The left-handed pitcher, born without a right hand, was given a standing ovation by Fenway Park fans after the win. (AP Photo/David M. Tenenbaum)

some said wasn't ready for the big leagues when the Angels put him on the roster as a 21-year-old rookie. And yet it is Abbott who expresses thanks for the opportunities he earned.

"I look at my career in terms of living up to ability," said Abbott, who went directly from college at Michigan to the major leagues with the Angels in 1989. "Regardless of how I was born, I was blessed. I was given a lot and had an obligation to live up to those talents. I know that my playing has touched people, and I'm incredibly thankful for that, too. I am extremely grateful to baseball for allowing me to have touched so many lives."

With constant practice and the help of his dad while growing up, Abbott learned to switch his right-hander's glove back and forth from his right arm to his left hand. It became natural for him, and he was a natural in other sports, as well.

Abbott not only was a standout baseball player in high school, he was also the quarterback of the football team and a forward on the basketball team.

"My dad wanted me to get into sports and get involved, but he wanted me to do it with sportsmanship and hard work," Abbott said. "He wanted me to do it the way other kids were doing it. There was no special pat on the back for 'great job just for trying.' He definitely had expectations of doing things the right way, but he was always more concerned with the lessons that sports held, and I'll always be thankful for that."

Abbott took his talents to the University of Michigan where he won the Golden Spikes Award as the best amateur baseball player in the country and the Sullivan Award as the best amateur athlete in the country.

The Angels drafted him in the first round of the June 1988 draft, but he didn't join the organization right away. He represented the United States on the 1988 Olympic baseball team and was the winning pitcher in the gold-medal game against Japan in Seoul, South Korea.

Despite Abbott's incredible success, the Angels found themselves having to defend the pick as being a legitimate baseball choice and not a publicity stunt.

"That particular year our goal was to come out of the draft with the best left-handed pitcher we could find in the first round," said Bob Fontaine Jr., the Angels' scouting director at the time. "I saw Jim pitch several times before the draft, and our only concern was if he could field his position. There was no question about his stuff and never a question about his makeup. It was clear how far he had come and how badly he wanted to play.

"A lot of people thought we did it for public relations value, but this was only my second year as scouting director and there was no way I was going to use the eighth [overall] pick for P.R. We took Jim solely on his ability to pitch."

Abbott won 12 games his rookie season in 1989, won 10 in 1990, and had his best season in 1991, going 18–11 with a 2.89 ERA. He fell to 7–15 in 1992 and was abruptly traded to the Yankees by general manager Whitey Herzog, who became impatient with contract negotiations.

Abbott was an unspectacular 20–22 in two years with the Yankees, but he did accomplish every pitcher's dream—he threw a no-hitter against the Indians at Yankee Stadium in 1993.

The Angels got him back in a trade in 1995, but Abbott struggled. He went 2–18 in 1996 and was released in spring training of 1997. Abbott took the rest of the season off but returned to the big leagues to pitch for the White Sox in 1998 and the Brewers in 1999.

As remarkable as Abbott's performance on the field was, it was his demeanor off it that touched so many and made a long-lasting impact. "I'd estimate that in Jim's first four years with the team, he personally met thousands of people with disabilities and probably had an emotional impact on every one," said Tim Mead, the Angels' director of publicity. "Everybody wanted a piece of Reggie

[Jackson] when he was with us, but no one has had the sustained impact that Jim did, and no one could have handled it better."

20 1961—Expanding Horizons

Gene Autry may have thought he had to stand on his head and jump through hoops in order to secure an American League expansion franchise, but the work was only just beginning.

Newly named general manager Fred Haney and manager Bill Rigney were commissioned to attend the expansion draft in Boston in December 1960 and form the 1961 Los Angeles Angels. The American League's eight existing teams had to submit a list of 15 players from their 40-man rosters who would be eligible for the draft.

The Angels and the other expansion team—the Washington Senators—would be allowed to pick 28 players, at least three players but not more than four from the existing clubs.

Haney and Rigney each had a different philosophy on their approach to the draft. Haney believed the Angels had to make a big splash, especially since they would be playing in the same town as the Dodgers, so they should draft as many recognizable names as possible. But Rigney leaned toward getting younger players and building for the future.

Haney and Rigney met somewhere in the middle and, helped by scouting reports from the Dodgers and Giants going into the draft, put together a team better than could have been expected.

They won the coin flip and got the first choice, selecting pitcher Eli Grba from the Yankees, and it was Grba who earned the victory in the franchise's first game on April 11, 1961, a 7–2 win over the Baltimore Orioles. Grba went on to win 11 games in '61.

Ken McBride, drafted from the White Sox, led the team with 12 wins and went on to win 24 games over the next two seasons.

The Angels also picked pitcher Dean Chance; who would win a Cy Young Award three years later in 1964; Jim Fregosi, who became a six-time All-Star with the club, and catcher Buck Rodgers, who was the club's starting catcher from 1962–68.

Center fielder Ken Hunt, drafted from the Yankees, played in a team-high 149 games and hit 25 homers with 84 RBIs. Catcher Earl Averill, taken from the White Sox, hit .266 with 21 homers.

Haney also got creative, using some of the players taken in the draft to make trades. The Angels drafted Jim McAnany from the White Sox, traded him to the Cubs for Lou Johnson, then traded Johnson to Toronto of the International League for Leon "Daddy Wags" Wagner.

Wagner led the Angels that first season in 1961 with 28 homers and 79 RBIs while batting .280. Haney also traded draftees Bob Cerv and Tex Clevenger to the Yankees for Lee Thomas. Thomas,

Original Angels

Here are the original Angels as selected by general manager Fred Haney and manager Bill Rigney in the 1961 American League expansion draft:

Pitchers: Dean Chance, Eli Grba, Fred Newman, Duke Maas, Tex Clevenger, Ned Garver, Bob Davis, Bob Sprout, Aubrey Gatewood, Ken McBride, Jerry Casale, and Ron Moeller.

Infielders: Julio Becquer, Steve Bilko, Eddie Yost, Ken Hamlin, Ken Aspromonte, Gene Leek, Jim Fregosi, Ted Kluszewski, and Don Ross.

Outfielders: Albie Pearson, Jim McAnany, Ken Hunt, Bob Cerv, and Faye Throneberry.

Catchers: Buck Rodgers, Red Wilson, Earl Averill, and Ed Sadowski.

who could play first base and the outfield, hit 24 home runs, drove in 70, and batted .284 in 1961.

A couple of the club's most productive players in 1961 came not from the major league expansion draft but a draft of minor league players. The clubs could pick two, and the Angels chose Steve Bilko and Albie Pearson.

Bilko, a first baseman, hit .279 with 20 homers and 59 RBIs, and Pearson, a small but spunky right fielder, led the team with a .288 batting average and 11 stolen bases.

The Angels wound up going 70–91 in 1961 but actually had a winning record (46–36) at home in L.A.'s Wrigley Field. All in all, not bad for a team not many expected would win even as many as 50 games.

Ken Aspromonte, the club's second baseman drafted from the Indians, predicted before the season that the 1961 Angels would "fool a lot of people. We've been called rinky-dinks and fringe players. Well, that's wrong. A lot of us are guys who only need a break. We're a bunch of angry men."

21 The Supernatural— Mike Trout

"Mickey Mantle."

Scouts have said watching Mike Trout's combination of power and speed reminds them of Mickey Mantle. No pressure, kid.

"The Supernatural."

That was the headline on the cover of *Sports Illustrated* in August 2012 that included a picture of Trout holding a bat behind his head. No pressure, kid.

The praise has come furiously, and it's all Trout's fault. His 2012 season was one that had historians thumbing through the record books, his numbers only surpassed by the sheer awe one felt when watching him play. And he just turned 21 on August 7, 2012.

"He's as advanced at his age as any player I've seen," Angels manager Mike Scioscia said. "He's still a work in progress—but what a work."

Trout finished the 2012 season as the American League leader in stolen bases and runs scored, and was second in batting average. He became the first player in major league history to hit .320 or better (.326) with at least 45 stolen bases (49), 125 runs (129), and 30 home runs (30) in one season.

He joined Tim Salmon (1993) as the only Rookie of the Year Award winners in Angels history, and he finished second in the AL MVP voting behind Detroit's Miguel Cabrera.

"He has special tools," Scioscia said. "I think his ability to change a game in so many ways, whether it's in center field or on the base paths or in the batter's box, you don't see many players that are so dynamic they can change games in so many different ways.

"He has a special package of speed, power, and strength. You are talking about a Rickey Henderson type, is what you are talking about with Mike Trout."

No pressure, kid.

His humble approach helped Trout through his rookie season as the hype grew as quickly as his numbers. He kept things simple, focused on his job, and let everything else take care of itself.

"My job is to get on base," said Trout, who finished 2012 with an on-base percentage of .399, the third best in the league. "If I have to hit with two strikes all the time, I will do it. I tell myself to shorten up and sometimes it helps me. I choke up, make that bat shorter, and I'm getting good results with it.

"Just making the pitcher throw pitches, seeing pitches, recognizing what he's throwing. I like to take a pitch and relay that information back to my teammates in the dugout."

Trout was drafted by the Angels in the first round of the 2009 draft out of Millville High School in Millville, New Jersey. Two years later, in 2011, he was in the big leagues.

Trout got 123 at-bats in 2011, staying under the limit of 130 to maintain rookie status for 2012. He didn't start the 2012 season in the majors, however, as an illness during spring training kept him out of action, and he began the year in the minors.

But by the end of April 2012, he was up in the big leagues to stay. Despite his sudden success, he's still a sponge, soaking up information from players including Torii Hunter and Albert Pujols. And even an All-Star and nine-time Gold Glove winner like Hunter is impressed.

"This guy is working the count, short swing, getting on base, hitting line drives, and he has speed," Hunter said. "You need a guy like that. I tell everyone that he is Rickey Henderson. He has all the intangibles. He can walk, steal bases, hit for average, hit for power. He plays defense and will only get better out there.

"If he stays healthy and focuses, he's on his way to the Hall of Fame."

No pressure, kid.

"There's always going to be pressure," Trout said. "Once you get on the field, you tell yourself it's just a game. You have been playing it since you were a kid.

"I just tell myself to be myself instead of going up there and trying to hit a home run every time. Just get on base, do my job, do what's best for the team. Get on base and let Albert, [Mark] Trumbo, and all the big guys get me in."

Good luck, kid.

22 "California" (i.e., Anaheim) Here They Come

Long Beach Angels. Gene Autry just did not like the sound of it.

The Los Angeles Angels' four-year stay at Dodger Stadium started out well when they moved in for the 1962 season, but it became increasingly clear the longer they stayed there that one stadium was not big enough for two teams.

After playing their first season in L.A.'s Wrigley Field in 1961, the Angels signed a four-year lease to play at Dodger Stadium, and Dodgers owner Walter O'Malley publicly proclaimed the Angels a welcome addition.

But Autry later said the Dodgers "dollared us to death." Besides having to pay the Dodgers a $350,000 "indemnification" fee, the Dodgers charged the Angels for things like landscaping, window cleaning, and upkeep of the parking lot even though the Angels received no compensation in parking revenue.

The Angels had the option to extend the lease three years beyond 1965, through the 1968 season, but Autry knew he had to find a new home for his team. In fact, when he first purchased the Angels, Branch Rickey, the former general manager of the Dodgers, warned Autry about the perils of sharing a city, let alone a stadium, with another team. Rickey pointed to Philadelphia (A's and Phillies), Boston (Braves and Red Sox), and St. Louis (Browns and Cardinals), where teams struggled to survive when sharing a city.

So Autry instructed his business manager Cedric Tallis to find a new home for his club, and Tallis soon found Long Beach, 30 miles south of Los Angeles but still accessible from Los Angeles and the surrounding areas that were on the brink of significant population growth.

Home Sweet Home

Anaheim Stadium opened on April 9, 1966, with an exhibition game between the Angels and the San Francisco Giants. It was completed at a cost of $24 million, and its centerpiece was the giant A-frame scoreboard that stood 230 feet high and prompted the stadium's nickname, the Big A.

Initially with a seating capacity of 43,250, the stadium underwent reconstruction in 1979 to create additional seating to accommodate the coming of the NFL's Los Angeles Rams. Seating capacity became 64,593 for baseball and more than 70,000 for football.

After the Rams left, renovations to return the stadium to a baseball-only park began in 1996 for an estimated cost of $100 million. The project was completed in time for the start of the 1998 season, and the stadium was renamed Edison International Field. The stadium was renamed again prior to the 2004 season to Angel Stadium after Edison opted out of its naming rights agreement.

The stadium has been host to three All-Star games (1967, 1989, and 2010), and four World Series games (Games 1, 2, 6, and 7 in 2002).

The biggest crowd ever to see a baseball game at the stadium occurred on October 5, 1982, for Game 1 of the American League Championship Series between the Angels and Milwaukee Brewers. That day there were 64,406 fans who witnessed the Angels beat the Brewers 8–3.

Negotiations seemed to go well until they hit a snag and neither side would budge. The city of Long Beach insisted the team should be called the Long Beach Angels. Autry refused, citing marketing limitations related to the Long Beach name. Autry's team would remain the Los Angeles Angels or be renamed the California Angels.

It didn't take long once Long Beach was eliminated before Anaheim got involved. Autry was already familiar with Anaheim because of his ties to Walt Disney, who had opened Disneyland there in 1955.

Anaheim and Orange County had been an agricultural region, but Autry realized the potential of a population explosion and even conducted a study that predicted a population belt stretching from Mexico to Santa Barbara, with Anaheim smack in the middle.

And what about the team's name?

"I don't give a damn," said Anaheim mayor Rex Coons. "Why should I? I know every broadcast, every dateline will have Anaheim in it."

Starting with the 1966 season, the California Angels were born.

1962

Ask most any Angels fan which is the greatest season in club history, and you're sure to hear "2002."

After all, it was the first—and so far only—World Series championship for the franchise.

But talk to some old-timers, and you'll get a different answer, World Series or no World Series.

"Anybody who played on that team back in '62 will tell you it was the greatest Angels season ever," said Dean Chance, a pitcher on that Angels team. "We had so much fun, and we were in the race all season."

The Angels ultimately finished 86–76 and in third place in the 10-team American League, 10 games behind the first-place Yankees and five games behind the second-place Twins. But they sure made things interesting along the way.

The Angels didn't get off to a necessarily hot start, playing .500 baseball for the first month of the season. But they got a sign it might be a special season on May 5 when Bo Belinsky threw a no-hitter.

They played well in May, winning 17-of-28 games, and by the start of June they found themselves only two games out of first place.

The Angels embraced their sudden success, and playing in brand-new Dodger Stadium brought in the Hollywood types. When the Yankees visited, the ballpark was full, and Marilyn Monroe even threw out the ceremonial first pitch before one of the games.

The Angels got big seasons from a variety of sources. Left fielder Leon "Daddy Wags" Wagner hit 37 home runs, drove in 107, and was named the MVP in one of two major league All-Star games that year.

First baseman Lee Thomas hit .290 with 26 homers and 104 RBIs, and second baseman Billy Moran hit .282 with 17 homers and 74 RBIs. On the mound, 21-year-old Chance led the team with 14 wins, Ken McBride won 11, and Belinsky won 10.

When the Angels swept a double header from the Washington Senators on July 4, they moved into first place, one-half game ahead of both the Yankees and Indians.

The 1962 season also saw the debut as a starter of a 20-year-old phenom named Jim Fregosi, who, along with 23-year-old starting catcher Buck Rodgers, formed a solid foundation with the club for the rest of the 1960s.

And manager Bill Rigney knew it.

"We were in first place on the 4th of July with this ragtag bunch," Rodgers said, "but Bill Rigney was a magician in finding out what guys cannot do. That's one thing he told me and Fregosi—he always talked to us like we were going to be managers, like he knew that—he said the biggest thing about managing is finding out what a guy cannot do, and then don't let him do it. We had platoon players, we had bullpen by committee, and all those things meshed into a ballclub, so pretty soon we said, 'You know, we're pretty good.'"

The 1962 season, however, also marked the beginning of what became a hallmark with the club over the years—the freak injury. Outfielder Ken Hunt, who hit 25 homers with 84 RBIs the year before in the Angels' debut season, broke his collarbone while warming up in the on-deck circle in April and played in only 13 games in '62. Then in August, pitcher Art Fowler, having a solid season out of the bullpen, was hit in the eye by a batted ball during batting practice at Fenway Park in Boston. He had a nasty gash above his left eye and didn't pitch again that year. He eventually lost sight in that eye. The very next day, McBride, who was considered the ace of the staff, was found to have a cracked rib. He missed six weeks, and even though he returned late in the season, he didn't win another game.

Still, with Rigney pulling the strings, the Angels were able to work some magic and were just four games out of first place after a 9–0 win over the Twins on September 11. But they ran out of steam from there, losing six in a row and 12 of their final 16 to come up short—a valiant try for a ragtag group of ballplayers.

1982

If baseball teams were judged by what they look like on paper, it would be difficult to argue that there has ever been an Angels team better than the club from 1982.

In January 1982, the Angels announced the free-agent signing of Reggie Jackson, making the club the first in baseball history to have four former MVPs on the same roster.

Of course, only one won his MVP while with the Angels—Don Baylor in 1979. The others were Fred Lynn (1975 with the Red Sox), Rod Carew (1977 with the Twins), and Jackson (1973 with the A's).

General manager Buzzie Bavasi didn't stop there. He traded Dan Ford to the Orioles for third baseman Doug DeCinces. He also traded for Tim Foli, who became the starting shortstop when Rick Burleson was injured in spring training.

Throw in returning players like second baseman Bobby Grich and catcher-turned-outfielder Brian Downing, and the Angels had the most-feared lineup in baseball. Not only did they have four MVPs, they had eight players in the starting lineup who were All-Stars at some point during their careers.

With a lineup like that, pitching didn't have to be perfect. The Angels had a decent starting staff led by Geoff Zahn who went on to win 18 games in '82.

"It was the most talented team I played on," Grich said. "And we were a smart team, too. Everyone knew how to play the game. I couldn't wait to get to the ballpark every night. It was fun. It was exciting."

These Angels, though, were not young. The starting lineup averaged 33 years of age, and the starting rotation averaged 34.

"What we have here is a very talented team that can't afford to let this opportunity get away," Downing said before the start of the season. "Many of us don't have a lot of years left."

The Angels got off to a fast start, winning 16 of their first 23 games and taking control of the American League West. But the race remained tight during the first half of the season, as the Angels held a one-game lead over the Royals at the All-Star break.

The Royals eventually passed the Angels and took over first place in late August and held the lead until the Angels finally caught them on September 19. The Angels regained first place the next day and held the lead the rest of the way, winning the division by three games with a 93–69 record.

The Angels offense had lived up to expectations. Jackson set a club record with 39 home runs and led the team with 101 RBIs. DeCinces hit 30 homers and batted .301, Carew hit .319, and

Tommy John delivers a pitch during the first game of a five-game ALCS against the Milwaukee Brewers on Tuesday, October 6, 1982, in Anaheim, California. John gave up seven hits, leading the Angels to an 8–3 win over the Brewers.
(AP Photo)

Downing, Lynn, and Baylor each hit 21 home runs or more and drove in 84 or more.

All that stood in the way of the club's first World Series appearance was the Milwaukee Brewers, winners of the AL East. They had an imposing lineup themselves, known as Harvey's Wallbangers in reference to their manager Harvey Kuenn. They had Gorman Thomas, Cecil Cooper, Robin Yount, Paul Molitor, Ted Simmons, and Ben Oglivie, and they led the league in runs scored and home runs.

The Angels won the first two games of the best-of-five series in Anaheim. In an 8–3 Game 1 victory, Baylor had two hits and drove in five runs, and Lynn had three hits, including a home run.

In a 4–2 Game 2 victory, Bruce Kison threw a complete-game five-hitter and got offensive help from Jackson, who hit what would be his only postseason home run as an Angel.

Needing to win one out of three in Milwaukee, the Angels faced an aging Don Sutton as the Brewers starting pitcher in Game 3, but Sutton kept the Angels in check in a 5–3 Brewers victory.

"The Brewers came to Anaheim flat as a door latch, and we just walked all over them," Grich said. "But by the time we got to Milwaukee, they were all rejuvenated. Don Sutton pitched Game 3, and it was overcast and tough to see the ball.

"Everyone came back to the dugout saying, 'I couldn't see the ball.' If they had turned on the lights, I think we would have won that game. Sutton was throwing 82 mph and couldn't break a pane of glass. We should have hammered him, but that was the great equalizer then, not turning the lights on, on a gray, overcast day."

It only got gloomier for the Angels from there. After losing Game 4 9–5, and Game 5 4–3, the second-guessing began. Angels manager Gene Mauch was criticized for not starting pitcher Ken Forsch, who had won 13 games during the regular season, in either Game 4 or 5. Instead, Mauch went with Tommy John (Game 4) and Kison (Game 5) on three days rest.

And in Game 5, another decision came back to haunt Mauch. With the Angels leading 3–2 in the seventh inning, the Brewers had the bases loaded with two outs and the left-handed hitting Cooper at the plate.

But instead of going to left-handed reliever Andy Hassler out of the bullpen, Mauch stuck with righty Luis Sanchez. Naturally, Cooper hit a two-run single that gave the Brewers the lead and eventually a win that sent them to the World Series.

Said Baylor, who left the Angels after that season and would come back to haunt the Angels in 1986 when playing for the Red Sox, "I had a lot of hurtful things happen in my career, but losing a series with that team...well, that one really hurt."

25 The Little General— Gene Mauch

Gene Mauch was a great manager, loved by Angels owner Gene Autry and respected by the players on the four teams he guided for 26 seasons.

Unfortunately, Mauch may be regarded as one of the biggest hard-luck losers in baseball history. In fact, he is by far the winningest manager to have never won a pennant, compiling a 1,902–2,037 won-lost record as manager of the Phillies, Expos, Twins, and Angels.

He was the manager of the division-winning Angels in 1982 and '86 when they came within one win of reaching the World Series before losing three straight in each series to drop each series.

Before his disappointment with the Angels, Mauch was also a tough-luck loser with the Phillies in 1964. With no division format

Angels manager Gene Mauch argues with home-plate umpire Dan Morrison after he is thrown out of the game for arguing over a pitch by Angels pitcher Mike Witt in the fourth inning against the Oakland A's on July 30, 1985, at the Oakland Coliseum. (AP Photo/Paul Sakuma)

then, Mauch's Phillies held a 6½-game lead in the National League standings with 12 games to play and a World Series berth on the line.

Mauch was second-guessed for his decision to start his top two starters—Jim Bunning and Chris Short—in seven of those games, six of them on just two days rest. The Phillies lost all of them—10 in a row in fact—before winning their final two games. By then, it was too late. They finished a game behind the National League champion St. Louis Cardinals in what became known as the Phold.

Eighteen years later, Mauch was managing the Angels in 1982 when they took a 2–0 lead in the best-of-five American League

Championship Series against the Milwaukee Brewers. Needing to win just one more game, the Angels lost all three and the Brewers went to the World Series.

Again, Mauch was second-guessed. He started pitchers Tommy John in Game 4 and Bruce Kison in Game 5 on three days rest and decided against using Ken Forsch in either of those games, though Forsch had won 13 games that season.

Mauch was also questioned for a move he didn't make in Game 5. The Angels led 3–2 in the bottom of the seventh, but the Brewers had the bases loaded with two outs. The left-handed hitting Cecil Cooper was up, and Angels' left-handed reliever Andy Hassler was ready in the bullpen.

But Mauch stuck with hard-throwing righty Luis Sanchez, who gave up a two-run single to Cooper and the Brewers would come away with a 4–3 series-clinching victory.

"I think most of us thought, 'Lefty vs. lefty, we'll take our chances,'" Angels designated hitter Don Baylor said. "Gene said he didn't want to risk a wild pitch, but that would have been only one run. The hit was two."

After the season, Mauch was stung by the second-guessing, much of it from his own players, but there was a more serious issue that led to his decision to resign. His wife, Nina Lee, was dying of cancer. "There were just some things that were more important [than baseball]," Mauch explained.

Nina Lee passed away in July 1983, and Mauch later returned to the club as director of player personnel. Following the 1984 season, new general manager Mike Port brought back Mauch to replace John McNamara for the 1985 season.

As disappointing as the failures of 1964 and '82 were for Mauch's teams, they would pale in comparison to 1986. They had a 3–1 series lead over the Red Sox and were one strike away from the American League pennant and a trip to the World Series when Dave Henderson homered off Donnie Moore and turned around the series, not to mention the direction of the franchise and so many lives within it.

Mauch's use of the pitching staff again came into question, but Mauch, as he was in '64 and '82, was defiant and stubborn.

"I've been disappointed, but I've never disappointed myself and never bored myself," Mauch said. "I don't give myself a pep talk this way, but in any of those years, you'd have to find me some SOB who could have gotten the '64 team or the '82 team or the '85 or '86 teams to the point I did, to a position where he could be disappointed. I knew I didn't always make the right decision, but I knew I had the best chance of anyone I knew of being right."

Mauch decided to resign as manager less than two weeks before the start of the 1988 season.

"Show biz," Mauch explained years later. "It wasn't my game anymore, the game I worshipped. People think that's BS, that you can't feel that strongly, but when I left that club, I left a jillion dollars on the table. I never received another cent of income, but it was never about money."

Mauch passed away from lung cancer in 2005 at the age of 79.

"Gene Mauch was the best manager we ever had and a dear friend," said Jackie Autry. "He loved the Cowboy and would have done anything to help him win. I really think he never recovered emotionally from the loss of his wife."

26 Speak Softly, Carry Big Stick—Garret Anderson

Many Angels players have basked in the spotlight in the franchise's 50-plus years, but the most successful Angel—at least, according to the numbers—stayed away from it as much as possible.

Garret Anderson is the Angels' all-time leader in games played (2,013), at-bats (7,989), runs scored (1,024), hits (2,368), total bases (3,743), extra-base hits (796), doubles (489), and RBIs (1,292), but he was never the face of the franchise. And that was his choice.

Anderson preferred to let his bat do the talking.

Fans and writers alike got on Anderson for his perceived lack of hustle or caring. As an example, Anderson rarely if ever dived for balls hit in the outfield. He admits his demeanor was low-key, but he insists he was as passionate about the game as anybody.

"I don't think I was misunderstood, I know I was misunderstood," Anderson said when he retired. "I'm sorry for that. I was who I was, going out and playing hard every day. I know I'm a quiet person."

Anderson finished second in the 1995 American League Rookie of the Year voting to the Twins' Marty Cordova. And in 1996 Anderson began a string of eight consecutive seasons in which he played at least 150 games.

It was the kind of quiet consistency that can often lead to being taken for granted. Despite his impressive numbers, he finished in the top 10 of the MVP voting only once, in 2002 when he was fourth.

The heart of his career came in the four seasons from 2000–03 during which he averaged 30 homers and 120 RBIs and batted .299.

Longest-Tenured Angels

1. Garret Anderson—15 seasons (1994–2008)
2. Chuck Finley—14 (1986–99)
2. Tim Salmon—14 (1992–2004, 2006)
4. Brian Downing—13 (1978–90)
5. Gary DiSarcina—12 (1989–2000)
5. Dick Schofield—12 (1983–92, 1995–96)
7. Darin Erstad—11 (1996–2006)
7. Jim Fregosi—11 (1961–71)

Six Hits, One Game
Two players hold the Angels' record for getting six hits in a game—
Garret Anderson (September 27, 1996) and Chone Figgins (June 18,
2007).
Anderson got his six hits in a 15-inning game, going 6-for-7.
Figgins, though, got his six hits in a nine-inning game, getting hit No.
6 in the bottom of the ninth, driving in the winning run with a triple to
finish the game 6-for-6.

Still, he was named to the All-Star team only three times, though
he made the most of it in 2003. That year he won the Home Run
Derby, and then in the All-Star Game he had a single, double, and
home run on his way to being named the MVP.

Angels manager Mike Scioscia was the American League
manager for the 2003 All-Star game. "He's one of the top five
hitters in the game, and a lot of people don't see it," Scioscia said
after that game. "He's not comfortable with it, but whether he likes
it or not, a lot more people are going to know about him now."

Anderson always said he wasn't one to dwell on his personal
achievements. "My proudest achievement can't be anything indi-
vidual because I can't share it with anybody," Anderson said. "The
proudest has to be the World Series. A lot of great players never
won one. I never got back to one. It's one of the things I hold near
and dear. It was seven months with those guys.... Those memories
I'll always keep close to me."

While many people outside the organization might have
overlooked Anderson, those in the Angels family insist he was
appreciated.

"Garret was an incredible player, one with a calm demeanor
and quiet confidence that allowed him to excel in this game,"
Scioscia said. "Garret's role in where the Angels organization is
today cannot be overstated. He had a tremendous passion to play
this game and a deep understanding of how to play to win, and that
was very important to this organization."

Division Dominance, 2004–09

Before the 2004 season, the Angels had won a total of three American League Western Division titles in the franchise's 43 seasons since 1961.

They won in 1979, '82, and '86, but they did not win the division in 2002 even though that year they went on to win the World Series. In 2002, the Angels won 99 games but finished as the American League wild-card entry, finishing behind the first-place Oakland A's.

But starting in 2004, the tough-luck Angels became a dominating force in the A.L. West, winning the division five times in six seasons. They won it in 2004, '05, '07, '08, and '09.

Only the 2006 season stopped the Angels from a remarkable six consecutive division titles. And that season wasn't exactly a bad one—they went 89–73, finishing four games behind the first-place A's in the West. They didn't win the wild card either, as the Detroit Tigers won 95 games to win the wild card on their way to reaching the World Series.

In 2004 the Angels and A's entered a season-ending three-game series in Oakland tied for first place at 90–69. In Game 1 of the series on October 1, the Angels sent Bartolo Colon to the mound against Oakland's Mark Mulder. It was no contest, as Colon shut out the A's on three hits through seven innings and second baseman Alfredo Amezaga—yes, Alfredo Amezaga—hit a grand slam in the sixth inning to turn a 4–0 game into an 8–0 game in an eventual 10–0 Angels victory.

The Angels knew a victory in the second game of the series would clinch the division crown and a loss would result in one final winner-take-all game, but the Angels removed any drama with a

5–4 win to clinch the division. They trailed 4–2 going into the top of the eighth inning but got a two-run double from Darin Erstad to tie it and an RBI single from Garret Anderson to put the Angels up for good.

The 2004 season was also the season of Vladimir Guerrero who won the club's second AL MVP award ever in his first year with the club. Guerrero hit .337 with 39 homers, 126 RBIs, and a league-high 124 runs scored. The elation of the division title soon ended, though, as the Angels were swept by the Red Sox in the American League Division Series.

In 2005 the Angels clinched the division title in Oakland again, this time a bit earlier, beating the second-place A's 4–3 on September 27 to go six games up with five to play.

The Angels won 95 games that year and had their second Cy Young Award winner in Bartolo Colon, who went 21–8. Offensively, the Angels were again led by Guerrero, who hit .317 with 32 homers and 108 RBIs.

The Angels beat the Yankees in the first round of the play-offs but lost to the White Sox 4–1 in the American League Championship Series that included the infamous "strikeout" of Chicago's A.J. Pierzynski.

In 2007 the Angels finally got to celebrate the division title at home, beating the second-place Mariners on September 23 to clinch the title. The Angels won 94 games and were again matched up with the dreaded Red Sox in the AL Division Series, only to be swept again in three straight games.

Guerrero (.324, 27 homers, 125 RBIs) led the offense, and the pitching staff had a solid 1-2 punch at the top of the starting rota-tion with John Lackey, who won 19 games, and Kelvim Escobar, who won 18 games.

But the disappointing loss to the Red Sox caused a shakeup upstairs, as general manager Bill Stoneman moved into a role as

Senior Advisor and Tony Reagins was promoted to fill Stoneman's place as the GM.

In 2008 the Angels put it all together, winning 100 games in the regular season for the first time in club history and finishing with the best record in the majors. They blew away the competition in the AL West, finishing 21 games ahead of second-place Texas. Guerrero again led the offense, and he got help from Torii Hunter who played his first season in Anaheim after signing a five-year $90 million contract.

The Angels had a solid five-man starting rotation, getting double figures in wins from all five—Joe Saunders won 17, Ervin Santana 16, Jon Garland 14, Lackey 12, and Jered Weaver 11.

But the playoffs again provided a sudden jolt—the Angels lost to the Red Sox in the AL Division Series, managing to avoid a sweep this time but still suffering a disappointing end to the season.

In 2009 the Angels dominated the division again, winning 97 games and winning the division by 10 games over the second-place Rangers.

Guerrero was slowed by injuries, missing 62 games, but the Angels had plenty of offense to pick up the slack. Kendrys Morales led the way with 34 homers and 108 RBIs, and the club also got production from Hunter, Bobby Abreu, Chone Figgins, Juan Rivera, and Mike Napoli.

The big news of 2009 was that the Angels finally broke through against the Red Sox in the playoffs, turning the tables and sweeping them in three straight games. But the Angels' attempt to reach the World Series for a second time was thwarted by the New York Yankees who beat the Angels in six games.

28 Kennedy for President

The Angels' 2002 World Series championship season featured plenty of heroes both during the regular season and in the play-offs, but it would be difficult to find a single performance bigger than that of Adam Kennedy in Game 5 of the American League Championship Series.

The Angels led the series 3–1 but trailed in the game 5–3 going into the bottom of the seventh inning. Kennedy had already hit two home runs in the game, but both of them came with nobody on base.

Scott Spiezio began the inning with a single and went to second base on a single by Bengie Molina. Up next was Kennedy, and Angels manager Mike Scioscia instructed him to bunt.

Yes, bunt.

Despite home runs in Kennedy's first two at-bats in the game, Scioscia had third-base coach Ron Roenicke give Kennedy the bunt sign. Scioscia's thinking was that a successful bunt would move the potential tying runs into scoring position at second and third. And the pitcher was Johan Santana, a hard-throwing lefty.

Kennedy, a left-handed hitter, often sat the bench during the season when the Angels faced a lefty, giving way to right-handed hitting Benji Gil. And in Game 3 of the ALCS, Kennedy did not play because Scioscia started Gil against the Twins' lefty Eric Milton.

Kennedy tried to bunt the first pitch from Santana but fouled it off. Scioscia then took off the bunt, but Santana threw another strike to get ahead in the count 0–2. Then Santana hung a curve-ball, and Kennedy crushed it, driving the ball deep into the seats in right-center field for a 6–5 Angels lead. It was the beginning of a

10-run inning in an eventual 13–5 win that put the Angels in the World Series for the first time in their history.

"My first reaction was that it didn't happen," Darin Erstad said. "I had to get on deck to get myself ready, and I nearly passed out."

Kennedy had achieved what only four players in baseball history had accomplished before—he hit three home runs in a post-season game. Kennedy joined Babe Ruth, Reggie Jackson, George Brett, and Bob Robertson in the exclusive club.

"It was pretty amazing," admitted the soft-spoken Kennedy.

After Kennedy's performance, there were signs at Edison Field held up by fans that said, "Kennedy for President." But Kennedy, the club's No. 9 hitter who led the team in batting average in 2002 (.312), saw himself as just one of the guys. "I just plug along and try to help," Kennedy said. "I'm just a regular player."

During that 2002 season, however, those "regular" players had extraordinary performances. None, though, was more dramatic than Kennedy's.

"That's what we're all about," Spiezio said. "Getting guys you don't expect to contribute. Like A.K. coming out and hitting three home runs in a game like that. You don't expect it, but he did it."

29 Wally Whirl

It began as "Wally World," but ultimately Wally Joyner's time with the Angels was nothing more than a six-year stretch that started red hot and fizzled amid some hard feelings. Joyner burst onto the scene in 1986 as the replacement at first base for Hall of Famer Rod Carew, who was initially bitter after Angels general manager Mike Port told Carew of the club's plans after the 1985 season.

Carew was 40, and his skills had diminished during the 1984 and '85 seasons, a .328 career hitter who failed to hit .300 both seasons as he struggled to stay healthy. Joyner was young (21) and inexpensive—he made $65,000 in 1986—something the cost-conscious Angels could appreciate.

The move could not have turned out better for Joyner and the Angels in the early months of the 1986 season. By the end of May, he had 16 homers and 41 RBIs while batting .305. *Sports Illustrated* did a feature article on the Wally World phenomena, and many fans thought Joyner would be an Angels star forever.

Joyner's appeal spread beyond the home fans in Anaheim and throughout the league, so much so that Joyner was elected the American League's All-Star starter at first base as a write-in candidate, beating out the Yankees' Don Mattingly who was coming off an MVP season.

Joyner's home-run production waned in June and July when he increased his season total to 21, but he still hit the ball well, holding a .315 batting average heading into August. But August was a different animal, as many young players who aren't used to the grind of the season find out.

Joyner even experienced the ugly side of New York when he was grazed by a knife thrown at him by a fan at Yankee Stadium. Fortunately, Joyner escaped injury. His performance on the field, however, took a few lumps. He batted just .232 in August and .239 in September/October as the club forged into their fateful playoff series against the Boston Red Sox.

Joyner and the Angels started off the series hot and won Game 1 8–1. Joyner went 2-for-4, including two doubles off Red Sox starter Roger Clemens.

The Angels lost Game 2 9–2, but Joyner went 2-for-4 again, including a home run off Bruce Hurst. Joyner went 1-for-3 with a walk in a Game 3 victory, but that would be Joyner's final playoff game in an Angels uniform.

Most Home Runs by Position in Angels History
Catcher: Mike Napoli—75
First base: Wally Joyner—116
Second base: Bobby Grich—137
Shortstop: Jim Fregosi—111
Third base: Troy Glaus—169
Left field: Garret Anderson—160
Center field: Jim Edmonds—114
Right field: Tim Salmon—249
Designated hitter: Chili Davis—108
Pinch hitter: Jack Howell—7

Joyner developed a staph infection in his right shin and was hospitalized, missing the rest of the series. The Angels never revealed the source of the injury, and speculation was that he might have been bitten by a spider, or it might have been the result of being spiked on the shin in Game 2.

Joyner had a huge year in 1987, hitting a career-best 34 home runs, driving in 117, and batting .285. He had decent but not spectacular seasons in 1988 and '89, missing half of the 1990 season with injuries, but he rebounded in 1991, hitting .301 with 21 homers and 96 RBIs.

Joyner was a free agent after the 1991 season, but he was still popular with the fans and many expected him to re-sign.

But Joyner made $2.1 million in 1991 and had also beaten the Angels in the arbitration process for two consecutive years. Lee Stevens, another up-and-coming minor leaguer waiting in the wings and seemingly ready for his big-league promotion, provided a cheaper option.

The Angels did offer Joyner a four-year deal worth $15.75 million, but Joyner instead opted to sign a one-year $4.2 million deal with Kansas City after negotiations with Angels general manager Whitey Herzog failed. But Joyner said it wasn't about the money and it wasn't about Herzog, implying a feud with owner Jackie Autry, who had to sign off on any deal.

"I think we all know who Whitey is and what he stands for," Joyner said at a tearful news conference announcing his signing with the Royals. "If he had control and was able to do what he wanted to do, it might have been different. What I found out, as far as myself was concerned, was that he did not have the power he thought he had with me."

According to published reports, it was Jackie Autry who refused to allow Herzog to structure Joyner's contract in such a way that he would get more money up front and less in 1994 when there could be, and ultimately would be, a players strike when no players would be paid. Herzog said the sides were only $500,000 apart, a mere half-million that ended Wally World with a thud.

Joyner ultimately returned to the Angels in 2001 and was excited to be back as Jackie Autry was no longer involved in the team's ownership.

"There's some unfinished business to do," Joyner said upon returning. "I can't think of a better place to finish out my career."

Unfortunately for Joyner, "finishing out" his career came sooner than he might have expected. He played 53 games in 2001 before being released in June, and he retired as an Angel with Wally World a distant memory.

30 Say It Ain't So, Bo— Bo Belinsky

He wasn't an angel—far from it. But no Angel made more of an impact on an organization by doing less on the field than Bo Belinsky.

Belinsky was 28–51 pitching eight seasons in the majors, including a 21–28 mark with the Angels from 1962–64. He was a bane to Bill Rigney, the Angels' first manager, but Belinsky's appeal stretched beyond the mound and Rigney couldn't do much about it.

During his time with the Angels, Belinsky dated Hollywood starlets like Ann Margret and Tina Louise, he was engaged to actress Mamie Van Doren, and he was a popular figure on the Sunset Strip. He was the center of attention at all the biggest Hollywood parties, and he could party with the best of them.

The Angels had just moved from old Wrigley Field in their expansion season of 1961 and drafted Belinsky in the annual draft of minor league free agents. He had already made a mark while in the minor leagues, developing a reputation as someone—as Angels scout Tuffie Hashem famously said—who had "a million-dollar arm and a ten-cent head."

The Angels took a chance on Belinsky anyway, drafting him from the Baltimore Orioles organization and offering him a contract for $6,000.

Belinsky had been pitching in the Venezuelan Winter League and was not aware of his selection initially. Upon returning to his home in Trenton, New Jersey, where he was known as a pool hustler more than anything, he was insulted by the offer when he learned of it.

"I thought it was a joke," Belinsky said years later. "I had played all those years in the minors, and they were offering me the minimum like I was a kid with no record. I told [Angels general manager Fred] Haney I wouldn't sign. I told Haney that if he didn't give me $8,500, then I'd forget about baseball. The hell with it. I had a few things going on in Trenton."

Belinsky didn't report for the start of spring training for the 1962 season, but Haney convinced him to come west and negotiate. Belinsky ultimately signed for the $6,000 provided the club would allow him to renegotiate at midseason.

Rookie pitcher Bo Belinsky gives out with a big smile after he blanked the Boston Red Sox with a two-hit 1–0 victory at Fenway Park on Sunday, May 21, 1962. The rookie southpaw, whose achievements include a no-hitter, threw out six batters himself as he boosted his record to 6–1 as only three balls traveled to the outfield. (AP Photo/Bill Chaplis)

The reluctant Rigney didn't start Belinsky until he had no other option, giving him the ball for a night game against Kansas City on April 19, 1962, at Dodger Stadium, the Angels' first year in Chavez Ravine.

Belinsky won. In his second start against Cleveland, he won again. In start No. 3, he beat Cleveland for a second time. And then in his fourth start, on May 5, 1962, vs. Baltimore, he threw a no-hitter.

"The night before my no-hitter I met this tall, thin, black-haired secretary out at a place on the Sunset Strip," he said. "We had a couple of drinks, and I wound up making it with her at her pad. She wasn't bad. I got home about 4:00 AM and that night pitched my no-hitter. I went back to look for her after the game and couldn't find her. I never found her again. She was my good-luck pitching charm, and when I lost her, I lost all my pitching luck."

However, he did win his next start to go 5–0, and Belinsky was the toast of the town.

"Everybody wanted me at Hollywood parties," he said. "Playing baseball seemed only incidental. It was a little too much,

Bo's Women

Bo Belinsky was known for his Hollywood party lifestyle, which included dating Hollywood starlets. Some of Belinsky's dates included:

Ann Margret
Connie Stevens
Tina Louise
Mamie Van Doren
Jo Collins

Belinsky was engaged to Van Doren, but the two never married. Belinksy married and later divorced Collins, who was a Playboy Playmate of the Year.

even for me. I mean, after hustling in pool halls and living on candy bars, this was something else."

The partying continued, but success on the mound did not. Belinsky finished the 1962 season 10–11 and was nearly traded at the end of the season. He fell to 2–9 in 1963, which included a stint in the minors. In 1964, he improved to 9–8, but by then the Angels had enough.

The last straw came in August of that year when he punched out a reporter in a hotel room, and he was traded to Philadelphia after the season. Belinsky, just 27 at the time, won only seven more games in the majors, the final victory coming while playing for Houston in 1967.

"I went from a major league ballplayer to hanging on to a brown bag under the bridge," said Belinsky, who died in 2001 at age 64. "But I had my moments, and I have my memories."

31 Tragedy in Gary, Indiana— Lyman Bostock

Lyman Bostock played less than one season with the Angels in his abbreviated major league career, but his impact was as powerful as any player who wore an Angels uniform. Bostock, 27, was shot in the face while sitting in the back seat of a car in Gary, Indiana, on September 23, 1978. He was a victim of simply being in the wrong place at the wrong time.

But Bostock's short life was a glimmer of light for those who knew him. Bostock moved with his mother from Gary, Indiana, to South Los Angeles at the age of eight, became a standout baseball player at Manual Arts High School, and went on to play at San Fernando Valley State College (now Cal State Northridge).

He was drafted in the 26th round by the Minnesota Twins in 1972 and reached the big leagues in 1975. He quickly made an impact, batting .282 in 98 games his rookie season before taking off the next two seasons in Minnesota.

He hit .323 in 1976 but actually had his 1977 salary reduced to $20,000 because the small-market Twins knew they would not be able to retain Bostock when his contract ran out after the 1977 season.

Bostock hit 14 home runs, drove in 90 runs, and batted .336 in 1977, finishing in second place to teammate Rod Carew (.388) in the American League batting race. Angels owner Gene Autry, anxious for that first championship, was more than willing to pay Bostock his fair value and signed the outfielder to a five-year $2.25 million deal.

Bostock turned down potentially more money from the Yankees and Mets to play close to home. "I was very close to signing with the Yankees," Bostock said after signing with the Angels. "But with all that controversy, I thought I might wind up being a vegetable. I'm not a flashy guy; I'm not a Joe Namath or Clyde Frazier."

Bostock, though, wasn't even Lyman Bostock once the 1978 season started. After an 0-for-4 game against Toronto on April 29, Bostock, whose average fell to .147, made an unthinkable offer. He wanted to return his salary for the month back to Autry, who flatly refused. "We wouldn't give him a raise if he had a good month," Autry explained, "so I'm not going to withhold his pay just because he had a bad one."

"I just can't make that kind of money and not produce," Bostock said.

So if Autry wouldn't take it, charity would. Bostock donated $36,000 to charity, some of which went to his church, Vermont Square Methodist in South Central L.A.

Bostock quickly turned around his season and began to hit as everyone knew he could. He hit .261 in May, .404 in June, .294

in July, .317 in August, and .302 in September, raising his season average to .296 by September 23.

With just a week left in the season and the Angels in Chicago to play the White Sox, Bostock got permission from the team to go to Gary to visit with his uncle and friends. One of the friends was a woman who was in a tumultuous relationship with her husband. The husband incorrectly assumed his wife was having an affair with Bostock and followed them in his car. At a stoplight, the man pulled out a shotgun and shot through the backseat window, killing Bostock.

At the funeral, Angels pitcher Ken Brett spoke on the team's behalf. "When he found the road to success, his first thoughts were to help the people who had helped him. We are all better people for having known Lyman and having him touch our lives."

"Lyman Bostock," former Angels outfielder Rick Miller said, "was one of the best people you'd ever be blessed to know."

Angels Tragedies
- Dick Wantz, a rookie pitcher with the Angels in 1965, died of a brain tumor at age 25 early in the season.
- Minnie Rojas, a relief pitcher with the Angels from 1966–68, was paralyzed in a car accident that also killed his wife and two of his three children following the 1968 season.
- Chico Ruiz, an infielder with the Angels in 1970–71, was killed in a car accident in 1972.
- Mike Miley, an infielder with the Angels in 1975–76, was killed in a car accident before the start of the 1977 season.
- Lyman Bostock, in his first season with the Angels after signing a $2.2 million free-agent contract, was shot and killed while riding as a passenger in a car in 1978.
- Donnie Moore, a relief pitcher with the Angels from 1985–88, shot and killed himself in 1989.
- Nick Adenhart, a starting pitcher with the Angels in 2008–09, was killed in a car accident while riding as a passenger.

32 Jim Fregosi

Throughout the Angels' first 10 years of existence, Jim Fregosi was the face of the franchise. Fregosi was the team leader on and off the field, in the clubhouse, and in the watering holes. He was like a son to owner Gene Autry and manager Bill Rigney, and he was the one player his teammates looked up to, even though he was younger than so many of them.

"When you have a little success as a player like I did, your confidence level changes and you begin to see what a team needs," Fregosi explained in Rob Goldman's *Once They Were Angels*. "The difference was I took such great pride in the organization that I wanted to do something to make it successful. I knew I had to take some leadership role because of the fact that there weren't any other players there who could do the job. I was an original Angel, and I was one of the first young players to really play well enough to have some leadership ability on the club. You lead by example, and I always played hard. The team saw I cared more about winning than about the individuality of the game, and players will generally gravitate toward that kind of player."

Fregosi was indeed an original Angel, drafted from the Boston Red Sox in the American League Expansion Draft in December 1960. Everybody loved and respected him, unless you played for an opposing team. When the Twins' Rod Carew slid hard into second base in one game, spiking Angels second baseman Bobby Knoop, Fregosi took it personally.

"A hundred dollars to anyone who takes Carew out," Fregosi said to his teammates. Nobody did, but years later when Carew played for the Angels and Fregosi was the manager, the play apparently hadn't been forgotten.

"We never really got along," Carew said. "I don't think he ever really forgot."

Fregosi was a natural, a gifted multi-sport athlete who prepped at Serra High in San Mateo, a high school near San Francisco that also produced Barry Bonds and Patriots quarterback Tom Brady. Fregosi was a big fan of Joe DiMaggio, who played for the Pacific Coast League's San Francisco Seals, and it was Fregosi's San Francisco connection that helped land him with the Angels.

San Francisco Giants general manager Chub Feeney had known about Fregosi and informed Rigney before the expansion draft that Fregosi was a "can't-miss" prospect, and he was right.

Fregosi was called up from the minors during the 1962 season at the age of 20 and was the Angels' starting shortstop through the 1971 season. He was a six-time All-Star and was recognized as the best shortstop in the league from 1964–70.

Off the field, Fregosi played just as hard and was just as success-ful. "No doubt about it, he had a swagger about him," said another original Angel, pitcher Eli Grba. "He could be classy and charming, and with his Italian good looks he became a target for the ladies.

"He could be arrogant and cocky, but not to the point where he was irascible. [And] to play in the big leagues at 19 or 20 like he did, you had to have some pizzazz!"

By 1971, some of that pizzazz had worn off. Fregosi had lost a step after having foot surgery, and Autry brought in a new general manager in Harry Dalton who cleaned house after the '71 season when the Angels went 76–86 and finished in fourth place in the AL West.

Dalton traded Fregosi to the Mets for Nolan Ryan, Leroy Stanton, Don Rose, and Francisco Estrada. The move turned out to be a good one for the Angels, but it stung Fregosi initially.

"Sure, I'll be leaving some of my heart behind," Fregosi said. "But after last year, this is the perfect year to make the move. It's obvious the Angels didn't want me, and I'm happy to go."

Angels All-Star Leaders
Games: Rod Carew, Jim Fregosi—6
Starts: Carew, Vladimir Guerrero—4
Hits: Carew—5
RBIs: Fred Lynn—5
Home runs: Guerrero, Garret Anderson, Lynn, Leon Wagner—1
Innings pitched: Nolan Ryan—4
Strikeouts: Chuck Finley—5

Bothered by a variety of injuries, Fregosi muddled through seven more major league seasons with the Mets, Rangers, and Pirates before he got an offer he couldn't refuse. Fregosi was with the Pirates in 1978, and with his playing career nearing an end, he got a call from general manager Buzzie Bavasi asking him to return to the Angels. Fregosi accepted the job as the Angels' manager, replacing Dave Garcia, and in 1979, he managed the club to its first division championship.

"I'll never forget Gene's eyes when I saw him after the game," Fregosi said of the division-clinching victory. "It was as if a black cloud had been lifted from his head forever."

The party soon ended, though, as the Angels lost 95 games the following year in 1980. And after a slow start in 1981, Fregosi was fired on May 28 and replaced by Gene Mauch.

Fregosi felt snubbed again, just like he did when he was traded 10 years earlier, but he tried to put things in perspective. "My goal when I came back was to win a championship, and we did that at least on a division level," he said. "We not only had to beat the other teams but had to tear away the reputation of always having been a loser, of being a hard-luck organization. No matter what happened to me later, I'll never forget the thrill of finally seeing that stadium filled, the look on the faces of the people who had been with the club for a long time when we finally won, and the positive reaction of the fans when we lost to Baltimore in the playoffs. You can live a lifetime and never be fortunate enough to experience any of that."

33 Saving the Best for Last— Mike Witt's Perfect Game

The 1984 season wasn't a memorable one for the Angels. They finished a mediocre 81–81 two years after a division title in 1982 and two years before another one in 1986. Before the final day of the season, about the biggest highlight for the Angels in 1984 was Reggie Jackson's 500th career home run on September 17.

Two weeks after Jackson's blast, the Angels were in Arlington, Texas, to take on the Rangers in the final game of the season on September 30, 1984. "What I remember most about that day was it was the last day of the season and everyone was glad the season was over," said Mike Witt, who pitched for the Angels from 1981–90. "The game was an afterthought in a lot of minds."

Witt, however, was beginning to come into his own. He was 24 and having a breakthrough season after going a combined 23–29 in his first three years with the club. He entered the final day with a 14–11 record, leading a less-than-overwhelming staff that included Geoff Zahn and Ron Romanick.

"I knew I wanted that 15th win," Witt said. "First and foremost, I wanted to win that."

Witt got his win, a 1–0 victory over the Rangers. But it was more than a win. It was perfect. Witt retired all 27 Rangers batters, throwing what was at the time the ninth perfect game in major league history during the modern era (since 1900).

"Throughout the game there were plays that I didn't know at the time would be big plays," Witt recalled recently, some 27 years after the game. "Looking at game tape, there were four or five plays that could have gone either way."

Witt remembered third baseman Doug DeCinces charging a ball, fielding it on one hop, and getting the out at first with a tough off-balance throw. Witt also remembered shortstop Dick Schofield going deep into the hole between short and third and getting the batter by a step.

Witt was also quick to note right fielder Mike Brown making a running catch in right-center field on a drive by Larry Parrish in the eighth inning. "There were no strike-threes in the dirt for [catcher] Bob Boone," Witt said. "And I remember the last out because it was a nice, easy two-hopper to Rob Wilfong at second base."

Witt said he felt good from start to finish. "I knew warming up in the bullpen before the game everything was working," Witt said. "I was talking to Charlie Hough [the Rangers' pitcher that day], and he told me in the third or fourth inning that he told his teammates, 'They get one run, and this one might be over.'"

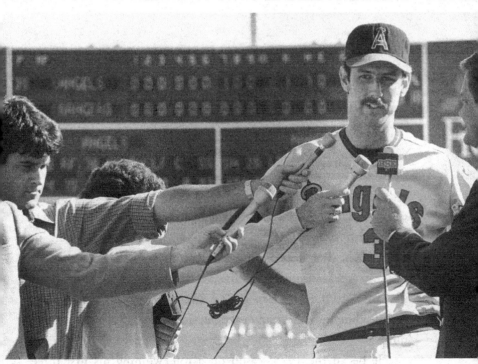

Mike Witt talks to the media with the scoreboard in the background showing his perfect game against the Texas Rangers at Arlington Stadium in Arlington, Texas, on Sunday, October 1, 1984. (AP Photo)

It took a while for the Angels to get that run, as Hough pitched well, too. In the top of the seventh, DeCinces led off with a single and went to second on a passed ball. Brian Downing's ground-out to second base moved DeCinces to third. DeCinces then scored on Reggie Jackson's fielder's choice ground-out, and that was it.

"I used to think no-hitters were thrown by guys who won 20 games and struck out 300 hitters a year," Witt said immediately after the game. "I have to think now I may be in that class."

Witt never won 20 games in a season, though he did have 18 wins in 1986, and he never struck out 300 in a year. He finished his career in a Yankees uniform—traded there by the Angels during the 1990 season—and he retired in 1993 after compiling 117 wins against 116 losses, and one flawless performance.

34 Nolan Ryan—No-No No. 1

Nolan Ryan threw a record seven no-hitters in his Hall of Fame career, the first four with the Angels.

On May 15, 1973, Ryan was 26 years old and in his second season with the Angels since coming to the club from the Mets along with Frank Estrada, Don Rose, and Leroy Stanton in exchange for shortstop Jim Fregosi. Ryan never won more than 10 games in a season during his five years with the Mets, but in his first year with the Angels in 1972 he went 19–16 with a 2.28 ERA while leading the American League in strikeouts (329) and shutouts (nine).

He began the 1973 season on a roll, winning his first three starts and throwing complete games in all three. The Angels lost his next two starts, Ryan received a no-decision in one and his first loss of the season in the other, and he took a 3–1 mark going into his sixth start of the season on May 2 against the Tigers.

Ryan won that game, throwing another complete game. But this one went 12 innings, and Ryan threw all 12 in a 4–1 win. The workload might have affected Ryan, as he lost his next two starts, including the second one in which he lasted only ⅓ of an inning before being knocked out of the game.

Because of his short start, Ryan was used out of the bullpen the next day, threw two innings of relief, and earned his first save of the season. After two days of rest, Ryan took the mound on May 15 to face the Kansas City Royals having already made eight starts and one relief appearance in a little over a month. The Royals were off to a good start, going 20–13 with the likes of Fred Patek, Amos Otis, John Mayberry, Cookie Rojas, and Lou Piniella.

The Angels were 16–13 and had Vada Pinson, Sandy Alomar, Bobby Valentine, and Frank Robinson at the top of their lineup. Jeff Torborg was Ryan's battery mate. The Angels got on the scoreboard with two runs in the top of the first inning, one coming on an RBI single by Bob Oliver and the second on an RBI single by Al Gallagher. Oliver made it 3–0 with a solo homer in the sixth inning.

Meanwhile, Ryan never threatened to throw a perfect game, walking the second hitter he faced—Steve Hovley—in the bottom of the first inning. He went on to walk three in the game while striking out 12.

The only real close call to a hit came in the eighth inning when pinch-hitter Gail Hopkins hit a soft liner toward shallow left field, but shortstop Rudy Meoli made an over-the-shoulder catch.

Ryan retired the side in order in the ninth to finish the no-hitter, getting Otis on a fly to right to end it.

The game was played under protest by Royals manager Jack McKeon, who argued that Ryan wasn't maintaining contact with the pitching rubber while pitching. The protest was denied and Ryan had no-hitter No. 1.

35 Nolan Ryan—No-No No. 2

Exactly two months after throwing the first no-hitter of his career, Nolan Ryan did it again, throwing a no-hitter at Tiger Stadium in the Angels' 6–0 win over the Detroit Tigers.

For those two months in between, however, it wasn't the Ryan Express mowing down hitters from city to city. In fact, the no-hitter brought Ryan's season record up to 11–11. Immediately after his first no-hitter on May 15, Ryan pitched on three days of rest and beat the Texas Rangers with a compete game. But Ryan lost his next three starts, although he didn't pitch poorly, by the scores of 4–1, 2–1, and 2–0. All three efforts were complete games.

Between no-hitters, Ryan made 13 starts and lost eight of them. And on July 11, the start before his second no-hitter, Ryan had one of his worst starts of the season, giving up six runs and lasting only six innings in a 7–1 loss to the Orioles.

The Angels were still in the pennant race at 45–43 and 4½ games out of first place in the AL West as they prepared to play the Tigers on July 15. Detroit had a pretty good team at 48–42 in the AL East.

The Tigers, however, didn't have anybody in their lineup that day hitting higher than Dick McAuliffe at .271. Norm Cash was the Tigers' cleanup hitter, and Jim Perry was their starting pitcher.

Ryan issued a two-out walk to Gates Brown in the first inning, but the second inning was a sign of things to come. Ryan struck out the side in the second inning, then struck out two in the third, and allowed a leadoff walk before striking out the next three batters in the fourth.

After Cash had struck out early in the game, he headed back to the dugout. The Angels catcher that day, Art Kusnyer, overheard a brief discussion Cash had with a teammate.

"Duke Sims, who's on deck, calls out to him, 'How's he throwing?'" Kusnyer said. "All Cash said was, 'Don't go up there.'"

Meanwhile, the Angels had taken a 1–0 lead in the third inning on a sacrifice fly by Vada Pinson. Otherwise, Perry kept the Tigers in the game—that is, until the Angels put up five runs in the eighth inning, getting a two-run pinch single from Winston Llenas, an RBI single from Bob Oliver, and another two-run single by Al Gallagher.

Ryan continued to work through the overmatched Tigers lineup. He walked four batters in the game but none got past first base, and he struck out 17.

"I think the Detroit no-hitter in '73 was probably the game where I had the most overpowering stuff," Ryan said when asked about all his no-hitters.

After a two-out walk to Brown in the sixth, Ryan retired the next 10 hitters in a row to finish it off, completing the no-hitter when he got Cash on a pop out to shortstop, but not before Cash tried to lighten the mood.

As Cash approached the plate for his at-bat in the ninth, he carried a table leg instead of a bat. "It was all square and knotted, and I say, 'You're not really going to use this, are you?'" Kusnyer said. "Nolan yells to [plate umpire Ron] Luciano, 'Hey Ron, check his bat!' Cash looks at Luciano, who says, 'Get that thing outta here. You can't use that!' Cash said, 'I can't hit it with my bat, so what do I have to lose?'"

While the Angels faded in the pennant race and finished the 1973 season 79–83 and in fourth place in the AL West, Ryan got better. He finished the season 21–16 with a 2.87 ERA and a remarkable 26 complete games. He also had 383 strikeouts and set a single-season record that still stands.

36 Nolan Ryan—No-No No. 3

The 1974 season was one of the Angels' worst in club history with a 68–94 record compiled by a team lacking punch and pitching. Frank Robinson was at the tail end of his Hall of Fame career. He led the team with 20 homers and 63 RBIs but didn't even make it to the end of the season in Anaheim because he was traded to the Indians in September.

Other than Nolan Ryan, the Angels had one pitcher who had more than seven wins—Frank Tanana, who won 14 but lost 19. In Ryan, however, the Angels had the most dominant pitcher in baseball. Despite pitching for a dreadful team, he won 22 games, threw 26 complete games, and led the majors with 367 strikeouts.

And on September 28, 1974, in his 41st and final start of the season, Ryan did it again. Ryan threw the third no-hitter of his career—his first in Anaheim—in a 4–0 victory over the Minnesota Twins. He struck out 15 and walked eight batters.

"I had made a silent goal to try and throw a no-hitter at home just to show the people I appreciate the way they have treated me," Ryan said after the game that day.

His toughest challenge was Rod Carew, the Twins' No. 2 hitter who was about to win his third consecutive American League batting crown with a .366 average. Ryan struck out Carew looking in the first inning and struck him out again in the eighth inning. In between, Carew drew two walks, one in the third and again in the fifth, but Ryan was able to pitch out of trouble.

The Twins had another future Hall of Famer on their team that day in Harmon Killebrew, but Killebrew wasn't in the starting lineup. Killebrew came up as a pinch hitter with two out in the ninth and drew a walk.

Nolan Ryan (30), center, is surrounded by teammates immediately after he struck out his final batter—giving him his third no-hitter—in a game against the Minnesota Twins at Anaheim Stadium on Saturday, September 28, 1974, in Anaheim, California. Ryan became the fifth pitcher in baseball history to accomplish this feat. (AP Photo/Jeff Robbins)

Ryan, possibly preferring to pitch to the next hitter, Eric Soderholm, struck out Soderholm to finish the game and earn no-hitter No. 3.

The performance of Ryan in 1974 was the lone bright spot in an otherwise dismal season. It was such a bad year that manager Bobby Winkles didn't survive—the club fired him in late July and hired Dick Williams. Winkles, though, saw enough of Ryan to form a strong opinion.

"Nolan was indestructible," said Winkles, the Angels manager in 1973 and part of '74. "He had the best work habits of any player I've ever seen in baseball. If you went out to the mound to remove him, he'd just say, 'Who would you rather have pitching to the next guy, me or the fella warming up in the bullpen?' So I'd leave him in."

That might explain why Ryan had 52 complete games in 1973 and '74 (26 in each season), the high marks in his career.

37 Nolan Ryan—No-No No. 4

Nolan Ryan threw his fourth and final no-hitter with the Angels on June 1, 1975, one of a major league–record seven in his career and probably the most significant.

It was his fourth no-hitter in just three seasons, two coming in 1973 and one in 1974. But Ryan was at his best those two seasons, winning 20-plus games and leading the majors in strikeouts each season.

In 1975, Ryan dealt with elbow soreness and started just 28 games after averaging 40 starts per season in '73 and '74. He faced a strong team in the Baltimore Orioles, who were coming off back-to-back American League East championships the previous two seasons.

The Orioles lineup that day featured Al Bumbry, Don Baylor, Bobby Grich, Lee May, Ken Singleton, and Brooks Robinson. Ryan was coming off losses in his previous two starts. Through three innings, Ryan struck out five, but he also walked three batters.

After the Angels took a 1–0 lead in the bottom of the third, Ryan then retired the side in order in the fourth, fifth, and sixth innings.

In the seventh, Ryan retired the first batter of the inning before Grich walked, and an error by Angels shortstop Billy Smith allowed the Orioles to put runners on first and second with one out. Robinson grounded out to third, the runners moving up to second and third with two outs and Elrod Hendricks coming up, but Ryan escaped the jam by getting Hendricks on a pop to third.

Ryan retired the side 1-2-3 in the eighth and got the first two batters in the ninth, bringing up Grich, who had reached base twice in the game on walks. Grich worked the count to 2–2 before Ryan fooled everyone at Anaheim Stadium that Sunday afternoon.

"Everybody in the whole stadium was thinking the same thing—fastball," said Bruce Bochte, the Angels' first baseman that day. "But instead, out floated this 75-mph changeup. Everybody just looked at it wide-eyed, including Grich, who watched as it went across the plate for strike three."

The fourth no-hitter tied Ryan for the major league record with Sandy Koufax. Six years later, Ryan would get no-hitter No. 5 while pitching for the Houston Astros against the Dodgers.

"I'm very proud that I have seven no-hitters and was able to throw four in a three-year span," Ryan would say years later. "But I would have to say the fourth one is the most memorable because it tied me with Sandy Koufax."

Ryan and Koufax, because both threw hard and were dominant during their heyday, inevitably drew comparisons, and there might not have been a better judge than Norm Sherry. Sherry caught Koufax during his playing days with the Dodgers and later was a coach and manager with the Angels when Ryan was in Anaheim.

"Ryan was a more physical pitcher," Sherry said. "He would use his legs and had a lot of drive and put a lot of terrific effort into throwing the ball. Koufax was more fluid and gave less exertion

Not Quite No-Nos

Nolan Ryan threw a major league record seven no-hitters in his career, including four with the Angels. But Ryan was close several other times, throwing 12 one-hitters, which is tied with Bob Feller for the most in major league history. Six of Ryan's 12 career one-hitters came while pitching for the Angels:

vs. Boston, July 9, 1972, in a 3–0 win.
vs. Yankees, August 29, 1973, in a 5–0 win.
vs. Texas, June 27, 1974, in a 5–0 win.
vs. Seattle, April 15, 1977, in a 7–0 win.
vs. Cleveland, May 5, 1978, in a 5–0 win.
vs. Yankees, July 13, 1979, in a 6–1 win.

than Ryan. Because of his large hands, Sandy was able to get more backspin, and his ball had more lift on it. Nolan held the ball deep in his hand and had a heavier type of action that would make the ball cut in and out and sometimes sink.

"People have always asked me who threw harder. My answer is when you throw like they did, what difference does it make?"

38 Chance of a Lifetime

Dean Chance grew up an Ohio farm boy dreaming of pitching in the big leagues like his idol, Cleveland Indians pitcher Bob Feller. Chance fulfilled his dream, pitching 11 seasons in the majors for five teams, but it was a single season with the Angels that made him an Angels legend.

Chance was selected by general manager Fred Haney in the 1960 expansion draft from the Baltimore Orioles. He won 14 games in 1962 and 13 in 1963, before putting up what some describe as one of the best single-season performances by a pitcher in baseball history.

The Angels were playing their home games in Dodger Stadium, and the Dodgers had Sandy Koufax and Don Drysdale. But Chance, just 23 years old, stole the spotlight.

Chance won the Cy Young Award after going 20–9 with a 1.65 ERA. He threw 15 complete games and 11 shutouts, but there was probably no better measure of Chance's complete dominance than his performance that year against the powerful New York Yankees.

The Yankees had won four consecutive American League pennants and were on their way to a fifth in a row in 1964. Their lineup, powered by Mickey Mantle and Roger Maris, struck fear into opposing pitchers. But with Chance, the fear factor flip-flopped.

"The Yankees would get one look at Dean," Angels outfielder Albie Pearson said, "and they would go run and hide.... When Dean pitched, the Yankees became a bunch of guys in pantyhose. They had no chance."

In five starts against the Yankees that season, Chance gave up one run in 50 innings, the only run coming in on a Mantle home run. Chance won four of those starts. Problem was, the Yankees' Jim Bouton threw 13 shutout innings himself, and the Yankees pushed across two runs in the 15th inning against the Angels' bullpen to win the game.

Chance was 6'3", 200 pounds, and had that farm boy strength. His delivery was a twisting, turning, and deceptive motion, and he glared menacingly toward the plate. But that success against the Yankees...well, it had some deep roots.

"I was a Cleveland fan as a kid," Chance said. "And I always had this kind of hatred for the Yankees. I loved beating them. And I loved pitching against them because there was always a big crowd, and there was always this electricity in the air. It felt like a big boxing match."

And it was Chance who always delivered the knockout blow.

"It wasn't enough to be loose [against the Yankees], you had to psyche up," Chance said. "They were the Yankees! You could never let up against those guys. Maris never got a home run off me, and I didn't have any trouble with Mantle. I just tried to overpower him."

Chance enjoyed his success on the field by partying off the field, often with fellow pitcher/partier Bo Belinsky, and it caught up to him slowly but surely. Chance won 15 games for the Angels in 1965, but he fell to 12–17 in 1966, the first season the Angels played at Anaheim Stadium.

Chance was a victim of poor run support in 1966, so he became trade bait for the team to bring in some much needed offense. He was traded to the Twins after the season for outfielder Jimmie Hall, first baseman Don Mincher, and reliever Pete Cimino.

Chance won 20 games for the Twins in 1967 and 16 in 1968, but he won only 18 more games during three more seasons playing for the Twins, Indians, Mets, and Tigers. He retired at age 30 in 1971.

"I guess we should all have taken better care of ourselves," Chance said after his retirement. "But when I look back, I feel I'm just luckier than the devil to get my required 10 years in the big leagues and get the maximum on the pension."

And that 1964 season was best among them.

"Amazing is how I'd describe him," said Buck Rodgers, Chance's catcher with the Angels. "I never saw a pitcher so overpowering. The greatest hitters in baseball—Killebrew, Maris, and Mantle—would just shake their heads in disbelief. Some were visibly scared—he was that overpowering."

39 Jim Edmonds and "The Catch"

Jim Edmonds was such a talented baseball player, some of his teammates figured he wasn't trying hard enough because he made things look so easy. A Southern California native, Edmonds was easygoing on and off the field. But hit a ball into the outfield gap, and the center fielder was anything but lackadaisical.

There would be no better example of Edmonds' talent with the baseball glove than on June 10, 1997. During what turned out to be another season without a trip to the playoffs, Edmonds made the play of the year. In fact, some said it might be the best defensive play ever.

It is known as The Catch, and it was compared to the over-the-head catch made by Willie Mays in the 1954 World Series. Mays caught a drive hit to straight-away center field by Vic Wertz of the Cleveland Indians at the Polo Grounds in New York.

Vic Wertz, meet David Howard.

David Howard had a non-descript major league career and played nine seasons with the Kansas City Royals and St. Louis Cardinals. He left after the 1999 season with a .229 career batting average.

But he got hold of a fastball from Angels pitcher Jason Dickson on June 10, 1997, driving the 1–1 pitch toward the fence in straight-away center field at Kansas City's Kauffman Stadium. Edmonds turned and raced straight to the fence and, with his back to home plate, dove and laid out his body horizontally, reaching out with his glove as far as he could.

"I was in trouble, I was beat," said Edmonds, who wound up with eight Gold Gloves in his career. "The ball was going to be over my head and they were going to score the go-ahead runs, so I went after it. I just ran as hard as I could and when I turned and saw it, I figured my only chance was to lay out for it."

Incredibly, the ball stuck in the webbing of his glove, and Edmonds rolled onto his back with his legs in the air. He smiled as he showed the ball to the umpires, who were as impressed as everybody else.

"That was one of the greatest plays ever," umpire Dave Phillips told the *Kansas City Star*. "That made Willie Mays' play look routine."

Edmonds himself, though, wasn't as impressed. In fact, he isn't sure it was the best catch he's ever made. "I made the exact same catch in Venezuela, playing winter ball in 1992, but nobody saw it so it was no big deal," Edmonds said a few days after the catch. "At the time, I didn't think it was that big of a deal. Then I saw it on TV a couple of times and, yeah, I'm pretty happy with the outcome. And it's gotten me some notoriety. But I'm sure I won't get to Jay Leno or anything."

Darin Erstad was a center fielder who had moved to first base that season and would eventually move back to center field after Edmonds was traded to the St. Louis Cardinals a few years later.

"I never show emotion on the field, but I couldn't stop laughing," Erstad said. "I mean, it's so amazing that you can't really say anything to describe it. You just shake your head. You have to understand everything that goes into it—the jump he got, the read on the ball, the route he took to get there, and his ability to hold it when he came down."

40 Fin to Win—Chuck Finley

A lot of colorful characters have worn Angels uniforms over the course of 50-plus seasons, but it would be difficult to find an Angel with a more self-deprecating sense of humor than Chuck Finley.

You might expect that from a quirky lefty who was buried in the bullpen and only got into games that were blowouts, which he was his first two seasons in the big leagues. But Finley soon became a quirky lefty who was a leader on the mound and in the clubhouse, and arguably the most successful pitcher in Angels history.

Finley played for the Angels from 1986–99, 14 seasons that left him as the franchise's all-time leader in wins (165), starts (379), and innings pitched (2,675). Only Nolan Ryan (2,416) had more strikeouts than Finley (2,151).

He was a five-time All-Star but never won 20 games in a season. He did win 18 games in a season twice, 16 three times, and 15 games twice. Not bad for a good ol' boy from Louisiana who reached the big leagues with the Angels during the eventful 1986 season and never looked back.

"I remember when I first came up, I was just trying to get my feet wet," Finley said. "I thought I would be up just long enough to get the itch out of my pants from the starch and the detergent used to clean them...watch them change the coffee pot four or five times and that would be it. I really loved the game of baseball, but when I first came up, I was so star-struck and so out there, wondering if I fit in here."

Finley not only fit in, he set the standard on the mound for Angels pitchers in the years to follow. His forkball was his out pitch, and for more than a decade he was the pitcher Angels fans wanted on the mound in a big game.

The Angels let Finley go after the 1999 season via free agency, and he finished his career with the Indians and Cardinals, compiling 200 victories, 63 complete games, 15 shutouts, and 2,610 strikeouts, which ranks 23rd all-time.

Finley, though, wasn't one of those bonus-baby can't-miss prospects. He wasn't drafted out of high school, and only one college showed any interest—Louisiana Tech. He accepted a scholarship there but lasted only one year in school.

"Chuck came to me [after his freshman year] and told me he was leaving school," said Pat Patterson, Louisiana Tech's coach at the time. "And Big Chuck [Finley's father] told me, 'He can quit, but if he does, I'm fixin' to put his butt to work daylight to dark six days a week.'"

Finley did quit, and Big Chuck put Finley to work on the family's 200-acre nursery, working 10-hour days six days a week making $4.75 an hour.

"I think it broke Dad's heart," Finley said of leaving school. "He said, 'You're walking away from free school? You're walking

Angels All-Time Career Pitching Leaders through 2011

ERA (minimum 1,000 innings pitched): Dean Chance, 2.83
Wins: Chuck Finley, 165
Innings: Chuck Finley, 2,675
Losses: Chuck Finley, 140
Hits allowed: Chuck Finley, 2,544
Games pitched: Troy Percival, 579
Home runs allowed: Chuck Finley, 254
Starts: Chuck Finley, 379
Walks allowed: Nolan Ryan, 1,302
Complete games: Nolan Ryan, 156
Strikeouts: Nolan Ryan, 2,416
Shutouts: Nolan Ryan, 40
Saves: Troy Percival, 316

away from baseball?' It was hard for him to swallow that I just wasn't happy, that I just wanted to go to work."

Finley soon returned to school—and baseball—at Northeast Louisiana State. He pitched well enough to be drafted by the Angels in 1985 and was in the big leagues after just 41 minor league innings, none above Class A ball.

When Mike Port, then the Angels' general manager, called Finley to tell him he was being promoted to the big leagues, Finley thought it was some kind of joke. But it was no joke—Finley left Quad City, Iowa, for New York where the Angels were in town to play the Yankees. A few days later, he made his major league debut at Anaheim Stadium against the Tigers.

"I got to the mound and I couldn't believe how bright it was," Finley recalled. "A night game in A ball, you turn on the porch lights. I couldn't believe how close [catcher] Bob Boone looked to me. I said, 'God, I know I can throw the ball right through him.'"

Finley spent 17 seasons under the bright lights of the big leagues—not bad for a good ol' boy from Louisiana.

Oh No, Mo!

Angels fans rejoiced when the team signed Albert Pujols to the richest contract in franchise history prior to the 2012 season, but those fans with a memory would have been wise to temper their excitement.

Pujols wasn't the first big-name, former-MVP, free-agent first baseman to sign with the Angels. There was also Mo Vaughn, whose time in Anaheim is not a highlight in Angels lore.

The Angels played relatively well in 1997 and 1998, finishing with a winning record each year and contending for a playoff spot. The Angels were close, many fans thought, and simply needed that final piece to the puzzle.

General manager Bill Bavasi was given the go-ahead from ownership to spend some money and get that piece to help put the Angels over the top and into the playoffs for the first time since 1986. Bavasi courted free agent pitcher Randy Johnson, but Johnson signed with the Arizona Diamondbacks. Bavasi pulled off the biggest move of the off-season when he lured East Coast native Mo Vaughn away from the Boston Red Sox.

Vaughn was an icon in Boston, a three-time All-Star and the American League MVP in 1995. In 1998, he had a monster season, batting .337 with 40 homers and 115 RBIs. Bavasi got Vaughn interested with a letter he wrote to him, and it didn't hurt that he offered $80 million over six years.

The Angels were excited about their chances in 1999, but on opening night against the Cleveland Indians before a sellout crowd at Edison Field and a national television audience, the Angels were struck again. In the top of the first inning, the second batter of the game, Omar Vizquel, hit a foul pop-up near the Indians' dugout on the first-base side. Vaughn drifted over near the dugout, looking to the sky, then fell into the dugout, landing hard and awkwardly on his left ankle.

Initially, Vaughn shook it off and stayed in the game. But after falling down while batting later in the game, he was removed and diagnosed with a severe high-ankle sprain. Interestingly, there had been a short fence at the top of the steps of both dugouts to help protect players in the dugout from foul line drives and prevent defensive players from falling into the dugout like Vaughn did. But Angels manager Terry Collins had the fences removed after the 1998 season because he had trouble seeing the field as clearly as he

Most Home Runs by an Angels Player in a Month
April: Brian Downing (1987)—9
May: Mo Vaughn (2000)—13
June: Tim Salmon (1996)—13
July: Juan Rivera (2006), Don Baylor (1979)—11
August: Bobby Bonds (1977)—12
September/October: Vaughn (1999), Vladimir Guerrero (2004)—11

wanted to. Soon after Vaughn's injury, the fences returned, but the damage was done.

Vaughn was hampered by the injured ankle all season, but he still managed to put up impressive numbers that year, batting .281 with 33 homers and 108 RBIs in 139 games. In 2000 he hit .272 with 36 homers and 117 RBIs, but he missed the entire 2001 season with a ruptured tendon in his left arm and was traded to the New York Mets prior to the 2002 season for pitcher Kevin Appier.

During spring training in 2002, some hard feelings between Vaughn and some of the Angels surfaced with barbs traded via the media from the Angels' spring training home in Arizona to the Mets' spring home in Florida. Angels reliever Troy Percival said, "We may miss Mo's bat, but we won't miss his leadership. Darin Erstad is our leader."

Vaughn responded harshly, saying the Angels "ain't done [expletive] in this game. They ain't got no flags hanging at [expletive] Edison Field, so to hell with them."

Ironically, the Angels went on to win the World Series that year. Vaughn played two injury-plagued seasons with the Mets and retired after the 2003 season.

42 A Life Too Short— Nick Adenhart

The Angels baseball team has suffered its share of on-field disappointments, falling short of playoff glory in dramatic fashion. But losses on the field pale in comparison to some of the tragedies the franchise has endured over the years.

Twenty years after Donnie Moore took his own life, the Angels family had another life taken away when pitcher Nick Adenhart was killed in an auto accident in the early-morning hours of April 9, 2009. The accident took place only hours after Adenhart, just 22 years old, made his season debut with the Angels and threw the best game of his career. He held the Oakland A's scoreless for six innings. It didn't seem to matter much that the A's eventually won the game—Adenhart had arrived.

A drunk driver drove through a red light and broadsided the car Adenhart was riding in, killing the driver, Courtney Stewart, and another passenger, Henry Pearson, at the scene. Adenhart died later at the hospital.

Another passenger, Jon Wilhite, suffered an "internal decapitation" but survived. The drunk driver, Andrew Thomas Gallo, was arrested and convicted on three counts of second-degree murder, two counts of driving under the influence causing great bodily injury, and one felony count of hit-and-run. He was sentenced to 51 years to life.

The Angels canceled their game the night of the accident, but many Angels players and staff met in the clubhouse that day and met with Adenhart's father, Jim, who had come to town to see his son pitch.

"A lot of these guys in here have never lost anybody in their family that's close to them," Angels center fielder Torii Hunter said. "I hate that this happened, but this is part of life. This is the real deal. That's why you've got to kiss your kids, kiss your family every day when you get up in the morning and before you leave for work."

The following day, the Red Sox were in town and Jered Weaver, Adenhart's best friend on the team, was scheduled to pitch. "There definitely was an empty feeling in the stadium," Weaver said. "I don't think anybody knew what to do. I don't think the fans knew, we didn't know…how could you?"

But the show had to go on.

"It's our job," Weaver said. "We had to go on. Once the game got going, and you were feeling the rhythm of the game again, it was baseball. The game was the same, but it was definitely different."

Weaver honors Adenhart's memory before each start he makes, writing "NA" in the dirt of the mound.

"The shock…I don't think you ever get over the shock," Weaver said. "Any time you bring it up, it's there. He was going to move in with me in Long Beach. He died on Thursday morning. We were going to move him in on Sunday."

Adenhart was just 21 when he made his major league debut in 2008, but by no means was his road to the majors without twists and turns. In fact, Adenhart had been projected to be a first-round draft pick out of high school, but in his very last high school game, before more than 20 scouts, Adenhart felt a pop in his elbow.

He needed reconstructive elbow surgery—Tommy John surgery—and his draft stock dropped dramatically. The Angels selected him in the 14th round but offered him an unusually high signing bonus for a 14th round pick—$710,000—in the hopes he would sign with them and not accept his scholarship offer to North Carolina.

The Angels' faith in Adenhart's abilities paid off when he reached the big leagues only three years after beginning his professional career.

"He just wasn't some extreme talent that was blessed," Angels manager Mike Scioscia said. "He fought to be here."

The Angels established the Nick Adenhart Pitcher of the Year award given to an Angels pitcher for outstanding performance throughout the regular season. And the Adenhart family created the Nick Adenhart Memorial Fund, which is designed to provide financial support to youth baseball organizations.

43 World Series 2002—Game 3

After watching the Angels and Giants combine for six home runs in Game 2 of the World Series, an 11–10 Angels victory at Edison Field, Giants manager Dusty Baker promised baseballs would not fly out of the park in Game 3 at San Francisco's Pacific Bell Park— not with that cool bay breeze making the air heavy and taking the steam out of fly balls.

He was right. The Angels did not hit a home run in Game 3. However, the Angels had 12 singles, three doubles, and a triple, and they put pressure on the Giants' pitchers in nearly every inning, running away with a 10–4 victory to take a 2–1 Series lead.

Darin Erstad had three hits, and Scott Spiezio drove in three runs. The Angels batted around in both the third and fourth innings, becoming the first team in World Series history to bat around in consecutive innings.

"Everybody wants to be an analyst, but nothing has affected this team all year," Angels hitting coach Mickey Hatcher said after the game. "It didn't bother them playing in New York, and it didn't bother them playing in Minnesota. I can't explain what's going on. We just watch and let 'em go."

Baker wasn't happy about it, but he was impressed.

"They were hitting; they've been hitting the last two games," he said. "I don't know, hopefully they hit themselves out, I hope. If you walk somebody, most of them have good speed and that allows [Angels manager Mike] Scioscia to do some things. Most of the guys over there are contact hitters. You don't strike them out very much."

The offensive onslaught came at a good time, considering Angels starting pitcher Ramon Ortiz looked jittery on the mound. He gave up home runs to Rich Aurilia and Barry Bonds in the fifth inning, but that wasn't totally unexpected because Ortiz gave up a major league–high 40 homers during the regular season.

"He had trouble with his rhythm," Angels catcher Bengie Molina said. "I think his wrist was hurting him. His fastball went from 95 [mph] to 88. I just tried to get him through five innings and let the bullpen take over."

Ortiz did get through five with the Angels holding an 8–4 lead. Brendan Donnelly and Scott Schoeneweis each threw two scoreless innings of relief.

The Giants held a lead early with a run in the first inning. Kenny Lofton led off the bottom of the first with a walk and stole second. He took third on an infield single by Jeff Kent, giving the Giants runners on first and third with one out and Bonds due up.

Ortiz walked Bonds intentionally, loading the bases and setting up a potential double-play with Benito Santiago coming up. Santiago obliged with a grounder to second, but it was hit too slowly and the only play was at first. Lofton scored to put the Giants up 1–0.

The Angels took the lead in the third inning with four runs—highlighted by a two-run triple from Spiezio. In the fourth, the Angels made things miserable for Giants starter Livan Hernandez and eventually the Giants bullpen.

The Angels scored four runs in the inning on four singles, two walks, and a double-steal pulled off by Erstad and Tim Salmon.

By the end of the fourth inning, the Angels were up 8–1 and on their way to their second World Series game victory in franchise history.

"The idea is to keep pressing, to keep pouring it on as much as you can," said Erstad, who wound up hitting .300 (9-for-30) in the 2002 World Series. "Regardless of the score, you can't lay back. It's like playing prevent-defense in football—it's not a good thing to do. So, if anything, we probably up our intensity a little bit [with a lead]. Killer instinct? I guess you can call it that."

44 Reggie, Reggie!

The Angels' first American League West Championship in 1979 will always be fondly remembered by Angels fans, but the team suffered a hangover that lasted for the next two seasons. They had one of their worst seasons in club history in 1980, going 65–95 and finishing 32 games out of first place. In the strike-shortened 1981 season, the Angels went 51–59 and again were postseason observers.

Owner Gene Autry and general manager Buzzie Bavasi made big moves in the winter following the 1981 season. They acquired Doug DeCinces and catcher Bob Boone, but the biggest splash was the signing of Reggie Jackson.

Jackson had already won five World Series rings with the Oakland A's and New York Yankees, and he brought with him a winning swagger.

The Angels already had a team of All-Stars in Rod Carew, Don Baylor, Bobby Grich, Fred Lynn, and Brian Downing—and

Reggie Jackson blasts a home run in the first inning of a game in Seattle on August 12, 1985, to tie as the eighth all-time home-run hitter. It was his 521st home run. (AP Photo/Barry Sweet)

brought in DeCinces and Boone—but it was Jackson whom Autry said brought something special.

"From the standpoint of excitement and drawing power, Reggie and Pete Rose are in a class by themselves," Autry said. "I've long admired the way he hustles and handles himself, and while we already have a number of players who have been on championship teams, Reggie adds yet another dimension. His desire should rub off."

Jackson signed for four seasons at $900,000 per year, but he would also get bonuses based on attendance.

"I don't know how many home runs Reggie will hit, but we're in the entertainment business and he's an entertainer," Bavasi said. "Either you love him or you hate him. The man has charisma. If we draw well, he has a chance to make a great deal of money, and so do we."

Jackson received 50 cents for each fan in attendance over 2.4 million. In 1982, the Angels drew a team-record 2.8 million, good for an additional $200,000 in Jackson's pocket. Soon after he signed, Jackson called Mauch and told him any problems he had with Yankees manager Billy Martin would not be repeated in Anaheim.

Mauch simply responded by saying he wanted Jackson to "play for me the way you did against me."

Jackson had his best season with the Angels that first year in 1982, hitting .275 with a league-leading 39 homers and 101 RBIs. The Angels won the division by three games and faced the Milwaukee Brewers in the American League Championship Series.

The Angels won the first two games of the best-of-five series only to lose the next three in a row. In the ensuing years, the disappointment of the 1986 playoff loss has drawn more attention, but the 1982 playoff loss stung the organization.

"I really thought our clubhouse was solid," Jackson said. "Bobby Grich did his thing. Doug DeCinces was a mature professional.

Rod Carew could hit underground in the dark. Freddy Lynn was an outstanding defender in center field. So we had a heck of a good ballclub with a lot of talent."

After the 1982 season, Jackson's only real personal highlight was hitting his 500th career home run on September 17, 1984. In five seasons with the Angels, he batted just .239 and hit 123 of his 563 career home runs.

Mauch and Jackson won two division titles together (1982 and '86) but suffered devastating playoff losses both seasons. Jackson had nothing but respect after his time together with Mauch and the Angels.

"I enjoyed playing for Gene Mauch because he was prepared all the time," Jackson said. "I went to the ballpark one time at 6:00 in the morning, and it was the first time I caught him out of uniform. He had his shirt on and he was sitting there in his underwear and street shoes. I never got to the ballpark before him, and I have nothing but positive things to say about him."

45 Most Valuable Vlad

Getting to the World Series and winning it, as the Angels did in 2002, was great for the franchise. It was a first, and it knocked the proverbial monkey off the team's back. But 2002 was the Angels' first playoff appearance in 16 years following the 1986 ALCS collapse. Would it be another 16 years until the Angels returned to the playoffs?

The Angels fell apart in 2003, falling to 77–85 and finishing 19 games out of first place in the American League West. Was it back to the same ol', same ol'?

Angels All-Time Career Batting Leaders*

Batting average: Vladimir Guerrero, .319
Extra-base hits: Garret Anderson, 796
Strikeouts: Tim Salmon, 1,360
Games played: Garret Anderson, 2,013
Doubles: Garret Anderson, 489
Stolen bases: Chone Figgins, 280
At-bats: Garret Anderson, 7,989
Triples: Jim Fregosi, 70
On-base percentage: Rod Carew, .393
Runs: Garret Anderson, 1,024
Home runs: Tim Salmon, 299
Slugging percentage: Vladimir Guerrero, .546
Hits: Garret Anderson, 2,368
Runs batted in: Garret Anderson, 1,292
OPS (On-base plus Slugging): Vladimir Guerrero, .927
Total bases: Garret Anderson, 3,743
Walks: Tim Salmon, 970
* Through 2012, minimum 1,500 plate appearances

Bill Stoneman, who became general manager before the 2000 season and hired Mike Scioscia, made a move that would help the Angels become a perennial winner for the years that followed.

Stoneman signed Vladimir Guerrero in January 2004 for five years and $70 million—a deal that took only a few days to get done. It was a deal that probably could not have happened had Disney still owned the Angels because there were too many upper management types who would have had to be consulted.

As it was, it took only a few phone calls.

Phone call No. 1: Stoneman called agent Arn Tellem to inquire about Rafael Palmeiro. Tellem responded with a question of his own, regarding another of his clients.

"How about Vlad?"

Phone call No. 2: Stoneman called owner Arte Moreno and convinced Moreno of Guerrero's potential value. It was a big pill to swallow considering the Angels had already committed $51 million to Bartolo Colon only a month previously. But Moreno agreed.

Guerrero thrived in obscurity with the Montreal Expos for eight seasons, a four-time All-Star who hit .323 overall and hit 34 or more homers five times, drove in 100 or more runs five times, and stole as many as 40 bases in a season.

With the Angels, he didn't disappoint, winning the club's second Most Valuable Player award (Don Baylor in 1979 was the other) in 2004, batting .337 with 39 homers and 126 RBIs. The Angels won the division.

Guerrero helped the Angels win division titles again in 2005, 2007, 2008, and 2009, being named an All-Star in four seasons and finishing third in the MVP voting in both 2005 and 2007.

Hall of Famer Cal Ripken called Guerrero the "best bad-ball hitter" he had ever seen, noting that Guerrero was such a free swinger he once hit a pitched ball after it bounced. Guerrero also was unusual in that he didn't wear batting gloves, explaining that it was a result of him helping his grandfather pull cows home bare-handed while he was a boy in the Dominican Republic.

In Guerrero's six seasons with the Angels, they won the division five times and Guerrero hit .319 with the club to surpass Rod Carew (.314) as the top hitter in franchise history. But after an injury-plagued season that limited him to 100 games in 2009, the Angels let Guerrero go and he made them pay.

Guerrero signed with the Rangers for the 2010 season and surprised nearly everyone in baseball. He played 152 games, hitting .300 with 29 homers and 115 RBIs, and he helped the Rangers end the Angels' run of three consecutive division titles.

46 Buy a Rally Monkey

If you don't have one, you don't know what you're missing.

It's more than a marketing tool for the club or a souvenir that gets buried in your kid's closet. As the giant scoreboard above the right-field seats proclaims, "Believe in the power of the Rally Monkey."

Throughout the concourses as Angel Stadium, the Rally Monkey is sold for $20, and a smaller, less-expensive version is also available. But it's not just your every-day stuffed animal. Coming in a variety of colors and adorned in an Angels uniform and cap, the Rally Monkey wraps its arms around the necks of children and adults alike.

Grab it the by tail and wave it around like you're waving a Terrible Towel or a Homer Hanky and watch the Angels' offense come alive. Or not.

Maybe it works better if the Angels' 3-4-5 hitters are due up, but no matter. It's the spirit of the Rally Monkey that counts.

These days, the Rally Monkey appears on the scoreboard late in games where the Angels trail in an effort to start a rally. It starts out with a clip from a popular movie, and eventually the Rally Monkey makes a cameo appearance, inserted into a scene in place of one of the movie's stars, getting a rise out of the crowd and even getting the opposing team's players to turn their heads and take a look.

"I kind of like the Rally Monkey, I do. It's funny," Dodgers manager Don Mattingly said. "I try and tell guys, 'You guys should like the Rally Monkey because when the Rally Monkey comes out, then you've got a lead.' I'd rather have a lead than be behind. I like the Rally Monkey. Think about it. When you see the Rally Monkey, you're usually ahead. I like it when he comes out."

Dodgers center fielder Matt Kemp is not convinced. "I don't like the Rally Monkey," Kemp said. "You're out there in the outfield, and the monkey just pops up on the screen. That's kind of scary."

Angels outfielder Torii Hunter saw the power of the Rally Monkey while playing for the Twins, especially when the Angels beat his Twins in the 2002 ALCS. Hunter signed with the Angels in 2008, and during his introductory news conference, he pulled out a Rally Monkey from underneath the table and said, "If you can't beat him, you join him."

The Rally Monkey was born in 2000 on a lark. At one point during the June 6 game against the Giants, two video board operators, Dean Fraulino and Jaysen Humes, played a clip from the Jim Carrey movie, *Ace Ventura: Pet Detective,* that showed a monkey jumping up and down.

Another Angels employee, Peter Bull, was roaming the crowd to monitor reaction and told Fraulino many fans seemed to enjoy the clip. They played the clip again, to more fanfare, then tried something different in the bottom of the ninth inning. With the Angels trailing, Fraulino superimposed the words "Rally Monkey" over the clip. The Angels rallied to win the game, and a star was born.

"At that point, we knew we had something," Bull said, adding that there are rules for when the monkey may appear. It can't appear before the seventh inning or when the Angels lead or trail by more than four runs. It can appear only at the start of an inning or during a pitching change, when the score is tied, or the Angels trail by four runs or fewer.

"It's got a role," Bull said. "It's like a closer. You wouldn't bring him in in the third inning."

"Fans in baseball these days are disconnected from the players," Fraulino said. "The Rally Monkey is a connection to the team. They can say, 'Hey, we can help you win.' And besides, who doesn't like a monkey, for crying out loud?"

The Rally Monkey's role with the club has expanded; it's also used in a summer reading program for children. They call the program Rally Readers.

47 There Is Crying in Baseball— Jered Weaver's No-Hitter

Moments after he beat the Minnesota Twins on May 2, 2012, with the ninth complete-game no-hitter in Angels history, Jered Weaver cried like a baby. Down on the field at Angel Stadium, near the on-deck circle, Weaver hugged his mom and dad, Gail and Dave, as well as his wife, Kristin.

"It was an unbelievable experience to be able to have them come down on the field and share some tears," Weaver said. "It's special for my dad to be here. It's been a long road, and he's been here all the way."

From their customary seats behind home plate, Gail and Dave cheered on their son but also chewed their fingernails along the way. "I get so nervous sometimes I have to go stick my head in a toilet," Dave said while sipping a beer in the clubhouse after the game. "It gets so nerve-wracking, and he's been close before. But after 8⅓ innings I figured he'd have a chance."

Weaver achieved what only five other Angels pitchers had done in more than 50 years—get 27 outs without giving up a hit, joining Bo Belinsky, Clyde Wright, Nolan Ryan, Mike Witt, and Ervin Santana in the no-hit club.

Weaver mixed his pitches well, keeping hitters off balance. He didn't overpower anyone he fooled them.

"I wasn't throwing 97 or 98 [mph] up there. It was pretty much the same [stuff] I've been throwing up there all year," Weaver said. "A lot of things got to go your way, and it happened. Balls were hit at people. It's just so surreal.

"I've been close once, in Seattle, and I had it broken up there in the eighth. It's funny, we were having this conversation about five days ago, and C.J. [Wilson] came up to me and said, 'Why don't you just go out there and throw a no-hitter,' and I was like, 'There's no way, there's no chance, this is a big-league game, and anything can happen.' It's funny that a week later it happened."

It wasn't funny to the Twins, but there were a few close calls. Jamey Carroll dropped a bunt in the third inning, testing third baseman Mark Trumbo, who was still trying to learn the position. But Trumbo fielded the ball cleanly and made a perfect throw to first baseman Albert Pujols.

Trevor Plouffe came close twice with hard-hit balls. With two out in the fifth he sliced a line drive to right field, but Torii Hunter made a nice running catch. And with one out in the eighth, Plouffe hit a line drive down the left-field line that hooked foul.

In the ninth inning, Carroll led off and hit a drive to left field but got under it just enough to allow Vernon Wells to run it down. For the final out of the game, Hunter raced to the warning track in right field to catch a liner hit by Alexi Casilla.

"I got to give it up to the defense, and obviously the offense, for making it a little more comfortable for me going through the game," Weaver said. "He put a charge in it, Casilla did, but Spider-Man [Hunter] was running stuff down. I wasn't worried at all. Torii is who he is. He's a nine-time Gold Glover, and I didn't have any doubt that he was going to run that ball down. The defense was exceptional for me, and [catcher] Chris [Iannetta] was throwing down the right fingers."

Hunter said there was no way he wasn't going to get that final out, even if it would have meant taking out the right-field fence. "That last hit, I had to get on my horse," he said. "I was like, 'Get it! Get it!' I came up with the ball; I didn't care if I knocked myself out. I was gonna do it for my boy. He pitched a tremendous game; this is a special moment for him."

Angels manager Mike Scioscia, who caught two no-hitters himself during his playing days (Fernando Valenzuela in 1990 and Kevin Gross in 1992), said Weaver did not pitch any differently than he usually does.

"I don't know if he had anything more [than usual]," Scioscia said. "He just changed speeds really well, and early in the game I think he established the fact that he could hit spots with his fastball. He was just relentless in repeating pitches and made those guys put the ball in play,"

Only two batters reached base in the game. Chris Parmelee struck out in the second inning but reached on Iannetta's passed ball. Josh Willingham walked in the seventh, but that was it.

48 Spring Training 2000— A New Era Begins

Immediately upon his hiring on November 18, 1999, new Angels manager Mike Scioscia made an impact. He revamped the coaching staff by bringing in fellow ex-Dodgers Mickey Hatcher (hitting coach), Alfredo Griffin (infield and first base coach), and Ron Roenicke (third base coach).

Scioscia would have considered Orel Hershiser to be his pitching coach, but Hershiser was still an active major leaguer. Instead, Scioscia and general manager Bill Stoneman agreed on Bud Black, who was working in the front office with the Cleveland Indians. Joe Maddon, Scioscia's bench coach, would be the only remaining link to past Angels coaching regimes. Maddon was a good resource for Scioscia. He had been with the organization since 1981 as a minor

Angels Milestone Wins

Win No. 1: April 11, 1961, 7–2 over Baltimore. Winning pitcher: Eli Grba

Win No. 1,000: September 29, 1973, 4–3 over Minnesota. Winning pitcher: Bill Singer

Win No. 2,000: September 17, 1986, 3–1 over Kansas City. Winning pitcher: Doug Corbett

Win No. 3,000: April 30, 2000, 5–2 over Tampa Bay. Winning pitcher: Kent Bottenfield

Win No. 4,000: June 14, 2011, 4–0 over Seattle. Winning pitcher: Jered Weaver

league coach and manager, and no one knew the Angels' players better.

Maddon was also the club's resident intellect, an avid reader who emphasized the use of computerized breakdowns of pitcher/batter matchups and defensive alignments based on opposing hitters' spray charts.

Soon after spring training for the 2000 season began, there seemed to be a new optimism in the clubhouse. However, there might have been lingering friction between first baseman Mo Vaughn and some of his teammates. The Angels engaged in a bench-clearing melee with the Indians in August 1999. After the game, Angels players watched the highlights on television in the visiting clubhouse at Jacobs Field and noticed that Vaughn had remained in the dugout and did not join his teammates on the field. Vaughn explained that as the designated hitter, he was in the clubhouse when the fight broke out, and by the time he got to the dugout, the fight had subsided.

Some Angels players didn't buy the argument, most notably Troy Percival, who confronted Vaughn in the clubhouse. It led to off-season rumors that Vaughn, who had completed just one year of a six-year $80 million contract, wanted to be traded. Vaughn, though, came to camp in 2000 with a new outlook.

"I read all this about me wanting to get traded," Vaughn said at the outset of spring training. "First of all, nothing I've ever started did I not finish. I'm not about to jump ship when things don't go the way they're supposed to go. I will always believe my choice to come here was the right choice. This organization took care of me, gave me an opportunity. Things don't always happen right away. Last year was a bad year, but we're in a different situation now."

With a new coaching staff in place and apparent harmony in the clubhouse, the Angels were poised to change the direction of the franchise. Even lifelong Angel Tim Salmon had questioned the team's direction following the 1999 season, but he changed his tune after a few days in Camp Scioscia.

"This is the first day toward redemption," Salmon said. "I was talking to some of the coaches and trainers and they were saying, 'Man, what a different attitude there is in there [the clubhouse].' This is a fresh start."

49 Skeeter's 1970 Season— Clyde Wright

They say lefties are a little different, and it would be hard to argue that statement if you ever got a chance to meet Clyde Wright—also known as Skeeter to his friends. A native of Tennessee who still has his southern drawl, Wright is an outgoing character with the gift of gab who has become an entertaining public speaker.

He pitched for the Angels from 1966–73, making his mark with the franchise in 1970 by throwing the club's first no-hitter at Anaheim Stadium and setting the single-season mark for wins with 22, since equaled by Nolan Ryan. Wright's 1970 season was among the best performances by a pitcher in club history. He went 22–12 with a 2.83 ERA and finished sixth in the Cy Young Award voting.

It was the only year of his career that he made the All-Star team, and of course, Wright was in the middle of a historic All-Star moment. Wright entered the game in the bottom of the 11th with the score tied at 4. He retired the National League hitters 1-2-3, getting Bud Harrelson on a fly out and Cito Gaston and Joe Morgan on ground-outs.

Wright remained in the game to pitch the bottom of the 12th with the score still tied at 4–4, and got two quick outs—getting first Joe Torre and then Roberto Clemente on ground-outs. Pete Rose followed with a two-out single to center and went to second on a single by Billy Grabarkewitz. Up next was Jim Hickman, who hardly had the same name recognition as those Wright had already faced in this appearance.

But Hickman, a fellow Tennessean, laced a single to center, and around third Rose came, eventually barreling into catcher Ray Fosse to score the winning run. Fosse injured his shoulder on the play and a promising career never panned out.

"If you watch it on television, every time Rose runs over Ray Fosse, everybody's looking at the play at the plate," Wright said. "But if you look behind the plate, there's ol' No. 38 backing up home, because I had a lot of practice backing up home, so I knew where to go."

Wright is also quick to note that the winning pitcher in the 1970 All-Star Game, Claude Osteen, the losing pitcher, Wright, and game-winning hitter, Hickman, were all native Tennesseans. "I kept it in the state. I'm proud of that," Wright said.

Eleven days before the All-Star Game, Wright threw his no-hitter against the Oakland A's in front of a small crowd of a little more than 12,000 at Anaheim Stadium on Friday night, July 3. Wright was perfect through four innings, then he walked Sal Bando to lead off the fifth. Two outs later, he walked Dave

Angels 20-Game Winners
Nolan Ryan (1974), Clyde Wright (1970)—22
Bartolo Colon (2005), Ryan (1973)—21
Bill Singer (1973), Andy Messersmith (1971), Dean Chance (1964),
Jared Weaver (2012)—20

Duncan, but he got Dick Green to hit into a force play at third to end the inning.

Wright settled into a groove again, retiring the next nine hitters—Tony La Russa, Bert Campaneris, and Felipe Alou in the sixth, Reggie Jackson, Bando, and Tommy Davis in the seventh, and Joe Rudi, Duncan, and Green in the eighth.

"You get through the seventh and you're sitting over there and nobody's talking to you," Wright said. "But I said, 'You got a chance at this thing.' So I get through the eighth and go out to the mound for the ninth and I say to myself, 'If somebody screws this up, I'm gonna hit them every time they come up again.'"

Wright walked pinch hitter Frank Fernandez to start the inning, and Campaneris followed with a scorching line drive hit right to Jim Fregosi at shortstop. Alou was up next and hit the ball hard, as well, a sharp ground ball to Fregosi who started the game-ending 6-4-3 double play.

"Curveball down and in and he hit a bullet," Wright said of Alou. "I'm one of the few guys who ever threw a no-hitter with only one strikeout. Twenty-six guys hit it! People said, 'What in the world?' But I said, they've all got brand-new gloves, break 'em in!"

The 1970 season almost never happened for Wright. After a 1969 season in which he went 1–8, Wright was waived by the club and no other team picked him up. Fregosi convinced Wright to pitch winter ball in Puerto Rico, where Wright developed a screwball and changeup.

"Pat Corrales was my catcher," Wright said. "Nate Colbert was the hitter. The count was 3–2. Pat puts down screwball. I shake it off. Pat puts down screwball again. I shake it off. He calls timeout and comes out to the mound. He says, 'Look, I'm gonna tell you something. If you throw it, and you throw it 3' in front of home plate, I guarantee you he's gonna swing at it.'

"I threw it and bounced it. He swung at it. From then on, I threw it 2–2, 3–2, 3–0, it didn't matter. But Corrales was the one that hammered me with that."

Wright won 16 games with the Angels in 1971, 18 in '72, and 11 in '73 before being traded to Milwaukee for the 1974 season. He was traded again in '75, going to Texas, and then he played three years in Japan before retiring as a player.

50 World Series 2002—Game 4

Any thoughts the Angels might have had of breezing to an easy World Series victory over the Giants in 2002 were erased in the eighth inning in Game 4 at Pacific Bell Park in San Francisco. The Angels had just won their second Series game in a row, not just beating the Giants but beating them up 10–4 in Game 3 for a 2–1 Series lead. So when the Angels jumped out to an early 3–0 lead in Game 4, there was no reason to believe the Angels wouldn't be able to hold it. After all, their bullpen had been fantastic throughout the playoffs.

The Angels offense was facing Kirk Rueter, a soft-throwing lefty, exactly the type of pitcher that would give the Angels hitters trouble. But the Angels pushed across a run in the second inning on three singles and a sacrifice fly by David Eckstein for a 1–0 lead. In the third inning, Tim Salmon led off with a single, and one out later he scored on Troy Glaus' two-run homer.

Angels starting pitcher John Lackey took a shutout into the fifth, but the Giants pushed across three runs on four singles, a sacrifice fly, and an Angels error, tying the game at 3–3.

It would come down to a battle of bullpens, and it was a battle for which the Angels were well-prepared. Ben Weber pitched a scoreless sixth, and Francisco Rodriguez pitched a scoreless seventh. Rodriguez came out to pitch the eighth and gave up a single to J.T. Snow to lead off the inning. Snow had his own moment in the sun with the Angels when he started the 1993 season with a bang.

Snow took second on a passed ball by catcher Bengie Molina, and it proved to be a key play as Snow scored on a one-out single by David Bell. The Angels couldn't score again, and the Series was tied at 2–2 after the Giants' 4–3 win.

"Well, you might be a little spoiled by Francisco because he's been incredible," Angels manager Mike Scioscia said of the 20-year-old phenom who had been called up from the minors in September, only a few weeks before the playoffs. "He's virtually gotten everybody out. We know that's not the life of a pitcher."

Snow said that facing Rodriguez in Game 2—even though Rodriguez got him out—helped him in Game 4. "We know he's good and he's got great stuff," Snow said. "But you better believe you can get him. You can't go up with negative thoughts in your head. Any time you see a guy for the first time, it's tough. Tonight, we made adjustments."

Snow said he was looking for a slider from Rodriguez because he noticed that Rodriguez threw more sliders than he or his teammates expected to see in Game 2. Snow got that slider and singled to right.

Rodriguez, though, said it wasn't the pitch selection, it was the location. "He was waiting for a slider, and he hit it well," Rodriguez said. "But it was down the middle. If it's down and away, he's not going to hit the ball like that."

Rodriguez got the first out of the inning when first baseman Scott Spiezio made a spectacular diving catch of Reggie Sanders' bunt attempt in foul territory, bringing up Bell.

Bell got a fastball up in the zone and hit a sharp grounder to the left of a diving Eckstein at shortstop to drive in Snow with what turned out to be the winning run. "When you throw a fastball up in the zone, it's going to go straight," Rodriguez explained. "If I throw the ball the way I usually do, it's middle-away."

As it was, the loss tied the Series and set the stage for a dramatic finish and the Angels' first World Series championship.

51 The Enforcer—Don Baylor

Don Baylor played for the Angels from 1977–82, was part of the franchise's first two division championships, and won its first MVP award, the only one in club history until Vladimir Guerrero won the award in 2004.

But Baylor's tenure in Anaheim was far from smooth, and the well-respected team leader often found himself in the middle of turmoil. Baylor came to the Angels as part of the first free agent class of 1977, leaving Oakland to join the Angels along with other free agents Bobby Grich and Joe Rudi.

Baylor received a signing bonus of $580,000 on top of $1.6 million for six years, making him one of the highest-paid players in baseball. So when things went wrong in '77, Baylor often found himself the target of the fans' frustrations.

"I remember Coach Del Crandall preparing me for the game every day with a 'Booooo!'" Baylor said. "Then I'd go outside and everybody in the stands started in on me. It was brutal!"

Of course, the problems of '77 were not all Baylor's fault. Grich hurt his back lifting an air conditioner at his home in Long Beach and wasn't the same all season. Rudi broke his wrist in June and was lost for the season.

The Angels' managers that season—first Norm Sherry and then Dave Garcia—were passive in their approach, and players took advantage of it as they caused chaos in the clubhouse. Baylor himself was bothered by a sore shoulder for much of the year, limiting him to the designated hitter spot—something he was not happy about considering his competitive nature.

The Angels finished Baylor's first year in Anaheim 74–88, hardly the result owner Gene Autry was looking for after committing to spending $5.2 million on his free agents. "I knew I was gonna have to win the fans back after '77," Baylor said. "I hit 25 home runs that year and still got hammered pretty good by the press. But the tough times I went through made me stronger. I could have cried about it, but instead I committed myself to turning it around."

Baylor had help turning it around, mainly from Buzzie Bavasi, who was hired by Autry as the club's new general manager. Bavasi traded Bobby Bonds to the White Sox for Brian Downing and pitchers Dave Frost and Chris Knapp. Also going to Chicago in the deal were pitcher Richard Dotson and outfielder Thad Bosley. Bavasi also signed outfielder Lyman Bostock to a free agent contract.

Another big move came midway through the '78 season when Autry and Bavasi decided to fire Garcia as manager and brought in Jim Fregosi to manage the club. Fregosi was just 36 years old and playing sparingly with the Pirates as his playing career was coming to a close.

"I read in the paper one day that Jim Fregosi made two errors in Pittsburgh and the next day he was our manager," Baylor said.

The team seemed to be headed in the right direction, but the season seemed insignificant when Bostock was shot and killed in

Don Baylor looks upward after slugging a grand-slam homer in the eighth inning against the Milwaukee Brewers on Saturday, October 9, 1982, bringing the score to 7–5 Milwaukee. But it was to no avail as Milwaukee went on to win 9–5. (AP Photo/ John Swart)

Most RBIs by an Angels Player in a Month
April: Don Baylor (1979)—28
May: Mo Vaughn (1999)—28
June: Vladimir Guerrero (2004)—30
July: Jim Edmonds (1995), Baylor (1979)—34
August: Kendrys Morales (2009)—33
September: Garret Anderson (2000), Vaughn (1999), Baylor (1978), Bob Oliver (1973), Frank Robinson (1973)—27
September/October: Vaughn (1999)—29

September while the club was in Chicago. "[The next day] I got to the park early, and when I got there, there was some damn photographer and he was taking a picture of Lyman's empty locker," Baylor said. "I threw him the hell out.

"Even after all these years, every time I go back to Chicago, I think about him. It was the end of the season and we were [still in the race], but after that happened the guys just wanted to get the season over with."

The Angels regrouped for the 1979 season, and Baylor was excited about Bavasi's next move—trading for Rod Carew.

Finally, most everything went right for the Angels on their way to winning the AL West title and qualifying for the playoffs for the first time in club history. And Baylor was the reason for it, both on and off the field. He hit .296 with 36 home runs and led the league in RBIs (139) and runs scored (120).

"He was the enforcer," Carew said of Baylor. "He wasn't a loudmouth or anything. He'd pick up guys in a professional way.... He had this sixth sense of when something needed to be done, and he did it."

52 Homegrown Hero— Bobby Grich

Somehow, some way, Bobby Grich was going to be an Angel.

Grich was drafted by the Baltimore Orioles out of Wilson High School in Long Beach in 1967. He was a first-round draft pick, the 19th player selected overall, and by 1970, at the age of 21, he had reached the big leagues. Grich had success with the Orioles, first taking over at second base for Davey Johnson and later becoming a three-time All-Star and four-time Gold Glove winner in Baltimore.

But it was just a matter of time.

When the players were granted the ability to become free agents after the 1976 season, Grich quickly became an Angel, signing a five-year, $1.55 million contract with the Angels. He turned those five years into 10 seasons with the Angels and was a member on the club's first three division-title teams in 1979, '82, and '86.

But Grich really became an Angel at heart before the Angels were even a major league team. The Los Angeles Angels, a Triple A team, played in the highly respected Pacific Coast League. In 1957 Grich's dad took him to a game at L.A.'s Wrigley Field.

Steve Bilko, who would become one of the original Angels with the major league club, was a power-hitting first baseman for the PCL Angels. And Grich wanted Bilko's autograph.

"When the game was over, I ran down to the dugout," Grich remembered. "All the other kids were around him, and I was in the back."

Grich was just 8 years old, but the tenacity that helped him become a major league All-Star was about to be revealed. Grich tore a strip of cardboard from a popcorn box and tied a pencil to the end of the strip. He reached and stretched over the crowd of kids and pleaded with Bilko to sign.

Members of the Angels Hall of Fame
Gene Autry
Bobby Grich
Jim Fregosi
Don Baylor
Rod Carew
Nolan Ryan
Jimmie Reese
Brian Downing
Chuck Finley
2002 World Series championship team

"He saw how adamant I was," Grich said. "In pencil, he autographed 'Steve Bilko' on this little piece of cardboard box. I was so thrilled and so excited that I grabbed it and ran all the way up the aisle, waving to my father, shouting, 'I got Steve Bilko's autograph! I got Steve Bilko's autograph!'"

Grich was in high school when the Angels moved into Anaheim Stadium in 1966.

"I was usually sitting about the fifth row, right in line with third base," he recalled. "Aurelio Rodriguez or Paul Schaal was the third baseman, and I was watching Fregosi, Knoop, Don Mincher, Bob Rodgers, Jose Cardenal, Albie Pearson. I had that lineup down. I loved the Angels, I loved Angel Stadium, and it was a dream and a goal of mine to play on that field some day, and to be able to play for the Angels was the crème de la crème."

Grich became an established major leaguer before he actually joined the Angels. With the Orioles, he was an All-Star by age 23 in 1972. In 1974 he had his best season in Baltimore when he was an All-Star, a Gold Glove winner, and finished ninth in the MVP voting.

After the 1976 season, Grich heard that the Angels had already signed Don Baylor and Joe Rudi to free agent contracts, and Grich wanted in. He called his agent and implored him to contact the Angels and get something done. It happened quickly, as the feeling was mutual. But Grich's homecoming was anything but a fairy tale. Before the season even started, Grich was injured.

Moving into a new apartment in Long Beach, Grich was lifting an air conditioner when his back went out. He was in traction for most of spring training and played in only 52 games that first season in Anaheim in 1977. But two years later in 1979, Grich had the best season of his major league career, hitting .294 with 30 homers and 101 RBIs.

Grich was confident off the field, as well.

"Grichie was always looking in the stands, and one day he spots this blond in the family pass section," Baylor said. "He gets one of the clubhouse kids to take her a note. He writes, 'My name is Bob Grich. I'd like to take you out. Please give me your number.' She writes back, 'I'd like to give you my number, but I'm married to the manager, Jim Fregosi.' Jimmy got a bigger kick out of it than anybody, and it just got better from there."

Grich became a three-time All-Star with the Angels and was a member of those three division championships, but his career ended with the disappointing Game 7 loss to the Red Sox in the 1986 American League Championship Series.

It was a bitter ending to a fantastic career, but Grich, like so many Angels fans, was able to forget about the failures of the past when the team won the 2002 World Series. Basking in the energy of a World Series victory rally that drew 100,000 people to Edison Field two days after the Game 7 win, Grich soaked it all in.

"All of the ghosts are gone," he said. "All the jinxes are gone, and the bad vibes are gone. There's nothing but blue skies ahead."

53 Fred Lynn's Grand Slam

There are some rarities in baseball—a triple play, a perfect game, an inside-the-park home run. But there is nothing more rare in major league history than an All-Star Game grand slam. There has been only one in history, and it was hit by a player wearing an Angels uniform.

Fred Lynn hit it in the 1983 All-Star Game at Chicago's Comiskey Park off Giants pitcher Atlee Hammaker, a lefty who was leading the National League at the break with a 1.70 ERA.

Hammaker entered the game in the bottom of the third with the American League already leading 2–1. Hammaker was knocked around in the inning, giving up a home run to Jim Rice and RBI singles by Dave Winfield and Rod Carew.

Carew's single sent Manny Trillo to third, and Carew took second base on the throw home. That brought up Robin Yount with first base open. But with the left-handed hitting Lynn on deck, National League manager Whitey Herzog instructed Hammaker to walk Yount intentionally, loading the bases with two outs for Lynn.

"It was a good strategy as far as lefty vs. lefty, and he was tough on lefties," Lynn said years later. "I never really had problems, especially when I was with the Angels, hitting lefties because I got a lot of strikes to hit. We had a lot of big right-handed hitters on our club.

"The lefties would rather pitch to me than some of the righties [Bobby Grich, Don Baylor, Doug DeCinces, Brian Downing]. So I got better pitches to hit; I didn't care if they were left-handed or not—if you throw it over the plate, I'm gonna hit it. Even against Atlee, I got a 2–2 slider that he got out over the plate, and that's what I was looking for. Had he thrown a fastball in, he'd have gotten me."

Instead, the slam put the American League up 9–1 in an eventual 13–3 victory.

"When it happened, it was a big moment just because the American League had finally won," said Lynn, who played football and baseball at USC before reaching the majors. "Prior to 1983, the National League owned us.

"At the time, I had no idea it was the only grand slam. All I knew is, we were going to win that game. I was pretty excited about that. Afterward, I found out, and I was like, 'Jeez, 50 years of All-Star competition and nobody's hit a grand slam?'

"That's a long time, but when you get down to it, it's not like the bases get loaded and they bring in some guy from the bully. It's a closer out there. You're facing the best of the best all the time. I think if it's going to happen, it's going to happen early in a game against a starter who's not quite into the game just yet. That's when you can get to some of these big starters. I don't think it's going to happen against a reliever."

It's a baseball rarity that Lynn, who played with the Angels from 1981–84, would like to keep as his own.

"Well, I have this hex that I put on the players. It's a voodoo chant," Lynn joked. "I've looked at All-Star Games since I've hit that home run. Very few times do bases get loaded. But when they do, it has my full attention. Never as much as when Mark McGwire came up with the bases loaded in Colorado. He hits a fly ball, it's a home run. I was thinking, 'Well, if McGwire does it, at least it'll be two 'SC guys.' But he didn't do it, so I guess the hex is still working."

54 World Series 2002—Game 5

Pressure? What pressure?

The Giants had just beaten the Angels 16–4 in Game 5 of the 2002 World Series, taking a 3–2 lead heading back to Anaheim for Game 6. If the Angels' players were feeling the heat, they didn't show it.

"That would make a good story if we won two, wouldn't it," Angels center fielder Darin Erstad said prophetically.

While it had been the Angels' offense that set all kinds of post-season records in 2002, it was the Giants' turn to unleash the heavy lumber in Game 5. Their 16 runs matched the second most in a World Series game in baseball history.

Jeff Kent had two home runs and a double to lead a Giants offense that totaled 16 hits overall. Rich Aurilia also homered for the Giants, bringing their World Series total to 12 homers, the most ever by a National League team and tied with the 1956 Yankees as the most by any World Series team. The Giants eventually set the World Series mark with 14 homers in the Series.

Kenny Lofton and Barry Bonds also had three hits apiece in the game at Pacific Bell Park in San Francisco.

"They had it going tonight," Erstad said after the game. "It was a little taste of our own medicine. But if you lose by one or by 12, it's still just one loss."

The Giants scored three runs in each of the first two innings for a 6–0 lead against Angels starting pitcher Jarrod Washburn. Washburn gave up six runs and six hits in four innings, easily the worst start of the season. He had gone 18–6 during the regular season but was just 1–2 with a 5.02 ERA in five postseason starts.

He made 37 starts in 2002, regular season and postseason combined.

"I've felt tired for the last month," Washburn said. "Tired or not, I'm expected to go out and do my job and I didn't. I let all these guys down in this room. I was terrible from the get-go. I feel terrible."

The Angels tried to make a game of it with three runs in the fifth off Giants starter Jason Schmidt and another run in the sixth. But the Giants blasted the Angels' bullpen in the later innings, scoring twice in the sixth and four times in both the seventh and eighth innings to win going away.

"The big key for us was adding on," Giants manager Dusty Baker said. "We didn't want to hold on to the lead, we wanted to add on to the lead, which we did. We know the Angels are a big comeback team. We also know they're a big-inning team, much like we are."

Now the Angels had their proverbial backs against the wall. But in the clubhouse that night, they almost seemed comfortable in that spot. After all, nobody expected much out of this group after it finished the 2001 season 41 games behind the first-place Seattle Mariners.

And in 2002, the team started 6–14, the worst start through 20 games in club history. Nobody panicked then, so nobody was going to panic now. "We've been through numerous games where we had tough losses or got blown out," Angels closer Troy Percival said. "But we've come back before. We've got two games we've got to win. There's not a guy in here who's going to panic."

Angels manager Mike Scioscia looked at Game 5 as a missed opportunity as much as a blowout loss. "Well, it was tough," Scioscia said. "We battled back. Actually, you look at the final score, it was a whoopin', no doubt about that. But the opportunity in the middle of the game for us to get back in it was there. We've felt good about that, obviously. But that's a flat-out whoopin'. You can't really put it into any more words."

55 Joe Maddon

Other than Gene Autry, there might not be a single person who's had more influence on the Angels organization without ever stepping into the batter's box or throwing a single pitch than Joe Maddon. In fact no one, except Autry, has been connected to the Angels longer than the 31 years Maddon spent playing, coaching, managing, instructing, evaluating, guiding, mentoring, and befriending anybody who had anything to do with the organization.

His playing career was short and uneventful. He was a catcher who never played above Class A ball after signing with the club as an undrafted free agent in 1975. But he soon found his calling when he began serving the organization as a non-player by managing Class A Idaho Falls in 1981, and he has done just about everything one can possibly do for a baseball franchise.

He's been a minor league manager and instructor, director of player development, minor league field coordinator and scout, major league bullpen coach, first base coach, bench coach, and interim manager. Maddon left the Angels organization after the 2005 season to become the manager of the Tampa Bay Rays. He has won the award as American League Manager of the Year twice (2008, 2011) and did the unimaginable by managing the club to the World Series in 2008.

So when asked to reflect on his 31 years with the Angels, Maddon needed a moment for some mental organization. "As a minor league player, the thing that stands out is that we were the best minor league organization at that time," he said. "It was all about winning, and it was all about the camaraderie among the players and the coaches that taught us.

"We had great coaching. I was taught really well at a very young age."

After Maddon made the transition to coaching, he began to shape the careers of young players who eventually became successful major leaguers. "In the early '80s when I got the job as a scout and a manager, I was taught well by Larry Himes, Marcel Lachemann, [and] Bob Clear probably more than anybody, how to do this, what I'm doing today.

"Moving forward, the thing that stands out is the World Series victory. It was a magical moment that helped prepare me for what I'm doing today. To participate in a World Series victory, that team…it teaches you how to go through the season and how to prepare for those tougher moments, those bigger moments, in a manner that you don't become overwhelmed."

Maddon is the son of an Italian dad, Joe Sr., who shortened the family name from Maddonini, and a Polish mom, Albina, affectionately known as Beanie. Joe Sr. passed away during the 2002 season, but Maddon made sure to honor his dad.

"Every game I give him a seat behind our dugout," Maddon said moments after the Angels clinched a playoff spot with a victory over the Rangers that September. That raucous celebration in the visiting clubhouse at The Ballpark in Arlington also gave Maddon a chance to reflect on his relationships with the players from that championship team.

"You try not to be overly emotional, but so many things go through your mind," Maddon said at the time. "Watching Garret [Anderson] walk up to the on-deck circle in the seventh inning, I flashed back to [Rookie League] Mesa, when I knew he didn't want to be there because he was better than everybody else. I remember watching [Tim] Salmon at Grand Canyon College and saw him as a freshman hit two home runs in a game."

Maddon made his mark with the Angels in many ways, including the quotes he posted throughout the clubhouse and on the lineup card each day. His favorite?

"I'm not sure if I have the wording exactly right, but it's, 'A mind once stretched has difficulty going back to its original form.' That's attributed to Einstein. I love that."

56 Bobby Valentine and a Chain-Link Fence

Bobby Valentine came to the Angels in what would be considered a blockbuster trade.

Following the 1972 season, the Angels sent Andy Messersmith and Ken McMullen to the Dodgers for Valentine, Frank Robinson, Billy Grabarkewitz, Bill Singer, and Mike Strahler.

Valentine had been a standout athlete in his home state of Connecticut and was even offered football scholarships to both USC and Notre Dame. But after the Dodgers selected him with the fifth pick overall in the first round of the 1968 draft, he chose baseball. He was a star among stars in a Dodgers minor league system that included Steve Garvey, Davey Lopes, Bill Russell, Ron Cey, Tom Paciorek, and Bill Buckner. He led the Pacific Coast League in hitting with a .340 average in 1970, and many people had him ticketed as the Dodgers' shortstop of the future.

Dodgers manager Walter Alston, however, favored Russell. After two seasons in Los Angeles, Valentine was sent up the freeway to Anaheim. Valentine was the Angels' Opening Day shortstop in 1973, and in the season opener against the Royals, he went 2-for-4 with a triple, an RBI, and a run scored. On May 17, he was hitting .302, and at age 23, it seemed his career was about to blossom.

But that day, center fielder Ken Berry was sick. So manager Bobby Winkles had to re-do his lineup, moving Valentine from shortstop and putting him in center field. Valentine's athletic ability allowed such a move.

But in the top of the fourth inning, Dick Green of the Oakland A's hit a drive to left-center field. Valentine ran hard, fast, and with a purpose, got to the warning track, and leaped into the chain-link fence. His spikes caught and his right leg was shattered, both bones in the lower leg were severely broken. Ironically, after Valentine was carted off, it was Berry who entered the game in center field, apparently feeling well enough to play.

"I ran as fast as I could into the wall, and the wall didn't go down," Valentine said years later. "It was the exact same break as Joe Theismann's. The only difference is that in 1973, medicine was a little different, and I came out of the cast with a leg that had a 20-degree bend one way and an 18-degree bend the other."

Valentine spent six months in a cast, and when the cast was removed, it was found that the bones had mended poorly.

Valentine was giving the option of having leg reconstruction surgery, but that meant another 12–18 months of rehab.

Valentine opted against the surgery but was never the same.

He hit .261 in 117 games for the Angels in 1974, then he was traded to the Padres late in the '75 season. He played five more seasons in the majors but never played in more than 86 games in a season. He bounced around from the Padres to the Mets to the Mariners, retiring after the 1979 season with a .260 lifetime average.

Valentine's baseball career was not over, though—not by a long shot. He has become a successful major league manager, managing both in Japan and the majors thanks to some advice he received from Tommy Lasorda not long after the accident. Lasorda had managed Valentine in the Dodgers' minor league system, and Valentine respected Lasorda's opinion.

"Lasorda was managing down in the Dominican winter league where I'd played for him five years before," Valentine said. "And I said, 'Tommy, all these people don't believe I can still play at the same level I did before I broke my leg. Why don't you let me come down and play for you, and you can tell me what you think.'

"We had a deal. And at the end of the season we went out for pizza and he said, 'Okay, I'll tell you. I think you should start thinking about coaching or managing.' And we both cried."

57 Wrigley Field

If a stadium could be loved, this one could. It sat right in the middle of an adoring neighborhood, as much a part of the community as city hall and the grocery store. It was Wrigley Field in South-Central Los Angeles, just like its namesake on the north side of Chicago.

Before the Dodgers came west, the best baseball in town was played at Wrigley Field, home to the Pacific Coast League's Los Angeles Angels. It wasn't the majors, but it was a look into the future.

Joe DiMaggio played there with the San Francisco Seals, Casey Stengel managed there with the Oakland Oaks, and Ted Williams played there with the San Diego Padres.

Philip K. Wrigley owned the stadium and his Cubs actually had their spring training off the L.A. coast on Catalina Island, but Wrigley missed the boat on the majors' westward expansion, and he sold the stadium to Dodgers owner Walter O'Malley.

When Gene Autry acquired the Angels for the 1961 season, he made a deal with O'Malley in which the Angels would play their first season at Wrigley then move into the newly built Dodger Stadium with the Dodgers starting with the 1962 season. O'Malley didn't feel threatened—Wrigley Field, with its large, Spanish-style clock tower, seated a maximum of 20,050. Indeed, the Angels drew a league-low in attendance that season, averaging less than 8,000 fans per game.

Of course, it was different when the Yankees were in town—the stadium filled each time Mickey Mantle, Roger Maris, and their teammates came to town.

Maris broke Babe Ruth's major league home run record that season with 61, and Mantle hit 54. Some figured Maris was able to break the record because he had the opportunity to play games in the cozy little ballpark. There were a total of 248 home runs hit at Wrigley that year, a major league record for home runs at one ballpark for a single season at the time.

But Maris hit only two there in nine games that season. He hit home run No. 3 on May 6 off Eli Grba, and he hit No. 50 off Ken McBride on August 22. Mantle also hit just two home runs at Wrigley.

Opening Day for the major league Angels at Wrigley Field came on April 27, 1961, and it attracted stars from Hollywood and politics alike. Tony Martin sang the National Anthem. Groucho Marx was there. So was Richard Nixon. Baseball commissioner Ford Frick and American League president Joe Cronin attended.

Baseball Hall of Famer Ty Cobb threw out the ceremonial first pitch in what would be his last public appearance. Cobb, 74, died of lung cancer three months later.

The Angels lost that home opener 4–2 to the Minnesota Twins, but Wrigley Field became a place of comfort for those expansion Angels. Even though they finished just 70–91 in their initial season, they were good at home, going 46–36 for a winning percentage of .561.

The final game ever played at Wrigley Field came on October 1, 1961, with the Indians beating the Angels 8–4. But the game was significant in that the last home run ever hit there came off the bat of Steve Bilko, who was a star with the PCL Angels at Wrigley Field before he was drafted by the club in the expansion draft.

Bilko's homer came in the ninth inning, and rumor has it that the round tripper was scripted. Bilko smacked the first pitch thrown to him by the Indians' Jim "Mudcat" Grant over the fence, and as he rounded third was seen to mouth the words, "Thank you" toward Grant.

Wrigley Field stood empty for a few more years, then it was demolished in 1966.

58 Frank Tanana Loves Frank Tanana

There was no bigger fan of Frank Tanana than Frank Tanana himself.

He had good reason to boast. A first-round draft pick of the Angels in 1971 who first reached the majors at age 19 in 1973, Tanana was still just 21 years old in 1975 when he was 16–9 with a 2.62 ERA and led the American League with 269 strikeouts. He threw hard on the field and played hard off it.

"My idol as a kid was myself," Tanana once said. He also said, "My ambition is to become the best pitcher in baseball. I may have already achieved it."

About his off-the-field exploits, Tanana said, "I went to an

Frank Tanana pitches during the first inning in the third game of the American League playoffs on October 5, 1979, in Anaheim, California, against the Baltimore Orioles. (AP Photo)

all-boys high school, and now I'm making up for it."

During the mid-1970s, Tanana and Nolan Ryan were the core of a team that didn't have much else, which led to the saying, "Tanana and Ryan, and a whole lotta cryin'." From 1974–78, Tanana and Ryan each won exactly 82 games for the Angels. Tanana also threw 13 scoreless innings twice in a game—once in 1975 and once in '76—only to receive a no-decision in each, becoming the only pitcher in baseball history to do so.

In 1977, Tanana was 12–6 with a 2.15 ERA at the All-Star break and was ticketed to start the All-Star Game. But he had thrown 14 consecutive complete games during one stretch, and that contributed to an inflamed triceps tendon. He was to be replaced on the All-Star roster by Ryan, who then refused the honor because he wasn't originally selected by American League manager Billy Martin.

That led to bigger changes starting in 1979, which turned out to be Ryan's last year with the club and a year that forced Tanana into becoming a different pitcher. Tanana missed two months of the season with a shoulder injury but was able to come back and pitch a complete game in the division-clinching victory in September.

"For us to win it and for me to pitch the clincher, well hell, it's unbelievable," he said. "I've never been this happy. It's like a script. It takes some of the sting out of all the BS I've had to go through this year, out of all the frustration of the last six years."

But it was also the beginning of Tanana's complete transformation as a pitcher. Because of his ailing shoulder, his pitching style was forever altered. The shoulder injury forced Tanana to go from being a fastball pitcher to becoming a soft-throwing pitcher who relied on an outstanding curveball. But the Angels weren't around to see it, unless they were in the opposing dugout.

The Angels traded Tanana following the 1980 season to the Red Sox, along with Jim Dorsey and Joe Rudi, for Fred Lynn and Steve Renko.

After the trade Tanana wound up pitching 13 more seasons for the Red Sox, Rangers, Tigers, Mets, and Yankees, compiling 240 major league wins, less than half of which (102) came with the Angels.

Almost parallel to Tanana's transformation as a pitcher was his transformation as a human being. His wild, off-the-field partying lifestyle gave way to becoming a leader within baseball's Christian community. He went on to serve on the Pro Athletes Outreach Board of Directors and is involved in the Home Plate and Career Impact ministries.

"Pretty soon the fancy lifestyle grew old and stale, and I became a very lonely man on the inside," Tanana wrote on thegoal.com. "I began to ask myself, 'Is this all I've got to look forward to for the rest of my life?'

"In my search for contentment, purpose and meaning in life, I began to attend a Bible study where I heard that God loved me and that I could get into heaven by believing in Him.... You see God wasn't a priority in my life at that time, and I really wasn't living for Him. I was living for my own selfish gain, and while I claimed to be a Christian, my Christianity was self-made."

59 Arte Moreno

Just call him Arte.

When Arte Moreno purchased the Angels from the Walt Disney Co. in 2003, he made it a point to be one of the guys. He wasn't "Mr. Moreno, sir." Upon meeting members of the media, Moreno was quick to say, "Call me Arte."

One of Moreno's first acts—insignificant as it seemed—was to lower beer prices at Angel Stadium. It was such a small thing, but the media ran with it and the fans, of course, loved it.

When he first purchased the team, Moreno would often walk through the concourse at the ballpark and mingle with fans, asking them what would make their ballpark experience better. He was the antithesis of the corporate giant ownership that was Disney. Moreno, like Gene Autry before him, was just another guy—a guy you'd want to have a beer with.

Moreno, however, ruffled some feathers in 2005 when he decided to change the name of the team from the Anaheim Angels to the Los Angeles Angels of Anaheim. It was all about tapping into

Angels owner Arte Moreno signs autographs before a spring baseball game against the Arizona Diamondbacks in Tempe, Arizona, on Saturday, March 15, 2008. (AP Photo/Jeff Chiu)

the broader-based L.A. market.

Of course, the city of Anaheim wasn't happy. And in fact, they made a deal with Disney in 1996 that the club's name would be changed from California Angels to Anaheim Angels in exchange for $20 million, which the city would contribute to the $100 million stadium renovation project that was eventually completed in 1998.

The city said calling the team Los Angeles Angels of Anaheim was a violation of the lease agreement that the city had with the team. Moreno's lawyers claimed that they lived up to the agreement because Anaheim remained part of the team name. Moreno figured it should be a no-brainer for fans if they knew a broader market base meant more revenue, which meant more money to spend on high-end players.

More high-end players mean more winning.

"For us, all of our media comes from the L.A. metro area, all the papers, all the TV, all the radio," Moreno said in a 2005 interview with Doug Miller of mlb.com. "In the total market, from the media perspective, and to represent the whole metro area, it will give us a good, solid economic balance. Anaheim is 300,000-plus people, Orange County is 3 million, and the metro area is 16.5 million people.

"For us to get an opportunity to market the entire metro area, long term, you have to do the right things. [The name change] will give us more viability in the long run."

Indeed, the Angels have broken the chains of the "mid-market" media tag that Jackie Autry insisted the club would always hold. Now the Angels have one of the highest payrolls in the major leagues and also doled out the second largest contract in major league history—guaranteeing Albert Pujols $240 million over 10 years.

As of 2012 Moreno was still waiting for it all to pay off in the form of a World Series victory, or even a World Series appearance. Under his guidance, however, the team has been a consistent winner. From the time Moreno bought the team in 2003 through 2009, the Angels won five division championships and reached the American League Championship Series twice.

Moreno is a pioneer, and his purchase of the Angels for $184 million made him the first Latino owner of an American-based professional sports franchise. Not bad for a kid who grew up the oldest of 11 children in a two-bedroom home in Tucson, Arizona.

He took over the family's *El Tusconense* newspaper for a while and also helped with the family's printing business. But where Moreno made his money was in the billboard business. Initially, he sold ads for Phoenix-based advertiser Eller Outdoor. He left Eller Outdoor and joined the competing billboard company Outdoor Systems in 1984, eventually becoming CEO, and turned it into the largest space-advertising firm in the nation.

When the company was sold in 1999 for $8.7 billion, Moreno pocketing nearly $960 million for himself. So when Disney let it be known the Angels were for sale a few years later, Moreno was ready. Not just financially ready, either. Moreno had already been involved in the business of baseball for years. He owned the minor league Salt Lake City Trappers in the late 1980s, and he helped found the major league Arizona Diamondbacks but was unable to buy out other investors. Eventually Moreno sold his shares of the Diamondbacks, but his love of both baseball and business led him to Anaheim—er—L.A.

60 1977 Free Agent Frenzy

The 1977 major league baseball season marked the beginning of a new era in the game, an era in which the players—under certain guidelines—could become free agents and not be contractually tied to a team for their entire career.

It was a boon for players who could now sell their services to the highest bidder. Owners of course, were not happy with the new reality, knowing that salaries would skyrocket.

Angels owner Gene Autry was no different than the other owners, but he also knew that if he didn't participate in the process, his Angels would be left behind. So after the 1976 season, Autry jumped in feet first.

"Gene was against the whole concept," said Harry Dalton, the Angels' general manager at the time. "He knew what effect it would have. But he asked me if our restraint would help create restraint throughout the game, I had to answer negatively.

"I told him that I believed it would only put us further behind, since most of our competitors wouldn't demonstrate the same restraint."

Autry told Dalton he could spend $4 million and Dalton then met with agent Jerry Kapstein, who represented 10 of the league's first free-agent class. Dalton's first agreement came with Don Baylor, signing him to a six-year $1.6 million contract plus a $580,000 signing bonus. Baylor had made $34,000 in 1976 with the Oakland A's and raised his average annual salary to $267,000 a year.

The next agreement came with outfielder Joe Rudi, a player Autry particularly liked, with a five-year $2 million contract with a $1 million signing bonus.

Just like that, Dalton had committed to spending $3.6 million dollars to two players, not to mention the more than $1.5 in signing bonuses. He figured his work was finished.

It wasn't.

Bobby Grich, who grew up in Long Beach as a big Angels fan, heard about the agreements with Baylor and Rudi and called his agent, Kapstein, and told him to see if there was a way he could go there, too. Grich had already established himself as one of the best second basemen in the game, coming off a season in which he was an All-Star for the third time in his career and had won his fourth Gold Glove.

Autry figured, "Why not?"

"I've already hocked the horse," Autry said. "I can always hock the saddle."

Grich signed for five years and $1.55 million, and the Angels were suddenly the favorites to win the American League West. Autry, however, soon found out that buying a championship wasn't as simple as signing the checks.

Grich hurt his back while moving into his new place in Long Beach even before the season began. He was bothered by back problems throughout the 1977 season and wound up playing just 52 games, hitting .243 with seven homers and 23 RBIs.

Rudi got off to a hot start, tying an American League record with 27 RBIs in April, but he suffered a broken hand when hit by a pitch on June 26 and didn't play for the rest of season, finishing with a .264 average, 13 homers, and 53 RBIs in 64 games.

Baylor played in 154 games and finished with decent numbers— .251 average, 25 homers, and 75 RBIs—but he got off to such a slow start that he was booed mercilessly by the hometown fans at Anaheim Stadium.

Angels manager Norm Sherry didn't even survive the season as he was fired in July, and he said a lot of the team's problems stemmed from the subpar performances by the new guys.

"We had been unable to use either Rudi or Grich, and we hadn't been getting help from Baylor," Sherry said. "You take those three guys away, and you have pretty much the same team you had [in 1976]."

The high hopes of 1977 ended with a thud, the Angels finishing the year 74–88 and in fifth place in the AL West.

61 Palm Springs—Spring Training or Spring Break?

One hundred miles east of Los Angeles sits Palm Springs, a desert resort community that seemed to have everything the Angels wanted in a spring training facility.

It had the Polo Grounds baseball facility. It had warm, dry weather, perfect for getting ready for the season. And it had a nightlife. The Angels players in those days played hard on the field, and they played hard off the field. Initially at least, new Angels manager Bill Rigney thought it was a great place to hold camp and credited general manager Fred Haney for making the decision.

"Fred had about five minutes to get organized and did a great job of finding that little park—then known as the Polo Grounds—in Palm Springs," Rigney said. "Fred felt it was close enough to L.A. for fans, sponsors, and media, and far enough for the players to realize they were in spring training.

"Everyone loved it. I mean, as long as we were in Palm Springs, I never had any trouble getting players to report early."

President Dwight Eisenhower, only a couple of months from leaving office in January 1961, was a frequent guest at the ballpark of Angels owner Gene Autry. Eisenhower was a resident of nearby Rancho Mirage.

Autry led a parade of players on bicycles down the street to the ballpark in a publicity stunt to get the party started in 1961, and boy, was it a party. "It was a four-week Mardi Gras is this chic resort mecca," said Dick Enberg, the longtime voice of the Angels.

The drinking was enough of an issue that manager Rigney felt it necessary to address it the following year in 1962 as spring training was about to begin. "Look boys, we've had one year in this

Presidential Pals

President Richard Nixon was a friend of Angels owner Gene Autry. After the Angels won the AL West in 1979, Nixon invited the team to celebrate the title at his estate in San Clemente, California, which sat on a bluff overlooking the Pacific Ocean.

Nixon wasn't the only former president that took a liking to Autry. President Dwight D. Eisenhower was a frequent guest of Autry's at the Angels' spring training ballpark in Palm Springs in the early 1960s. Eisenhower, who left office in January 1961, owned an estate in nearby Rancho Mirage.

President Ronald Reagan attended the All-Star Game at Anaheim Stadium in 1989, and he spent a few minutes in the television booth providing some color commentary.

town, and I know how it is," Rigney told his players. "I enjoy it, too. But until we get in good shape, no drinking, and I mean no drinking for anybody, for two weeks! We're a new ballclub, and for some of you this is a second chance. For some of you, it's a first chance. So let's dry out and get in the best shape we've ever been in in our lives. Okay?"

It was a nice thought, but it didn't work.

Catcher Buck Rodgers roomed with first baseman Steve Bilko, who was a veteran of the old Pacific Coast League and wasn't about to miss out on living the big-league lifestyle. Bilko filled the bathtub in their room with cans of beer, and Rodgers said the tub was never empty all spring.

"We never took a shower or a bath in that tub all spring," Rodgers said in Rob Goldman's *Once They Were Angels*. "The older players were always in our room—Eli Grba, Ken Hunt, Ned Garver. Some of us younger players—Jim Fregosi and Lee Thomas—we'd all hang out together. When I got back after dinner, Bilko would be in his bed snoring up a storm so bad the windows would rattle."

Pitcher Ryne Duren might have been the club's biggest partier of all. One early morning in spring training, Duren decided to hit golf balls from the back patio of his room onto the roof of pitching coach Marv Grissom's room.

"Kind of an early starting time, don't you think, Ryne?" Grissom quipped.

Palm Springs was a glamorous spot for the new club, which stayed at the Desert Inn before Autry eventually bought his own hotel in town.

The Angels continued to make Palm Springs their spring training home until moving to Tempe, Arizona, in 1993. The Palm Springs facility eventually became outdated and too small. Many clubs were moving their camps to Arizona, and it simply became a logistical nightmare to bus the team several hours to Arizona every day just to play a game or for other teams to bus to Palm Springs.

The Angels' last spring training in Palm Springs in 1992 gave many Angels a chance to reflect. Scott Bailes, an Angels reliever on that 1992 team, had T-shirts made up that said, "Last Hurrah in Shangri-La."

"The thing I've missed most is spring training in Palm Springs," Grich said about his life after baseball. "It was my favorite time of the year, with the intimate crowds, the relaxed atmosphere, the great weather, the chance to see some of the young players, and Gene Autry watching from that tunnel under the stands, right there next to the dugout.

"It was a beautiful place to play, and there was no more wonderful view than to stand out at second base and look at that small grandstand with all those tank tops and shorts, and snow-capped San Jacinto in the background."

62 K-Rod Saves the Day (62 Times)

They say it takes a certain mentality, a certain fearlessness, to be a closer. It also takes an ability to make pitches that leave batters shaking their heads as they walk back to the dugout after striking out.

In Francisco Rodriguez, the Angels found both, and he was the perfect successor to Troy Percival, the Angels' all-time saves leader. Rodriguez, however, did something Percival never did. In fact, Rodriguez did something that no pitcher in major league history—since the save became an official statistic in 1969—has ever done.

Rodriguez recorded 62 saves in 2008, breaking the previous record of 57 set by Bobby Thigpen of the White Sox in 1990.

Rodriguez burst onto the scene in September 2002, a late-season call-up by the Angels as they made their playoff push. Rodriguez was just 20 years old but stifled hitters with a fastball-slider combination that made him nearly impossible to hit.

He was so good in those last couple of weeks of the 2002 season—he had 13 strikeouts while allowing three hits in 5⅔ innings—that the Angels found a way to get him on their postseason roster. He worked his way into the club's primary set-up role during the playoffs and established himself as the league's next great closer.

Of course, the Angels still had a good one in Percival, so Rodriguez settled for the role of set-up man in 2003 and '04. But Rodriguez stepped into the closer's role for the 2005 season, and he led the league with 45 saves. He led the league again in 2006 with 47 saves, and he saved 40 in 2007.

Going into the 2008 season, the Angels were again expected to win their division. For a closer, obviously, that's big because saves

Francisco Rodriguez throws against the Detroit Tigers in the ninth inning of their game in Detroit on Saturday, September 2, 2006. Rodriguez got the win with 1⅔ innings of relief, striking out four and extending his shutout streak to 23 outings in the Angels' 7–2 win. (AP Photo/Paul Sancya)

only happen when a team has a lead going into the ninth inning. The 2008 Angels won the division again and won a franchise-record 100 regular-season games. Rodriguez was on hand to finish off 62 of them.

There was a sign of things to come when Rodriguez had saves in each of his first three appearances of the season. He was consistent throughout the season—he had 11 saves through April, 21 through May, 32 through June, 44 through July, and 53 through August.

Thigpen's 18-year-old record seemed bound to fall. And it did.

Rodriguez tied the record with save No. 57 on September 11 and set a new record with save No. 58 on September 13. He got four more saves for good measure to push the mark to 62, and he was tagged for only six blown saves all year.

Rodriguez left the Angels to sign with the Mets after the 2008 season, then he was traded to the Brewers during the 2011 season. As of 2012, he was closing in on 300 career saves. Getting so close has allowed Rodriguez to look back and reflect on how—and who—made it possible.

Percival is at the top of the list.

Percival finished his career with 358 saves, and 316 of them were earned with the Angels. When he got save No. 300, he made a point to show Rodriguez the significance of the accomplishment.

"When he took the picture with the bullpen and the baseball, he told me, 'Make sure when you get yours, you invite me, because I want to be in that picture,'" Rodriguez said. "And I laughed like, 'Yeah, right. I'm not a closer. You're the closer.' And he said, 'Yeah, but you will be.'

"I was like, 'No chance,' and he said, 'Son, you will be. Make sure you call me when you get your 300th because I want to be there.'"

Midway through the 2012 season, Rodriguez had 294 career saves, and had to start thinking about getting in touch with Percival and fulfilling his wishes.

"I need to start making phone calls," Rodriguez said. "I will find a way to get him here. He was my mentor. He was a guy coming in and taught me everything I know about being a closer, and has been really, really helpful."

63 Bus Crash

Bob "Buck" Rodgers was an original Angel, playing with the team at its inception in 1961 through the 1969 season. He was a favorite of owner Gene Autry's, which is why Rodgers eventually found his way back to the organization as the club's manager more than 20 years later, in 1991.

His tenure as the club's manager from 1991–94 was unremarkable, and his biggest accomplishment during that time might have been simply surviving the accident when the team bus crashed off the New Jersey Turnpike in the early morning hours of May 21, 1992.

Rodgers was the most seriously injured of the 12 Angels players and staff who required medical attention after the first of two team busses traveling from New York to Baltimore veered off the road and into a grove of trees about 20 miles from Philadelphia.

Rodgers suffered a broken right wrist, a shattered right elbow, a broken left knee, and two cracked ribs. The most serious injuries were to his right arm, which required six hours of surgery.

Almost one month after the accident, Rodgers held a news conference in the backyard of his Yorba Linda home. "I remember going down a mountain and a forest of trees coming through the windshield," he said while sitting in a wheelchair. "I thought I had it made and that I would walk away with nothing until we hit that last tree. I was in the front pew like a sardine.

"When we got down to the bottom and hit the tree, I knew my elbow was hurt. It was hanging down, just swinging. It was a bag of bones."

Despite his injuries, Rodgers' sense of humor was intact, recalling his interaction with a young paramedic immediately after the accident. "There was a young guy tromping all over my foot," Rodgers said. "He said, 'I found one! I found one, but I think he's dead.' I said, 'I'm not dead, just get off my damned foot.'"

Rodgers did not return to the dugout for more than three months after the crash, finally resuming his duties as the club's manager on August 28, 1992. He could have chosen to come back earlier, but he would have had to do so in a wheelchair—something he wouldn't do.

"I think a manager has to have a certain presence around the clubhouse, and I don't think coming back on crutches or in a wheelchair, you can have that," he said.

Others injured in the crash included infielder Alvin Davis, traveling secretary Frank Sims, and head trainer Ned Bergert. Davis and Bergert were tested for possible kidney damage, and Sims had cracked ribs. Bullpen catcher Rick Turner had a gash under his left arm that required 26 stitches. Remarkably, only one player ended up on the disabled list—infielder Bobby Rose went to the 15-day disabled list (DL) because of a sprained ankle.

"It was like being in a big washing machine or a heavy duty dryer, just thrashing around," said shortstop Gary DiSarcina, who suffered bruises and a sore back. "Then it got real dark, and all I heard was moaning and groaning, and there was luggage and food all over the place. It seemed like it took an hour to realize where we were."

After the crash, a second team bus stopped on the side of the road and several players went to help before paramedics arrived. Pitchers Chuck Finley, Jim Abbott, and Bert Blyleven were lauded for helping pull people out of the mangled bus.

"I saw Chuck Finley running around the bus grabbing people," DiSarcina said, "and the thought crossed my mind, 'Chuck wasn't on this bus.'"

A year after the accident, the National Transportation Safety Board ruled that driver error was the cause of the crash saying: "The probable cause of this accident was the failure of the fatigued intercity bus driver to keep his vehicle on the roadway."

64 Tim Salmon's First Day in the Majors

Tim Salmon was the Angels' first Rookie of the Year in 1993, but the 1992 season was a big one for him, as well. He began the season in big-league camp, then he went on to win *Baseball America's* award for the Minor League Player of the Year. But Salmon did not finish out the season with Class AAA Edmonton.

On August 20, 1992, Edmonton was in Calgary for a game, but just before the game Edmonton manager Max "Mako" Oliveras told Salmon he was being taken out of the lineup. The Angels had called and Salmon was headed to the big leagues the next day. His destination—Yankee Stadium in New York.

Salmon had to fly first to Toronto before getting a connecting flight to New York. He was anxious, wanting and hoping to get to Yankee Stadium in time for the game. He landed at about 4:30 PM and was directed to take a cab directly to the ballpark.

"When I finally arrived, the taxi dropped me off right in front of the stadium entrance," Salmon said in his book, *Always an Angel*. "There I stood with two big equipment bags and no idea where to go next. When fans streaming into the stadium realized that I was a new player, they began to shout, 'Who are you?' 'You somebody special?' 'Sign this for me?' Getting into the clubhouse was quickly becoming difficult.

"Then out of nowhere some burly cop came over and asked me suspiciously, 'Are you a new player? Follow me.'"

Salmon made it to the Angels clubhouse while the team was on the field taking batting practice. But his first order of business was to meet John Wathan, the Angels bench coach who had become interim manager. Earlier that year manager Buck Rodgers was injured when the team bus crashed going from New York to Baltimore.

Wathan welcomed Salmon then told him he was in the lineup batting cleanup. No pressure.

Chad Curtis, a rookie with the Angels and a teammate of Salmon's at Grand Canyon University, led Salmon to the field to get in a few swings before the game. He met with some of the writers and had a quick bite before taking the field. "My stomach was churning like a garbage disposal when the game started," Salmon said. "But as soon as I stepped into the on-deck circle to await my first major league at-bat, all my nerves instantly disappeared. When I put the weighted donut on my bat and started taking some swings to get loose, a sense of peace came over me. I had done this before. Sure, the venues were much different, but the game was the same."

The Yankees pitcher was Shawn Hillegas, and he got two quick strikes on Salmon. But Salmon took the next four pitches for balls and worked a walk. He ended up striking out twice, lined out to left, and grounded out to shortstop. He was 0-for-4 with a walk, but he was a big leaguer.

The game was over, but his big-league duties were not. After the game, instead of taking the team bus back to the hotel, Curtis invited Salmon to go with him and two other Angels players—Greg Myers and Rob Ducey—to meet and sign autographs for fans in Yankees owner George Steinbrenner's luxury box at the stadium.

After a couple hours, Salmon left the stadium with $2,000 cash and a sign of the future.

"So long, Skippy Peanut Butter!" Salmon said to himself. "The first thing I did was call room service. It isn't cheap in New York;

just a cheeseburger and Coke set me back $25. But I didn't have to worry about that any more."

Indeed. Salmon would go on to earn more than $70 million in his career, all 14 seasons with the Angels.

He only needed to wait one more day for his first major league hit—a single to center field off Yankees pitcher Melido Perez. Unfortunately for Salmon, prankster pitcher Bert Blyleven picked up the baseball and wrote on it.

Blyleven wrote: "A 60-hopper that barely trickled through the infield."

"I still laugh every time I see it in my trophy case," Salmon said.

Welcome to the big leagues.

65 The Eck Factor

There might be no one in the history of major league baseball who defines "unlikely hero" more than David Eckstein.

Eckstein became the World Series MVP with the St. Louis Cardinals in 2006, but by that time, the diminutive blond-haired Florida native had already established himself as a winner on the baseball field. Eckstein was generously listed at 5'8", but he admitted he was no more than 5'7", putting him at a disadvantage by so many scouts who look for size first. When he arrived for his first major league spring training with the Boston Red Sox in 2000, he was mistaken for a clubhouse attendant.

But what so many overlooked was the size of Eckstein's heart. After all, Eckstein was voted "most helpful" by his senior class at Seminole High School in Sanford, Florida, in 1993.

During the 2000 season, Eckstein was playing in the Red Sox minor league system when the club put him on waivers in order to clear a spot on their 40-man roster. The Red Sox likely figured that no team would claim him and Eckstein would remain in the organization.

But on the advice of his scouts, Angels general manager Bill Stoneman claimed Eckstein off waivers, discounting Eckstein's lack of size. "It didn't keep us from taking a chance, but I would venture to say it would keep other teams from taking a chance," Stoneman said. "Scouts today are looking for the biggest, fastest, strongest guys. But the one thing we talk to our scouts about is heart, how he plays with the tools he has. It showed up in our reports, and it showed up when he arrived in spring training [in 2001]."

Eckstein was ticketed for another season in Triple A in 2001, but an injury to second baseman Adam Kennedy during spring training cracked open the door for Eckstein, who then kicked it wide open. "I've loved the guy from Day One," Angels teammate Darin Erstad said. "If there's a definition of team player, it's that guy. He knows his role and maximizes his ability in that role."

And the surprises kept coming. Eckstein had been a second baseman all of his career, but infield coach Alfredo Griffin saw something in Eckstein that no one else did—he saw a shortstop. Benji Gil had been the Angels' primary shortstop in 2000 and appeared to be the Angels' choice again for 2001. But Griffin spoke up during a spring training meeting.

"Alfredo was convinced Eck could play shortstop," Angels manager Mike Scioscia said. "He felt Eck could do it. There were probably 20 coaches, scouts, and player development people in the room, and everybody thought he was nuts. But in his mind, he could make him a shortstop."

Eckstein kept the starting shortstop position the following year in 2002, and early on that season, there were signs good things were in store for Eckstein and the Angels. Eckstein, anything but a power hitter, hit a grand slam in back-to-back games on April 27 and 28 against the Toronto Blue Jays.

Eckstein, though, was never someone who craved the spotlight.

"The biggest thing I tried to do when I stepped on the field was to find a way to help the club win," he said. "Whatever that meant on any given day, I would put myself in a position to do it. I never worried about my stats, and I never worried about anything other than finding a way to make myself valuable on the field."

66 Little Man—Albie Pearson

Long before there was David Eckstein, there was Albie Pearson.

Pearson was just 5'5" and 140 pounds, but like Eckstein, he defied the odds and proved the skeptics wrong during a successful major league career. But it wasn't without twists and turns.

Pearson's major league career was at a crossroads after the 1960 season. He was the 1958 American League Rookie of the Year with the Washington Senators, but he had been traded to Baltimore when he hurt his back and was assigned to Miami, one of Baltimore's minor league affiliates.

So Pearson, a Southern California native who was a baseball and football star at El Monte High School, made a plea to new Angels general manager Fred Haney once Pearson learned that Los Angeles had landed an expansion team.

Pearson wrote a letter to Haney. "Mr. Haney: I'm Albie Pearson. I was Rookie of the Year in the American League. I've been sent down to Rochester, [which had just replaced Miami as Baltimore's top farm club] but I want you to know my back is well and I can play. I want to come home and play in Los Angeles where

I was born and raised. Please consider this letter as you make your draft. Sincerely, Albie Pearson."

With the 30th and final pick in the expansion draft, Haney and new Angels manager Bill Rigney selected Pearson, and it was a choice they would not regret. Pearson was the Angels' starting right fielder in 1961 and moved to center field in 1962. In 1963, Pearson hit .304, which ranked fourth in the American League. And in doing so, he became the Angels' first-ever .300 hitter.

Pearson had a strong arm and good speed, which made him a good outfielder. But he was also a student of the game and studied hitters closely.

"I had to think way ahead," Pearson said. "I had to be very sensitive in deciding how to play hitters. I would watch them and study their strengths and weaknesses.

"With Mickey Mantle, I could tell in batting practice by the way he held his hands if he was hurting physically or if he had too much to drink the previous night. If he was tired, he would lower his hands and have trouble handling the ball. So during the game I might move on him. Play a couple of steps the opposite way."

Pearson was popular with his teammates and the fans—not just Angels fans, but fans from other teams, as well. "I was popular mainly because of my lack of size," Pearson said. "I never heard a 'Boo' in my life. I was the hero for the guy who never made it. They always saw me as the underdog because I was competing at the highest level against guys a foot taller. I got many, many, many letters saying, 'I got a kid and he's little or he's small.'"

Pearson's bad back eventually forced his retirement in 1966, but Pearson was anything but finished making a big impact. Known as being devoutly religious during his playing days, Pearson established a youth foundation to raise money for abused children in Riverside, California, soon after retiring from baseball.

In 1972, he became an ordained minister and traveled throughout the world helping build churches and support missionaries.

In 2002, he was invited to watch the Angels in the World Series from a private suite, and he met Eckstein, the Angels' shortstop who was similar to Pearson not only in his stature but also with his selfless and giving nature.

"David is a giant compared to me," Pearson said. "I had a chance to shake his hand and let him know that he is such a great player. David is an overachiever, a winner. He is the kind of player who knew how to handle situations."

Just like Pearson.

67 Go to Disneyland

Amid the exultation on the field after the Angels won Game 7 of the World Series in 2002, there was no Angels player who turned to the camera and proclaimed, "I'm going to Disneyland!"

In a sense, they were already there.

The Angels have had three owners in their existence, starting with Gene Autry's long reign and most recently with billionaire businessman Arte Moreno. In between, the Angels were owned by the Walt Disney Co., which took operational control of the club in 1996 and acquired controlling interest upon Autry's death in 1998.

Disney sold the franchise to Moreno in 2003, ending its short stint in Major League Baseball but not without making an impact—Disney was the owner when the Angels won their first, and to date only, World Series.

Disney also owned the National Hockey League's Anaheim Mighty Ducks at the time, part of its effort to broaden its entertainment scope in Orange County and around the world. While

Disney has since sold both the Angels and Ducks, Disneyland remains "The Happiest Place on Earth."

Autry and Disney had a history long before Disney assumed control of the club. Autry had named Walt Disney himself to the Angels' board in 1960, and Disney served on the board until his death in 1966. Disney had also been one of the proponents of the Angels' move from Los Angeles to Anaheim.

Disneyland and Angel Stadium are separated by only three miles, and it's safe to say that without Disney, Angel Stadium might never have been built in Anaheim.

Disneyland opened in 1955, but Anaheim wasn't Disney's first choice. The original plans for the park were for eight acres next to the Burbank studios where his employees and families could go to relax and enjoy themselves. But World War II put those plans on hold. During the war, Disney's vision for this "magical park" began to expand, and it became clear that eight acres would not be enough.

His search for a new location ended in Anaheim when he bought a 160-acre orange grove near Interstate 5 and Harbor Boulevard. Hundreds of citrus trees and 15 houses were cleared, initiating construction of Disneyland in 1954.

Disney himself planned the details of each "land" within the park.

Adventureland was made to be an exotic tropical place in a far-off region of the world. "We pictured ourselves far from civilization, in the remote jungles of Asia and Africa," Disney said.

Frontierland was made to relive the pioneer days of the American frontier.

Fantasyland was created with the goal of making dreams come true. Said Disney, "What youngster...has not dreamed of flying with Peter Pan over moonlit London, or tumbling into Alice's nonsensical Wonderland? In Fantasyland, these classic stories of everyone's youth have become realities for youngsters—of all ages—to participate in."

Tomorrowland was created as a look at the marvels of the future, but Disney was worried about the concept and said, "Right when we do Tomorrowland, it will be outdated."

All of it would not be accessible without first strolling down Main Street. Disney wanted to relive what he considered the typical turn-of-the-century Main Street experience.

"For those of use who remember the carefree time it re-creates, Main Street will bring back happy memories," Disney said. "For younger visitors, it is an adventure in turning back the calendar to the days of grandfather's youth."

68 1966—Home Alone

Playing their home games in Dodger Stadium from 1962–65, the Angels were truly the little brother in the Los Angeles baseball family. It was *Dodger* Stadium, after all.

After their search for a new Southern California city and new ballpark landed them in Anaheim, the Angels finally gained a sense of identity. The California Angels now had a ballpark to call their own and would be free to establish their own history away from the Dodgers. Granted, the Dodgers were still No. 1 in Southern California, but the Angels finally had a home.

"The important thing is that having our own park with our own fans will mean a great deal for team pride," shortstop Jim Fregosi said. "There won't be 10,000 people in the stands listening [on the radio] to the Dodgers."

The Angels drew fewer than 600,000 fans at Dodger Stadium in 1965, and they drew 3,300 fans in their Dodger Stadium finale.

So general manager Fred Haney figured it was important to make an immediate splash in their new digs.

In the off-season before the 1966 season, Haney acquired veterans like catcher Ed Bailey, first baseman Norm Siebern, pitcher Lew Burdette, and third baseman Frank Malzone.

Haney had remembered the excitement created after a fast start in 1962, and he wanted to re-create that feeling. "We must make a good showing," Haney said. "And that constitutes a first-division finish. From the stands we looked dead last year [1965]. We have to recapture the spirit and attitude of three years ago."

Manager Bill Rigney was intent on cracking down on some of the Angels' purported partying lifestyle, saying in spring training that he "will not allow this team to leave its desire on the golf course or bar."

The Angels didn't come out of the gates blazing, but they weren't buried early, either. A victory over the Red Sox on May 15 put the Angels six games over .500 at 17–11, but they immediately lost six in a row. They hovered around .500 for the next month, then got hot, winning 11-of-13 to improve to 38–31 and were within seven games of first place in the American League.

Only five players—Dean Chance, Albie Pearson, Fred Newman, Jim Fregosi, and Buck Rodgers—remained from the Angels 1961 expansion team, but they got a boost from second baseman Bobby Knoop, who was in his third season with the Angels.

Knoop was a good fielder, making up a solid double-play combination with Fregosi at shortstop. But Knoop didn't have much pop at the plate, hitting .242 and averaging seven homers and 41 RBIs those first two seasons in 1964 and '65.

He had the best season of his career in 1966, hitting 17 homers with 72 RBIs and leading the league with 11 triples. He was an All-Star and won the first of his three Gold Gloves.

A shutout thrown by Clyde Wright on July 17 put the Angels a season-best nine games over .500 at 49–40. They were in third place in the AL but were still 10 games out of first.

They faded in August and September and finished in sixth place at 80–82, 18 games behind the American League champion Baltimore Orioles. Though they didn't win as much as they would have liked, Rigney worked wonders with a club that struggled offensively all season and saw a dramatic decline in pitcher Dean Chance, who won the Cy Young Award only two years earlier. Chance suffered from a "mysterious infection" most of the year and was traded after the season.

Overall, a relatively competitive club and the new ballpark helped bring in the fans—the Angels drew 1.4 million fans in their debut season at the "Big A."

69 Leading Off—Darin Erstad

Darin Erstad, meet Heinie Manush.

Who?

Exactly.

Erstad's 2000 season was so spectacular that he was introduced to the baseball history of Heinie Manush, who played in the majors some 70 years earlier. Erstad got off to a fast start in 2000, and he never slowed down. Throughout the year, there were records broken and milestones reached. When he got his 100th hit in his 61st game of the season, it was the fastest anyone had reached 100 since Manush did it in 60 games in 1934.

"Who the heck is Heinie Manush?" Erstad asked when told about the record.

For much of the season, Erstad remained on a pace to break the all-time single-season hits record of 257 set in 1920 by George Sisler. It was broken by Ichiro Suzuki (262) in 2004.

Darin Erstad hits a two-run home run against the New York Mets in the sixth inning at Shea Stadium in New York on Friday, June 10, 2005.
(AP Photo/Gregory Bull)

Erstad's approach was as much nose-to-the-grindstone as it gets. A former football player who played on Nebraska's NCAA championship team in 1994, Erstad kept his head down and his batting average up.

However, Erstad seemed amused and maybe sometimes annoyed when asked about numbers. He said he never thought about the results, just the process. "I'm not good with the stats sort of thing," he said. "But if it's the last game of the year and I have 256 hits and we're in a pennant race and we have a runner on second, I know what I'm doing—I'm moving the runner over."

Maybe that's the type of attitude it takes to put up the numbers Erstad put up in 2000. He wound up with 240 hits, batted .355, hit 25 home runs, and scored 121 runs. He also became the only player in baseball history to drive in 100 runs in one season from the leadoff spot. He also won a Gold Glove that year playing center field.

"Darin's motivation has not changed since he put on a baseball uniform as a little kid," said Mike Scioscia, whose first season managing the Angels came in 2000. "He's all about winning."

Erstad, though, was never one to tout his exploits. "As a hitter, I'm not going to explain much," he said. "You find a rhythm, you find a groove, and the ball finds a hole. It's amazing. It's like they're throwing it where my bat is."

As the season neared an end, there were some people who called for Erstad to be named the league's MVP. However, it didn't help that the Angels finished out of the playoff picture.

The top names thrown around for MVP were Jason Giambi, Frank Thomas, and Carlos Delgado, and it was Giambi who ultimately won the award. Scioscia, obviously, had his favorite.

"There are tremendous guys having tremendous seasons with huge impacts for their teams, and I'm not taking anything away from them," Scioscia said. "But looking at where we'd be without Darin and the intensity he brings, his RBIs, his hits and runs, the number of runs he's saved defensively.... I don't think there's a player in the league who has had more of an impact. I've seen a lot of names for MVP. To me, Erstad is at the top of the list."

Erstad finished eighth in the voting, and though he never had a season to match his accomplishments of 2000, he was a leader on the 2002 team that won the World Series and he also played on the division championship teams in 2004 and '05.

He finished out his final three seasons playing for the White Sox and Astros and is now the baseball coach at his alma mater, Nebraska.

70 Imagine Mark McGwire Hit 70 Home Runs for the Angels

It didn't happen. But it should have and could have—steroids or not.

Before he set the baseball world on fire with his dramatic chase of Roger Maris' home run record in 1998 with the Cardinals, Mark McGwire played for the Oakland A's. McGwire's career was blossoming in Oakland, but it seemed clear during the 1997 season the small-market A's would not be able to keep the burly slugger as he approached free agency.

McGwire is a Southern California native, and his son lived in SoCal with his ex-wife, so coming to play for the Angels seemed like a perfect fit.

The Angels and A's talked trade, and it seemed they might be able to reach a deal. The A's were to send McGwire and third baseman Scott Brosius to the Angels for center fielder Jim Edmonds, third baseman Dave Hollins and a pitcher—either Jarrod Washburn or Jason Dickson.

Tony Tavares, the Angels president under Disney at the time, said the deal never got that far. Tavares said the A's refused the Angels' request to talk to McGwire's agent, knowing that McGwire was due to become a free agent after the 1997 season and needed to gauge McGwire's likelihood to sign.

And besides, as Tavares was famously quoted as saying, no player was worth $10 million a year. Those words came back to haunt him because the payoff for a franchise with a player chasing—and then breaking—Maris' home run record would be immeasurable.

"Hindsight is 20-20," said Bill Bavasi, the Angels' general manager at the time. "I would have loved to see McGwire hit 70 home runs in an Angel uniform.... I definitely think there would have been the same frenzy in Anaheim that there was in St. Louis. I'm also confident that I could have convinced Disney that he was worth $10 million a year, but the bottom line was that we weren't going to make a trade of that magnitude without talking to the agent and receiving contractual assurance that he wasn't going to leave at the end of the year."

Instead, McGwire was traded to the Cardinals for Eric Ludwick, T.J. Mathews, and Blake Stein; not nearly as much as the Angels supposedly offered. And of course, in 1998 he hit 70 home runs to break Maris' record, which had stood for 37 years. McGwire remained in St. Louis for the rest of his career, wearing Cardinal red, not Angel red.

But give the Angels credit for learning their lesson. Maybe there was a player out there who *was* worth $10 million a year.

The Angels competed in 1998, battling for a division title most of the season until falling out of the race in the last week of the season. They finished 85–77, three games out of first place.

They figured they needed one more piece or, as it was, one "Mo" piece. Suddenly, $10 million a year was doable, and the Angels signed Mo Vaughn to a six-year $80 million contract.

That didn't turn out so well, but Bavasi insisted that Disney was always willing to do what it took financially. "They've never been afraid to spend the money as accused," he said at the time. "There's a change in action but not a change in philosophy. We just haven't seen the players we thought were the right fit for the right type of money. If we had seen a player like Mo Vaughn last year, he would have been signed. That's easy to say, but it's true. Players like him don't come around very often."

Though McGwire's status in the game eventually changed with allegations of steroid use, seeing a 70-homer season in Anaheim would have been an unforgettable experience. But we can only imagine.

71 Home Run Havoc— Kendrys Morales

The Angels have had more than their share of bizarre injuries. Whether it was Mo Vaughn falling into the dugout and severely spraining his ankle, or both Gary DiSarcina (forearm) and Chuck Finley (orbital bone) breaking bones in freak spring training accidents, it seemed to become some kind of sick joke.

Even success resulted in injury. Take Angels relief pitcher Jim Barr, who broke his hand in an altercation celebrating the 1979 American League Western Division championship. Barr's injury knocked him out of the playoffs.

But after the Angels won the World Series in 2002 and began to reach the playoffs regularly, it seemed maybe that jinx was lifted. That is, until they experienced one of the most bizarre incidents in their history and perhaps in all of baseball history.

It was May 29, 2010, and the Angels were one of the hottest organizations in baseball. They had won three consecutive AL West titles and five of the previous six. They had started the 2010 season a bit slow and were four games out of first in the West at 23–27 as they took the field that Saturday afternoon against the Seattle Mariners.

The game featured a great pitching matchup between the Angels' Jered Weaver and the Mariners' Felix Hernandez, and the game lived up to the billing. The Mariners scored once on a throwing error by Erick Aybar in the fourth inning. The Angels tied the game in the eighth inning on a solo home run by Bobby Abreu.

By the 10th inning, both Weaver and Hernandez were through for the day, and it became a battle of bullpens. Neither team scored in the ninth inning, and the Mariners did not score in the top of the 10th.

But in the bottom of the 10th, the Angels got something going. With one out, Maicer Izturis doubled to right field off Mariners reliever Brandon League. Abreu was walked intentionally, and then Reggie Willits reached on an error to load the bases for Kendrys Morales.

Morales was the Cuban refugee who emerged with a fantastic season the year before, hitting .306 with 34 homers and 108 RBIs in 2009. On the first pitch from League, Morales launched a towering drive to center field, and the ball cleared the fence for a game-winning grand slam.

Morales circled the bases like he had many times before while his teammates gathered around home plate, ready to celebrate. Morales tossed his helmet aside, approached the plate, and jumped on it.

The celebration was on, but it was soon clear that something was wrong. Morales was still on the ground. He had landed awkwardly when he hit the plate and snapped his left ankle.

While the Angel Stadium crowd filed out still buzzing with excitement, a motorized cart rolled to the plate and took Morales away. The break in his ankle was so severe that he missed the rest of the 2010 season and all of the 2011 season. He had two surgeries and when he returned in 2012, he was relegated to the designated hitter spot.

"It'll change the way we celebrate," Angels manager Mike Scioscia said immediately after the game. "It sure was exciting, but you always wonder if it's an accident waiting to happen.... It's definitely not the mood we would expect in the clubhouse after a win, but when something like that happens, it's definitely disturbing."

"The screams just went to silence," Angels center fielder Torii Hunter said. "I've never really seen that before. I've seen a kicker kick a field goal, jump up, and hurt his knee, tear his ACL. I've never seen it in baseball."

Morales not only had to deal with the injury, he had to deal with the strange nature in which it happened. "We were just

9-for-9

The Angels accomplished a rare statistical feat on August 18, 2009, when at the conclusion of their game—No. 117 of the season—against the Indians at Jacobs Field, all nine hitters in the lineup had a batting average of .300 or better.

The lineup:
Chone Figgins—.308
Bobby Abreu—.310
Juan Rivera—.310
Vladimir Guerrero—.313
Kendrys Morales—.303
Torii Hunter—.307
Maicer Izturis—.300
Mike Napoli—.300
Erick Aybar—.313

It marked the first time since 1934 that every player in the starting lineup finished a game with a batting average of .300 or better at least 100 games into the season.

caught up in the emotion of the game, the victory," Morales said. "Yeah, I think [about] what would have happened had I not jumped, but it was an accident. It happened. All I can do is move on."

72 Bill Stoneman

From 1961 through 2011, the Angels reached—and won—the World Series exactly one time. The general manager in charge of putting together that 2002 team was a guy many fans wouldn't recognize, and that's just the way he'd want it.

Bill Stoneman preferred to stay behind the scenes and out of the limelight, he endured criticism before, during, and after his tenure as GM, but his results speak for themselves. He not only put together the 2002 team but he also set the club in a direction it finds itself now—a perennial contender.

But the road to Anaheim was anything but direct for Stoneman, who figured his baseball career was finished when shoulder problems forced him out of the game in 1974.

"I never thought I would come back to baseball," Stoneman said. "I had some success as a player, but my last year and a half in the major leagues was awful. I had hurt my shoulder and really never recovered. The power was gone from my arm. I used to have a good fastball and a good curve ball—both were gone. It just was not a whole lot of fun going out there, getting your brains beat out most of the time. Occasionally, you had enough to fool somebody, but usually I didn't.

"Because the previous year and a half was not a lot of fun, I just wanted to distance myself from the game. I had a college degree [B.S. in Business from the University of Idaho], and I also had a master's degree [M.Ed. from the University of Oklahoma] and decided to put it to work."

Having played most of his career with the Montreal Expos, Stoneman returned to Canada to work for a highly respected financial institution, Royal Trust, before a chance meeting after taking in an Expos game in 1983 resulted in his return to the game as a member of the Expos' front office.

Stoneman gained a reputation as being somebody who could work well with a limited budget, and with the Expos, the budget was extremely limited. He caught the attention of Angels president Tony Tavares in 1999 when the Angels were searching for a new general manager following the resignation of Bill Bavasi.

Stoneman, though, was immediately tagged a bean-counter, and many Angels fans figured a penny-pincher wouldn't make winning a priority. "A lot of people think I'm an accountant. I'm not," Stoneman said after his hiring. "A lot of people think I'm a lawyer. I'm not. I'm really a baseball guy. I had an opportunity to work with general managers and had involvement in player personnel decisions without having to be the guy to pull the trigger.... I have a player's background and a business background. This is the marriage of those two things together."

Stoneman looked forward to having a bigger financial base with which to work. "Believe me, coming from a $15 million payroll to whatever it's going to be here is going to be very different from what I'm used to," he said. "And very welcomed....I know small payrolls, and the Angels don't have a small payroll."

Stoneman's first big move with the Angels was hiring a manager, and he surprised some people with the choice of Mike Scioscia, who had left the Dodgers organization.

He was often criticized for not making trades, but Stoneman made some shrewd moves that paid dividends throughout his tenure as the club's GM. He traded for Chone Figgins and Adam Kennedy, signed David Eckstein off waivers, and signed free agents Vladimir Guerrero and Bartolo Colon.

Stoneman was indeed more than a bean-counter, and his major league career includes a feat accomplished by only 25 other players in major league history. Stoneman is on a list that includes Nolan Ryan, Sandy Koufax, and Bob Feller, among others, who have thrown more than one no-hitter in the majors. Stoneman threw both of his pitching for the Montreal Expos—against the Phillies on April 17, 1969, and against the Mets on October 2, 1972. He was a National League All-Star in 1972, but just two years later, shoulder problems ended his playing career.

The Expos had sold Stoneman to the Angels at the start of the 1974 season, but Stoneman knew his shoulder wouldn't cooperate. "The general manager was Harry Dalton, and he was only 30 years old," Stoneman said. "Harry made me an offer to stay in baseball, that is, go to Triple A and see if I could go and straighten out, but I knew the power was gone and I told Harry that I appreciated the opportunity but I thought it was time to get a job outside of baseball."

Stoneman did, but he would come back 25 years later with a second chance to help lift the Angels to the top of the baseball world.

73 The Disney Era

Baseball had been a game to Gene Autry. He loved what happened between the lines and his interaction with the players. They were his drinking buddies, his pals. But as the years went by, it became more and more clear that Major League Baseball, first and foremost, was a business.

Toward the end of the 1980s and into the 1990s, the business of baseball became increasingly difficult. The Angels were losing money and could not see the situation improving. By this time, Jackie Autry was a strong presence in the Angels' front office when it came to making financial decisions. Gene was in his eighties and he knew he could sustain losses for only so long.

It became a decision between declaring bankruptcy and selling the club.

Two potential buyers emerged as the top candidates. One was Peter Ueberroth and his group. Ueberroth was the former commissioner of baseball, and he was also in charge of running the 1984 Summer Olympics in Los Angeles. He was an Orange County resident and had a good relationship with Gene Autry.

Major League Baseball, however, was becoming more and more dominated by the corporate world. The Walt Disney Co. had long-range ties with Autry and the Angels. Walt Disney himself encouraged Autry to move the team to Anaheim from Los Angeles in the early 1960s. Disney buying the Angels simply made sense. Disney had purchased the NHL Anaheim Mighty Ducks a few years earlier.

It was all about "synergy"—a Disney term. The company would have Disneyland, the Ducks, and the Angels all within a few square miles. And if Autry were to sell to a different ownership group, that group might move the Angels out of Anaheim.

"We just never had the funds to package or leverage the way Disney does, the synergy Disney has," Richard Brown, the Angels' president under Autry at the time, said in Ross Newhan's *The Anaheim Angels: A Complete History*.

"Disney can do so many more things through cross-ownership and cross-sponsorship. Disney can say, 'Buy a ticket to an Angels game for $50, and we'll throw in a trip to Disneyland.' We'd say, 'Come see the Angels play for $15 and then go to Disneyland on your own. Say hi to Mickey for me.'"

Ultimately, both Disney and the Ueberroth group agreed to pay $130 million for the Angels. However, Ueberroth was not willing to tack on an additional $10 million to pay for past debts incurred by the Autrys. Disney did agree to pay the extra $10 million and agreed to buy the team for $140 million in 1995.

The deal was approved by MLB in 1996 with Disney paying $30 million up front and taking over operational control with the option to complete the purchase upon Autry's death, which took place two years later.

Disney's marketing gurus immediately went into overdrive. They changed the team's name from California Angels to Anaheim Angels. They changed the uniform style and colors, introducing the color teal to Major League Baseball.

They also initiated a $100 million stadium renovation plan that was finished in time for the 1998 season.

It was corporate ownership in the truest sense of the word. Disney chairman Michael Eisner showed up at the news conference to announce the deal wearing an Angels jacket and a cap promoting the Disney movie *Angels in the Outfield* that was released in 1994.

Eisner, though, wasn't like Autry when it came to his visibility around the park, except during the Angels run through the playoffs and World Series in 2002. In 2003, Disney sold the club to Arte Moreno for $184 million.

Moreno, like Autry, was visible in the early years of his ownership, he was often seen on the field and even in the concourses of the stadium, mingling with fans.

"Mr. Moreno comes down before batting practice, shakes our hands, and asks us how we're doing," former Angels coach Joe Maddon said. "That leaves us really believing he cares, whereas [Disney], you'd never see them unless something good was happening or maybe something really bad was happening. From an employee perspective, you'd much rather see the family touch as opposed to the corporate touch."

It was under Disney ownership, however, that the Angels won the franchise's first—and so far only—World Series.

74 Brian Downing

If there was ever an underdog who defied all odds to become a successful major leaguer, it was Brian Downing. He was cut from his high school team and his junior college career consisted of him mostly warming up the pitchers as part of the team's "taxi squad."

And even when he did reach the major leagues, he found the worst luck. On the first pitch of the first inning in his first major league game, Downing, playing third base, made a catch while sliding into the dugout. He severely injured his knee and was out for two months.

Downing was the epitome of hard work. Despite his failures as a player in high school and junior college, Downing was impressive enough at an all-comers tryout for the Chicago White Sox to get signed at the age of 18.

Four years later, at age 22, he reached the big leagues.

His career with the Angels started in 1978 after a trade in which Bobby Bonds was sent to Chicago. Downing's first season in

Baltimore Oriole Eddie Murray is out at home plate as he slides past catcher Brian Downing on Friday, October 5, 1979, in Anaheim during the third game of the American League playoffs. Murray tried to score off a ball hit to center field by Rich Dauer. The throw was from Angel Rick Miller. (AP Photo)

Anaheim was nothing to get excited about—he hit .255 with seven homers and 46 RBIs.

But after the season, Downing, who built a batting cage in his backyard, became a committed weightlifter and significantly changed his body. He also altered his stance, and the results were immediate.

Downing was a major contributor to the team's 1979 American League West title when he hit .326 with 12 homers and 75 RBIs. He was also named to the All-Star team for the only time in his career.

"He was one of the first players to get into weightlifting and totally loved it," Angels pitcher Bert Blyleven told the *Orange County Register*. "[And it] should be said he did it without the juice. He was a quiet teammate, but once you got to know him, he was a great friend who loved playing the game."

Though he started out as a catcher, Downing eventually became an outfielder, and his ability to draw a walk resulted in his becoming a productive leadoff hitter.

Downing hit 20 or more home runs in a season six times and drove in as many as 95 runs one season. He spent 13 of his 20 big-league seasons with the Angels and was part of their first three division titles in 1979, '82, and '86.

But Downing was disillusioned when the club decided to let him go after the 1990 season. Downing said he simply would have appreciated being told ahead of time that the club had no plans for him.

He wound up playing two seasons with the Texas Rangers, and he had trouble forgiving the Angels for a while. "I'm very conflicted about a lot of things," Downing said in 2009.

Although he is an Orange County native, he didn't return to the Big A until he was invited to throw out the first pitch before a playoff game in 2002. It would be another seven years before Downing showed up again, that time to be inducted into the Angels Hall of Fame.

For years, Downing was the all-time Angels leader in numerous categories, before eventually being passed by Garret Anderson and Tim Salmon. As of 2012, Downing ranked third all-time in games played, at-bats, runs, hits, total bases, extra-base hits, doubles, home runs, RBIs, and was second in walks.

Still, the humble Downing has trouble seeing himself in a Hall of Fame that includes the likes of Rod Carew, Nolan Ryan, and others. "I was always glad to be part of a team with a bunch of players," Downing said, "but I never wanted to be *the* player."

Downing now lives on a ranch in Texas, home of his new favorite team, the Angels' AL West rival Texas Rangers.

"The Rangers just remind me of the type of team there was when I went to Anaheim," Downing said. "They had never won, then they were in the playoffs. Now Nolan Ryan is running things, and I root for him."

75 Go to Spring Training

There might not be a better segment of a Major League Baseball season than spring training. Optimism abounds, even for fans of teams that will ultimately finish in last place. The ballparks are small and intimate, the players are more accessible, and the weather is warm.

The Angels trained in Palm Springs from 1961–92 but moved to Tempe, Arizona, in 1993 after the facility formerly used by the Seattle Mariners was renovated. It has since been renovated again.

While Florida was the spring training hub of so many teams for many years, Arizona has turned into the place to be with an influx of new, state-of-the-art facilities.

Go see the Angels in spring training and you should visit not only the Angels' home park in Tempe but all the others that are within a half-hour's drive of central Phoenix. Fifteen teams train in the region's 10 spring training facilities. The games are played primarily in the daytime—when baseball was meant to be played. And that leaves time for a nightlife for fans who plan to stay for a while. Old-town Scottsdale, a Barry Bonds home run away from the Giants' facility in town, is a great place to spend an evening.

There are many restaurants within walking distance on or near North Scottsdale Road, like Oregano's Pizza Bistro, AZ 88, Daily Dose Old Town Bar & Grill, and The Mission. But a favorite is Bandera, right on the corner of N. Scottsdale Rd. and E. 1st Street. It has the best homemade cornbread you'll ever eat.

This is how Bandera describes itself at urbanspoon.com: "Bandera features an exciting exhibition kitchen with a large, full-service wrap-around bar centered in the room. All of our grill items are cooked over live wood. Popular dishes include our iron skillet cornbread, wood-fired rotisserie chicken, grilled artichokes, center-cut filet, and our famous banana cream pie."

Get there early because there's usually a wait, but saddle up to the bar for a refreshment and there's a good chance you'll eventually see a ballplayer or two come in for a meal.

But make sure you don't make it too late of a night because the early birds get the autographs at the ballparks. Players arrive early for a morning workout, and the ballparks usually open for fans to watch. When players make their way from one field to another within the facility, it can be a good time to snare an autograph or two.

Oh, and while you're there, take in a few games. You'll see a mix of major league stars, stars of the future, and even some you'll never see again.

76 1995 Collapse

What made the 2002 World Series championship so special was that it dulled the pain of so many failures from the past. And the failure freshest in the minds of Angels fans when the club finally won in '02 was the collapse of 1995.

The '95 Angels were stacked with young talent, particularly on the offensive end. Garret Anderson hit .321 with 16 homers and 69 RBIs and was second in the American League Rookie of the Year voting. Tim Salmon had the best season of his career, hitting .330 with 34 home runs, 105 RBIs, and 111 runs scored. Jim Edmonds was becoming the best defensive center fielder in baseball and hit .290 with 33 homers, 107 RBIs, and 120 runs scored. And J.T. Snow hit .289 with 24 homers and 102 RBIs.

The Angels also had a veteran presence in the clubhouse with designated hitter Chili Davis, who hit .318 with 20 homers and 86 RBIs. The club traded Chad Curtis for leadoff hitter Tony Phillips, who walked 113 times, scored 119 runs, and hit 27 home runs.

On the mound, the Angels had a solid 1-2 punch with Chuck Finley and Mark Langston, who each won 15 games. Closer Lee Smith had 37 saves and had Troy Percival setting him up, going 3–2 with a 1.95 ERA and 94 strikeouts in 74 innings.

Pitching-coach-turned-manager Marcel Lachemann might have been uncomfortable as the lead guy, but the pitchers loved him because he was what they call a player's manager.

It was all so perfect—until August 3.

The Angels had a game with the Seattle Mariners that day, and the Mariners were in third place, 13 games out of first. The Rangers were in second, 11 games out. The Mariners took a 10–2 lead going into the bottom of the seventh inning.

Jorge Fabregas led off the inning with a walk and went to second on a single by Gary DiSarcina, the Angels' shortstop who was deemed the heart and soul of the team by his teammates.

Up next was Phillips, who hit a grounder to second base. DiSarcina slid hard into second base in an effort to break up the double play. He was successful—the throw to first was too late to get Phillips.

DiSarcina, though, said he heard "something like a pencil breaking" when he grabbed the base with his hand as he slid by. He figured it was only a sprain, but it was worse—torn ligaments that required surgery and forced DiSarcina to miss the rest of the season.

"It took my breath away," backup shortstop Spike Owen said when he heard the news.

Losing DiSarcina would be a blow, but this team was too good, too talented to fall apart. That was the thinking, and general manager Bill Bavasi was sticking to it. "This hurts us, but I wouldn't call it a devastating blow," Bavasi said at the time. "I'll make the argument that Gary is the best shortstop in the league right now, but we never thought we could go wire to wire without losing a key component. If we can't still win, we're not as good as we think we are."

DiSarcina agreed. "This team is too good to go down the tubes because of one player," he said. "Having a good year makes it worse, and with the team playing like it is makes it twice as bad. It's going to be tough to sit there and watch."

Initially, the Angels held their own without DiSarcina. On August 16, they still led the division by 10½ games over the Rangers and 11½ over the Mariners. They lost six of their next eight, reducing their lead to 7½ over the Rangers. But the Mariners, the team that would eventually catch and pass the Angels, were still 11½ games out on August 24.

Then it started.

The Angels lost nine in a row, and their lead over the Mariners, now in second place, was just 5½ games on September 3. Ten days later, they began another nine-game losing streak, and by the time that was over, their lead was gone and they were two games behind Seattle.

The Angels managed to win their final five games of the regular season to tie the Mariners and force a one-game playoff in the Kingdome against Randy Johnson. It didn't go well, as the Mariners won 9–1. This one would sting for a while.

DiSarcina evaluated the collapse from his seat on the bench.

"We lost that intimidation, that edge, the feeling that we were going to go out and hammer teams," he said. "We lost the feeling of what it's like to win."

77 The Colossal Comeback

It was one of those games that all teams have during a season, no matter how good they might be.

For the Angels, their game against the Detroit Tigers on August 29, 1986, seemed to be one of those games. The '86 Angels team was talented, and it won the AL West. And as any baseball fan would know, they came within one strike of reaching the World Series. But on that late summer Friday evening, the Angels turned "one of those nights" into the team's greatest comeback ever.

The Angels led the division by 4½ games and were trying to hold off the Texas Rangers for another month or so. But Angels starting pitcher Kirk McCaskill got knocked around early in the game against the Detroit Tigers, giving up five runs in three innings to put the Angels in a 5–1 hole.

Chuck Finley, who would go on to set numerous club records for pitching, was in his rookie season, having been brought up three months earlier. He replaced McCaskill to start the fourth inning but had similar success—or a lack thereof.

Finley pitched scoreless innings in both the fourth and sixth, but in the fifth he gave up three runs, and the Tigers increased their lead to 8–1. The Angels managed to push across two runs in both the sixth and seventh innings, but as they headed to the bottom of the ninth, the outcome seemed just a formality as the Tigers led 12–5.

Dick Schofield led off the bottom of the ninth inning with an infield single, but Rick Burleson lined out to center field for the first out. Wally Joyner followed with a walk, and then Brian Downing singled to center.

With the club down by seven runs, Schofield was naturally held at third on Downing's single, loading the bases. Next up was Jack Howell, who entered the game defensively in the top of the ninth in place of Doug DeCinces. DeCinces was 36 years old and trying to get through the season in one piece.

Howell, 25 at the time, was a bench player and spot starter in '86 and was hitting just .248 on the season. But Howell was in the right spot at the right time this time, hitting a double to right field that scored two runs and made it 12–7.

Not wanting to take any chances, Tigers manager Sparky Anderson then replaced pitcher Randy O'Neal with closer Willie Hernandez. Hernandez immediately gave up RBI singles to George Hendrick and Bobby Grich, and suddenly the Tigers lead was just 12–9.

Hernandez got the second out of the inning when Gary Pettis grounded into a force play, but Ruppert Jones, batting for Jerry Narron, drew a walk to load the bases.

Schofield stood in the on-deck circle, while Reggie Jackson sat on the bench next to manager Gene Mauch. Would Mauch send up Jackson to pinch hit for Schofield? Granted, Jackson's skills were declining and he was in his final season with the Angels, but surely he had more power in his little pinky than the singles hitter Schofield.

Jackson remained seated, and Schofield made his way to the plate. He took strike one, then flailed at a screwball and fell behind in the count 0–2. But Schofield got a pitch to hit and turned on it, hitting it over the fence in left field for a game-winning grand slam. Final score: Angels 13, Tigers 12.

Even a grizzled vet like Mauch had to be impressed with the eight-run, ninth-inning rally.

"I've seen a few of them over the years, and that's lots and lots of years," Mauch said, "but I don't think I've ever seen anything like that one. In fact, I know I haven't. That's an all-timer, boys. That's an all-timer right there."

78 Batting Champ or Chump?—Alex Johnson

Rod Carew won seven batting titles during his Hall of Fame career, but none of them came during his seven years with the Angels. In fact, there has only been one Angel to win a batting championship, but he is not among the most recognizable names that have put on an Angels uniform. And he wasn't someone beloved by the fans, the media, or even his own teammates.

And there were a lot of teammates.

During Alex Johnson's 13-year major league career, he played for the Phillies, Cardinals, Reds, Indians, Rangers, Yankees, and Tigers. And he also played three seasons with the Angels from 1970–72—mostly nondescript seasons other than 1970 when Johnson hit .329 to win the American League batting title.

Johnson went into the final game of the 1970 season against the White Sox trailing Boston's Carl Yastrzemski by .0005 percentage points in the batting race. He needed two hits in the season's final game to secure the batting crown.

He grounded out in his first at-bat and singled in his second. In his third at-bat he beat out an infield single and was taken out of the game by manager Lefty Phillips to ensure the title.

Both Johnson and Yastrzemski hit .329, but Johnson was .0003 higher—.3289 to .3286.

"When I got to first, I heard a lot of noise and saw the scoreboard lighting up," Johnson said. "Suddenly I saw Jay Johnstone running out of the dugout toward me. He's yelling, 'You've got to leave the game! You've got to leave the game! Lefty says you've got to leave the ballgame whether you want to or not!' It totally surprised me. Then I looked at the scoreboard, and my name was ahead of Yastrzemski's. So I put two and two together."

There was a reason, though, that Johnson played for so many teams despite his talent. His teammates and managers were upset about what they perceived as a lack of hustle. Johnson came to blows with Angels teammate Chico Ruiz one day in the batting cage, and Ruiz had been a friend of Johnson's when the two were teammates with the Reds.

Johnson also had a scornful relationship with the baseball writers. "It was difficult covering the club because you would walk into the clubhouse and here would come this stream of epithets directed at the writers," said Ross Newhan, who covered the team for the *Long Beach Press-Telegram* and *Los Angeles Times* and has since been inducted into the Baseball Hall of Fame.

Johnson had a particularly surly relationship with *Herald Examiner* writer Dick Miller, but it seemed to work both ways. Johnson once poured coffee grounds into Miller's typewriter, but it came as retaliation for Miller hiding some of Johnson's bats.

In an interview with Newhan, Johnson explained his anger was a result of what he perceived as racial injustice. "Hell yes, I'm bitter," Johnson said. "I've been bitter since I learned I was black. The society into which I was born and in which I grew up and in which I play ball today is anti-black. My attitude is nothing more than a reaction to their attitude. But they [white people] don't keep their hatreds to themselves. They go out of their way to set up barriers, to make dirty little slights so that you're aware of their messed-up feelings."

79 G.A.'s All-Star Ambitions

Whether you're a little leaguer or a major leaguer, it's nice to be recognized for your accomplishments. In any league, that recognition comes when a player is named an All-Star.

Some deserving players never quite get there. Tim Salmon, the Angels' all-time home run leader, put up some big numbers over the years. But Salmon was a slow starter, so his numbers midway through the season—when the major league plays its All-Star game—might have fallen below All-Star standards.

Such was not the case for Garret Anderson in 2001. He had established himself as a big-time player in 2000 when he hit .286 with 35 homers and 117 RBIs, and he was off to a good start in 2001.

At the All-Star break that year, he was hitting .279 with 15 homers and 62 RBIs. Anderson wasn't a media star, so he didn't expect to be voted in as a starter by the fans. But he thought he had established himself enough to be chosen by Yankees manager Joe Torre who, as the manager of the defending AL champions, was the All-Star manager that year and would pick the reserves.

The phone call never came, and Anderson was disappointed.

"There's politics involved, and that takes the fun out of it," Anderson said at the time. "I thought I had a case last year, but I didn't get picked. There were a lot of guys like that; I wasn't the only one. The coaches take care of their own, and it kind of takes the luster out of it."

Anderson then said it would be "cool" to make an All-Star team some time during his career, but he didn't dwell on it. "I'm more proud of playing well over the course of a whole season, not just half the season," he said. "But if I do good enough and make it one year, so be it."

Turns out Anderson didn't have to wait that long.

He was named to the All-Star team in 2002, the first of his three All-Star selections. But he didn't settle for simply being named to the team. As an All-Star in 2003—he was a starter along with teammate Troy Glaus—Anderson had the kind of All-Star experience most players can only dream of.

On the Monday before the All-Star Game, the Home Run Derby took place, and Anderson, though not known as a pure home run hitter, accepted his invitation to participate. He reached the finals against Cardinals slugger Albert Pujols, and Anderson won nine homers to eight. Garret Anderson was the Home Run Derby champion.

It only got better from there in the game itself.

Anderson, batting fifth and playing left field, struck out in his first at-bat in the second inning against Giants pitcher Jason Schmidt. Then Anderson singled in the fourth inning off Cubs pitcher Kerry Wood.

In the sixth inning with the AL trailing 5–1, Anderson hit a two-run home run off Cardinals pitcher Woody Williams, and Anderson followed that up with a double in the eighth inning off Dodgers closer Eric Gagne, sparking a three-run rally that lifted the AL to a come-from-behind 7–6 victory.

One night after winning the Home Run Derby, Anderson was the All-Star Game MVP, becoming the third Angel to win the award. Leon Wagner won it in 1962 when the league played two All-Star Games, and Fred Lynn won it in 1983 thanks to hitting the only grand slam in All-Star Game history. For Anderson, it was recognition at the highest level, even though he was never one to actively seek it out.

Said Angels manager Mike Scioscia, "Whether Garret likes it or not, he's on that stage now."

80 Talk Baseball with Kurt Loe

Walk into the Angel Stadium press box, and he's there. For more than 2,200 games since 1985, Kurt Loe has been there in his wheelchair, fired up for each game like it was his first.

Loe, who was born in 1959, is as much a fixture at Angel Stadium as the Big A itself, and his passion for the team and the game are unmatched. The cerebral palsy that has limited him to that wheelchair is no match for Loe's passion for life. And for Loe, life is baseball.

"I live all winter for this stuff," Loe said. "I deal with whatever I have to deal with. And I get through it. I do what I have to do. I'm rewarded by being able to come out to the ballpark again."

Loe graduated from nearby Cal State Fullerton in 1983 and began working for local weekly newspapers. He began covering Angels games in 1985, and in 1991 he started writing for the in-stadium program, *Angel Magazine*.

He has featured all the big names—and some not so big—who have come through Anaheim. And along the way he has formed tight relationships with team personnel, players, coaches, and other reporters.

Loe cannot use his left arm and has limited use of his right arm. But he's able to keep score—pitch by pitch—on his iPad. Technology has certainly made things easier, even though the scowl on Loe's face may say something different.

As he types that day's lineup into his iPad, he has questions. "Trumbo needs to be hitting cleanup, and why isn't Bourjos in there?" Loe might say. Loe knows the club as well as anybody because he sees them on the field and in the clubhouse after the game. He knows what makes them tick.

The key to a good relationship with Loe? Don't feel sorry for him. "He's only restricted by the fact he can't walk around," former Angels coach Joe Maddon said. "The guy has everything else going for him. He never says, 'Why me?' He never plays on his plight. He doesn't dwell on that."

The Angels keep tabs on his attendance, knowing that he will be at every home game unless he's physically sick. He hasn't missed many, and he even received a special acknowledgement when he reached game No. 1,000 years ago.

On the pregame press notes of August 4, 1997, mention is given to Loe attending his 1,000th game. Handwritten on the notes in black ink was a personal message: "Kurt, the first 1,000 is the hardest." It was signed, "Cal Ripken Jr."

"Joe Maddon's idea," Loe said.

Of all the players who have come and gone during Loe's days at the ballpark, there is one who stands out head and shoulders above the rest: Chuck Finley. Finley took a special interest in Loe, talking to him regularly, calling him when he was in the hospital, making sure his metal drinking mug was filled with Loe's favorite beverage after each game.

It was a blow to Loe when the Angels didn't re-sign Finley after the 1999 season as Finley moved on and signed with the Indians.

"I knew I'd miss him," Loe said. "But I thought I'd get over him. I still haven't. He took me inside of his life. He treated me like a friend. It doesn't get better than that."

Asked to give his list of top 10 Angels (players or coaches) to come through the organization, Loe hemmed and hawed. His list, which has nothing to do with performance on the field and everything to do with his personal relationship with them, is as follows:

1) Finley; 2) Maddon; 3) Deron Johnson; 4) Doug Rader; 5) Mike Scioscia; 6) Bobby Knoop; 7) Marcel Lachemann; 8) Troy Glaus; 9) Torii Hunter; 10) Jim Edmonds.

81 Jack H. and Tony C.—One Pitch, Two Careers Ruined

On August 18, 1967, the paths of two very different baseball players crossed, forever altering their futures—and their lives—for the worse.

Tony Conigliaro was an outgoing, flashy, superstar-in-the-making with the Boston Red Sox. He was a hometown kid, just 22, and the sky was the limit. He was cocky and brash, and the hometown Boston fans loved him.

As a 19-year-old rookie in 1964, he hit the first pitch thrown to him in the majors for a home run. In 1967, he became the youngest player (22) in baseball history to hit his 100th career homer.

Jack Hamilton was a journeyman pitcher with the Angels, "a quiet and nice guy" according to Angels catcher Buck Rodgers. Hamilton was just 28 in 1967, but the Angels were already his fourth major league team, having played for the Phillies, Tigers, and Mets before the Mets traded him to the Angels in June '67.

Hamilton was having his best season in '67, winning 8-of-10 decisions as the Angels took the field on August 18. Conigliaro had hit 20 home runs and driven in 67, then he singled in the second inning off Hamilton in that game.

Hamilton retired the first two batters in the bottom of the fourth, bringing up Conigliaro. Then came the pitch. It was a fastball, though some argued it was an illegal spitball, that sailed up and in and hit Conigliaro on the left side of the face. Conigliaro was wearing a helmet, but it did not have an earflap, and the ball hit Conigliaro flush.

"It was a 'squish,'" said the Red Sox's Rico Petrocelli, the on-deck hitter. "Like a tomato or melon hitting the ground."

Conigliaro suffered fractures to his cheekbone and eye socket and had a severely damaged retina. Some players at the time thought Conigliaro's eyeball had come out of the socket. As blood poured out of Conigliaro's ears, nose and mouth, Hamilton walked toward the plate, but Rodgers shooed him away.

Rodgers and others defended Hamilton, who had hit only one batter with a pitch all season before Conigliaro. "Tony always leaned over the plate," Rodgers said. "Actually, his elbow and his head were on the inside part of the plate."

"The pitch Jack threw was up and in, but it wasn't that far in," said Jay Johnstone, an Angels outfielder at the time. "Because Tony had actually taken a stride toward the plate, looking for something out over the plate. Whether he was thinking breaking ball or looking for something outside, he never moved. It was a sickening sight."

As for allegations the pitch was a spitball, Rodgers again was quick to defend Hamilton. "Unfair, completely unfair," Rodgers said.

Angels pitcher Clyde Wright said it didn't matter what pitch was thrown. "If it was [a spitball], big deal," Wright said. "It's a pitch, a lot of people threw it. It got away from him. There was no intent for Jack Hamilton to throw at him."

Conigliaro later said he thought he was going to die that night. As it was, he missed the rest of the 1967 season and all of the 1968 season. He returned in 1969 and hit 20 homers with 82 RBIs while batting .255. In 1970, he hit a career-high 36 homers with 116 RBIs while batting .266.

But all was not well. His vision continued to deteriorate, and the Red Sox traded him after the 1970 season to, of all teams, the Angels. He had one miserable season with the Angels in 1971 (74 games, four homers, 15 RBIs, .222 average) and announced his retirement in July of that year.

He signed as a free agent in 1972 with the Red Sox but lasted only 21 games and was released. Ten years later, at the age of 37, he had a debilitating heart attack. He died in 1990 at the age of 45.

Hamilton tried to visit Conigliaro in the hospital the day after the beaning but was turned away. Billy Conigliaro, Tony's brother, reportedly said he believes Hamilton was throwing at Tony. "I couldn't take a baseball and throw it at somebody's head on purpose," Hamilton said recently. "I don't have the guts.... I really don't care what the public thinks about me. Accidents happen. If I thought about it all the time, it would bother me. I know in my heart I didn't mean to throw it."

Hamilton was out of baseball only two years after the beaning, his career ending even before Conigliaro's. "He was known as a head-hunter, and I think it affected the way he threw the ball," Rodgers said. "He started guiding the ball, aiming the ball."

Johnstone concurred. "It think it made him a little more conscious of pitching inside," Johnstone said. "When you lose the ability and have fear of throwing inside, you lose some of your sharpness."

82 1999—A Pivotal Season

The new era in Angels baseball that began in 2000 under general manager Bill Stoneman and manager Mike Scioscia would not have happened if not for the implosion that was the 1999 season.

Big things were expected of the Angels in 1999. The Angels had back-to-back winning seasons under manager Terry Collins in 1997 and '98 and figured they were close to finally getting over the hump and ending their playoff drought.

General manager Bill Bavasi got the go-ahead from Disney ownership to spend some money, and he identified his first target—pitcher Randy Johnson. Johnson, though, spurned the Angels in favor of the Arizona Diamondbacks, partly because he lived in the Phoenix area.

Bavasi's next target was Red Sox first baseman Mo Vaughn, who was the American League MVP in 1995. It took the biggest contract in club history—$80 million over six years—but it got the job done. Vaughn, many thought, was the final piece for the Angels.

Of course, no Angels fan needs to be reminded what happened next. On Opening Day, the second batter of the game, Cleveland's Omar Vizquel, hit a foul pop-up that drifted near the Indians' dugout on the first base side. Vaughn fell into the dugout and severely sprained his ankle, hampering him for the entire season.

As bad as things seemed at the time, Vaughn actually put up good numbers in 1999—.281, 33 homers, 108 RBIs. But there was some underlying dissension building within the club throughout the season, and it eventually boiled over.

Players complained to management about Collins, who had been hired by team president Tony Tavares after the 1996 season because of his no-nonsense approach that was a direct contrast to previous manager Marcel Lachemann, who employed a more laid-back approach.

Tavares and Bavasi, though, supported Collins. Tavares even likened the Angels clubhouse to a day care center, and at one point he had the big screen televisions removed from the clubhouse as some sort of punishment.

Collins, however, lost the team soon after a game on August 31, 1999, against the Indians at Jacobs Field. The Angels held a 12–4 lead going into the bottom of the eighth inning when the Indians put up a 10-spot, the final runs coming in on a home run by Richie Sexson off Troy Percival.

David Justice followed Sexson, was immediately hit by a pitch from Percival, and a bench-clearing fight ensued. After the game the team watched highlights in the clubhouse, and many of the Angels players noticed that during the chaos, Vaughn was still in the dugout and didn't join his teammates on the field.

According to players in the clubhouse, Percival confronted Vaughn, but Vaughn explained that as the designated hitter that day, he was in the clubhouse when the fight broke out. And by the time he got to the dugout, the melee had subsided.

The next day, a number of players went into Collins' office and said they wouldn't play that day if Vaughn was in the lineup. Feeling he had no choice, Collins benched Vaughn.

Less than a week later, on September 3, Collins tearfully announced his resignation.

"I kicked butts, patted butts, and tried everything I knew to motivate them, but a manager today only has one hammer—and that's the lineup card," Collins said. "I love managing. I'll miss coming to the park and putting the uniform on, but I won't miss the bickering that went on this year."

Then it was Bavasi's turn—he resigned as general manager four weeks later. Bavasi, at one time the club's director of player development, had a personal interest in many of the Angels' major leaguers in '99 because he had a role in their rise through the minor league system.

But some hinted, Tavares chief among them, that Bavasi was too closely tied to those players and it affected his judgment in evaluating them. Tavares felt sweeping changes needed to be made, but Bavasi stood firm. "Am I too attached to these players?" Bavasi asked, repeating a reporter's question. "Maybe. However, I don't believe I ever allowed that attachment or those emotions to get in the way of doing what was best for the team."

Ironically, when Stoneman took over, he seemed to agree with Bavasi's evaluations of many of those players, who ultimately made up the core of the World Series champions three years later in 2002.

83 Troy Glaus— World Series MVP

Scott Spiezio's Game 6 home run and Garret Anderson's three-run double in Game 7 are the highlights many Angels fans remember about the 2002 World Series victory. But the player holding up the Series MVP trophy was somebody who never sought the spotlight.

Troy Glaus found himself on top of the baseball world when he was named the MVP of the 2002 World Series—not because of one hit necessarily, but because of what he did over the course of the seven games. Glaus hit .385 (10-for-26) with three home runs and eight RBIs in the 2002 Fall Classic. He had at least one hit in every game except Game 7 (he walked twice in Game 7), and he had at least two hits in four of the seven games.

He homered twice in Game 1 and once in Game 4. But his biggest hit of the series came in Game 6 after the home runs by Spiezio and Darin Erstad cut the Giants' lead to 5–4. Glaus'

Trivia
Question: Who holds the Angels' single-season record for home runs?

Answer: Troy Glaus with 47 in 2000.

two-run double in the bottom of the eighth off Robb Nen put the Angels up 6–5 and capped the biggest rally in Angels history.

Glaus was never one who enjoyed talking about himself, especially when it came to the 2002 Angels. "I don't think we were the most talented team in those playoffs," he said. "But we were playing the best at the time, and it was as good a run as I've seen a team have for a month.

"Our offense, our pitching, our defense…everything just clicked at the right time. I knew once we were in the playoffs that anything could happen, and we were clicking on all cylinders for the whole month. It was a run I'll never forget."

The Angels expected big things from Glaus when they drafted him in the first round (third pick overall) in the 1997 draft out of UCLA, where he was a big (6'5") shortstop and drew comparisons to another big shortstop—Cal Ripken Jr. But the Angels had an established shortstop at the time in Gary DiSarcina, and the club was confident enough in Glaus' raw athletic ability that he would be able to handle a move to third base without a problem.

Just one year after being drafted, Glaus reached the big leagues in 1998. He played his first full big-league season in 1999 at age 22 and hit 29 home runs, setting the stage for a memorable season in 2000. At just 23 years old, Glaus was named to the first of his four All-Star teams and went on to hit 47 home runs, breaking the Angels' previous club record of 39 set by Reggie Jackson in 1982.

Glaus, by the way, also hit 41 home runs in 2001 and through 2012 was the only Angel in club history to hit 40 or more in a season.

That 2000 season was special to the Angels for more than Glaus' 47 home runs. Glaus teamed up with Mo Vaughn (36),

Anderson (35), and Tim Salmon (34), to help the Angels become the first team in American League history to have four players with at least 30 home runs in a season. The Toronto Blue Jays also accomplished that feat the same year.

Darin Erstad also had a remarkable season in 2000, getting 240 hits, batting .355, and hitting 25 home runs with 100 RBIs.

"I made a combination of adjustments that year and had gained a lot of experience, knowing the pitchers I was hitting against," Glaus said of his 2000 season. "Those factors all helped me get better as a player, but I also got better by just being in our lineup.

"Hitting is very contagious, and we had guys that were hitting homers and stealing bases, and it all just kind of funneled down to everyone else and helped us all have great years."

Glaus was slowed by injuries in 2003 and 2004 with the Angels, then he left the club to sign with the Diamondbacks as a free agent in 2005. Once healthy again, he put up good power numbers outside of Anaheim, hitting 37 homers for Arizona in 2005, 38 for Toronto in 2006, and 27 for St. Louis in 2008.

He retired after the 2010 season at age 34 with 320 career home runs—182 of those with the Angels.

84 Bill Rigney—The Original Angels Manager

Bill Rigney wasn't their first choice, but he ultimately showed that he was the best choice for a franchise just starting out. Gene Autry had been awarded the Los Angeles Angels in 1960, and he quickly had to get to work putting together a team. Fred Haney was hired, and Haney, Autry, and Bob Reynolds, Autry's business partner, got busy in deciding who to hire as the club's first manager.

Their choice: Casey Stengel.

Stengel had been fired by the Yankees following the 1960 season and had the name recognition that would help an expansion team like the Angels, especially in a town they shared with the popular Dodgers.

Autry and Stengel had lunch, during which Autry made his offer. Stengel, who had a home in Glendale, a suburban city near Los Angeles, offered up a couple of reasons why he couldn't do it. One was that he had become a director and stockholder of a Glendale bank, and he would be required to put in some time at the bank. Another was that he had a deal with the *Saturday Evening Post* to serialize his life story. One of the agreements of the deal was that Stengel needed to remain out of baseball until the story was published.

Later, it was said that the reason Stengel turned down the Angels was because he had a secret deal to manage the expansion New York Mets one year later starting in 1962—and Stengel did in fact become manager of the Mets.

The Angels then turned their attention to a couple of other candidates—Leo Durocher and Rigney. They ultimately settled on Rigney, who had been fired by the San Francisco Giants during the 1960 season.

Rigney didn't quite have the star-power name of a Stengel or Durocher, something even Autry could attest to. When introducing Rigney at a Welcome Angels banquet in Palm Springs before their very first spring training, Autry called Rigney, "Phil Wrigley," mistaking his new skipper for the owner of the Chicago Cubs.

Rigney, though, made his mark.

Before Mike Scioscia came along, no Angels manager in the history of the franchise provided as much stability from the manager's chair. Rigney managed the club from its inception in 1961 until he was fired during the 1969 season, a longer tenure than any Angels manager other than Scioscia. The team went 625–707 under Rigney, who won the American League Manager of the

Trivia
Question: Who hit the first home run in Angels history?

Answer: Ted Kluszewski on April 11, 1961, in Baltimore's Memorial Stadium during the first inning off Orioles pitcher Milt Pappas.

Year award in 1962. But Rigney was so much more than what the numbers might reflect.

He was a favorite of both the players and the writers who followed the team—a rarity indeed. Ross Newhan, who covered the Angels in the 1960s for the *Long Beach Press-Telegram* and *Los Angeles Times*, said this about Rigney is his book, *The Anaheim Angels: A Complete History*:

"Rigney was criticized for his tendency to display a quick hook with starting pitchers, to burn out hot relievers, but he consistently seemed to draw more out of the Angels than they were capable of giving. His strategic moves were seldom questioned, and he was definitely a newspaperman's manager, providing stories on games that otherwise weren't worth more than a sentence.

"He ripped players, managers, and umpires. He exhibited emotion, sensitivity, and humor. He worked hard to provide something other than a cliché. He enjoyed being with the writers socially."

Quite possibly Rigney's greatest asset was his ability to relate to the players—no easy task with the Angels teams of the 1960s, which were populated with players who partied to an extreme level. "One thing Rig could do was get along with every player," said Marv Grissom, the Angels' pitching coach from 1961–66. "He was able to develop a personal relationship with all of them."

Rigney, who spurned numerous offers to manage other clubs during his time with the Angels, was fired by general manager Dick Walsh in May 1969 and replaced by Lefty Phillips. Rigney went on to manage the Minnesota Twins and the Giants again, winning the AL West with the Twins in 1970.

"Bill Rigney—'Rig' we called him—had his hands full with us young kids," said pitcher Dean Chance, who won the Cy Young Award with the Angels in 1964. "But he was tremendous. He played hunches; he knew his players."

Rigney credited much of his managerial success to Durocher, whom Rigney succeeded as the Giants manager in 1956.

"I learned a lot from Leo Durocher," said Rigney, who died in 2001 at age 83. "I learned about the hit-and-run, about gambling, and going against the percentages. You can't play it the same all the time."

85 The Closer—Troy Percival

The image will be ingrained in the minds of Angels fans forever.

Troy Percival, arms raised, back arched, anticipating a catch by center fielder Darin Erstad for the final out of Game 7 of the 2002 World Series. Percival's screams of elation are drowned out by the thousands of fans in the seats, but no matter.

The Angels were the World Series champions, and Percival was there to close it out.

Percival had 316 of his 358 career saves pitching for the Angels, not including the three saves he earned in the 2002 World Series. Only seven other pitchers have registered more career saves than Percival since the save became an official statistic in 1969.

But that's not exactly what the Angels had in mind when they drafted him out of UC–Riverside in the sixth round of the 1990 draft. Big and burly, Percival had the body of a catcher.

He was assigned to the Boise (Idaho) Hawks of the Northwest League, a lower level of Class A ball. The team was managed by

Tom Kotchman. Percival caught 28 games for the Hawks that year and displayed a good arm from behind the plate.

His bat, however, was a bit of a problem. Percival had 16 hits (all singles) in 79 at-bats for a .203 average. He struck out 25 times. Something had to be done. Angels coach Bob Clear, seeing Percival's arm, suggested a switch to the mound. And Percival didn't fight the move.

"When I went 22 days without even sniffing an at-bat in low A ball, I thought I had nothing to lose," he said.

The only person who seemed to fight the switch at the time was Joe Maddon, who was a minor league instructor in charge of coaching the catchers. "I remember a meeting when we discussed making this guy a pitcher or putting him behind the plate," Maddon said. "I thought it was paramount to lean toward the scouts [who signed Percival as a catcher]. But I was voted down.

"Clear was the strongest voice. I remember him seeing Troy on the mound with the same delivery you see now. He said, 'Don't make it pretty; leave him like he is.'"

The very next season at Boise, Percival—the pitcher—got into 28 games and went 2–0 with a 1.41 ERA and 12 saves. He had an overpowering fastball, which helped him strike out 63 batters in just 38⅓ innings.

"I think when they drafted me, they probably had it in the back of their heads that I was not going to end up as a catcher," Percival said. "[Clear] would tell me I was the worst hitter this organization has ever seen. He told me I had to get on the mound and pitch.

"I finally did it, and then our pitching coaches basically taught me how to pitch. They knew I had the mentality, and they taught me the technique. I took off my catcher's gear, and they molded me into the pitcher they wanted. They let me be aggressive, and they fine-tuned my mechanics so that I could pitch a little bit longer. I loved every minute of it."

Angels fans did, too…well, maybe not every minute, as Percival had a knack for making things interesting. But such is the job of a closer. "It's like the guy who shoots two free throws with one second left and his team down by a point," Angels manager Mike Scioscia said. "It's like the field-goal kicker trying to kick a 47-yard field goal with one second left and his team down by two points. Everything is magnified."

Percival, though, was someone who was a leader in the club-house and trusted by his teammates when the game was on the line.

"He's the ultimate security blanket," said Erstad, Percival's teammate for nine seasons. "When he comes in, the game's pretty much over. It's nice to know if you get a one-run lead it's a done deal."

86 Bo Knows the Angels

There has been only one person to play for both Southern California teams. No, we're not talking about the Angels and Dodgers. We're talking about the Angels and Raiders.

Bo Jackson's athletic career is the stuff of legends. He was the Heisman Trophy winner at Auburn in 1985 before embarking on a dual career—NFL player for the Raiders and MLB player for the Kansas City Royals.

In 1987, he hit 22 home runs with 53 RBIs during the summer for the Royals, then jumped right into the NFL season in the fall and rushed for 554 yards on 81 carries (6.8 yards per carry) and four touchdowns for the Raiders.

His best all-around year came in 1989. He led off the major league All-Star Game at Anaheim Stadium with a towering home run off Giants pitcher Rick Reuschel and was named the game's MVP. He went on to hit 32 home runs with 105 RBIs and 26 stolen bases for the Royals and then joined the Raiders after the baseball season and enjoyed his best season in the NFL. He rushed for 950 yards and averaged 5.5 yards per carry. He had four touchdowns.

He had another productive year for both teams in 1990, but in the NFL playoffs that year against the Cincinnati Bengals, Jackson dislocated his hip and never played in the NFL again. He did, however, return to baseball despite having hip replacement surgery.

Jackson played for the White Sox for two seasons before signing with the Angels for an otherwise forgettable 1994 season. The season was cut short because of a strike, and there was no World Series. Not that the Angels would have played in it. The Angels went 47–68 that year, a .409 winning percentage that was the worst in club history except for the even more forgettable 1980 season when the club had a winning percentage of .406 (65–95).

Jackson provided some intrigue to a team that was led offensively by Chili Davis and Tim Salmon and on the mound by Chuck Finley, who led the team with a paltry 10 victories.

Jackson hit .279 with 13 homers and 43 RBIs in 75 games. After the final game before the strike, a number of reporters chatted in the parking lot when a dark sedan with tinted windows screeched to a halt in front of them.

The power window went down, and Jackson stuck out his head.

"So long, boys," Jackson said.

And with that, Jackson's athletic career was over even though he was only 32 years old.

Jackson, however, said it was his choice, not his body saying no. "I was at home for eight months," Bo said, referring to the time between the end of the strike-shortened 1994 season and spring training of '95. "I had the opportunity to take my kids to school. I was able to go to parent-teacher conferences. I was able to take my family out for dinner on a Friday evening instead of being at the ballpark playing a game during the summer. I got used to that. I got spoiled. It wasn't a case of, 'I couldn't play anymore.' I didn't want to play anymore.

"I think there comes a time in everybody's life where you get tired of being the employee. You want to be the employer, and that's what I was striving for."

87 Bob Boone

He was done, finished, kaput.

Bob Boone finished the 1981 season with the Philadelphia Phillies having been limited to 76 games because of injuries. He was 33, but he might as well have been 43 considering he had already spent 10 major league seasons as a catcher—the most physically demanding position in baseball.

So the Phillies did what all baseball teams do when they're done with you. They sold Boone to the Angels. Boone already had a World Series championship ring that he had earned with the Phillies in 1980. But he had something to prove to the Phillies, to the Angels, to everybody.

"I was kind of kicked out of Philly where the word was that I was over the hill and couldn't throw anymore, and Mike Schmidt, my good friend, said, 'Why don't you let them trade you?'" Boone said. "I came to the Angels with a lot to prove in 1982. I needed to show them what I was made of, especially on that special team with guys who all knew how to play the game, had 8-to-10 years of experience and everybody has a big baseball card when you flipped it over."

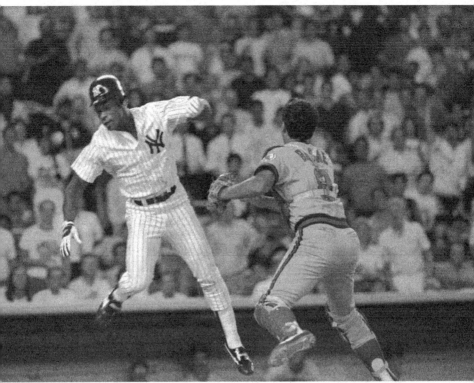

Catcher Bob Boone kept New York Yankee Rickey Henderson from touching
the plate as Henderson tried to score on Claudell Washington's hit in the
first inning at Yankee Stadium on Tuesday, August 17, 1988, in New York.
Henderson was tagged out by pitcher Willie Fraser, and the Angeles won 15–6.
(AP Photo/Ron Frehm)

Boone was part of the Angels division championship teams in
1982 and '86, and he was more than an afterthought on a team
that had four former MVPs in 1982—Rod Carew, Don Baylor,
Reggie Jackson, and Fred Lynn—as well as All-Stars up and down a
lineup that also included Bobby Grich, Brian Downing, and Doug
DeCinces.

Boone wasn't washed up after all—he was named to the All-
Star team in 1983 and won four Gold Gloves with the Angels,
including one at age 40 in 1988. (He also won a Gold Glove at age
41 with the Royals).

All in the Family
Catcher Bob Boone played for the Angels from 1982–88 and is part
of only four grandfather-father-son combinations in major league
history.
    Boone's father, Ray, played in the majors, as did his sons, Bret
and Aaron.
    The other combinations include the Bell family: Grandfather
Gus, father Buddy, and sons David and Mike; the Coleman family:
Grandfather Joe, father Joe, and son Casey; and the Hairston
family: Grandfather Sammy, father Jerry, and sons Jerry Jr. and
Scott.

He caught Mike Witt's perfect game in 1984 and was as
durable as they come behind the plate, playing at least 122 games
in all of his seven seasons in Anaheim. He played in 139 or more
games in his first five years with the Angels.

But Boone is like any Angels player who played for the team
during the mid-1980s. They are disappointed because they feel
they had a team that was good enough to not only get to the World
Series, but win it. Boone was in the middle of the things in 1982
and in particular '86 when the fateful pitching moves were made
by manager Gene Mauch in the ninth inning of Game 5 against
the Boston Red Sox.

Boone expressed a unique perspective of Dave Henderson's
crushing home run in Game 5 when the Angels were one strike
away from reaching their first World Series.

"It was a really weird day; atmospheric conditions were such
that balls were going out in that area [left-center field]," Boone
said. "Dave hit his good—it was a legitimate home run—but if you
hit it up in the air that way, it was going out.

"Before that, though, with two outs in the top of the ninth
inning of Game 5, Mauch took out pitcher Mike Witt and brought
in reliever Gary Lucas. Witt was tremendous. But Rich Gedman
was coming up, and he was the only guy that hit Witt. So Mauch

brought in Gary Lucas, who hadn't hit a guy with a pitch in 100 years, and he hit Gedman. It was unbelievable.

"Then the dam broke."

Boone, whose father, Ray Boone, played in the majors, as did Bob's sons, Bret and Aaron, left the Angels after the 1988 season and played two more seasons with the Kansas City Royals.

He eventually became a manager, first with the Royals for three seasons (1995–97) and then with the Reds for three more (2001–03).

Oh My!—Dick Enberg

Quite a few announcers have broadcast games for the Angels over the years, but one stands out as the voice of the Angels. Dick Enberg was the Angels' announcer for 11 seasons—from 1969–78 and again in 1985. No broadcaster put in more years with the club until Terry Smith reached his 11th season in 2012.

Enberg became known for his signature exclamation—"Oh my!"—but unfortunately for him and for Angels fans, he never used it to describe an Angels victory that put them into the play-offs. However, he was there for all four of Nolan Ryan's no-hitters, Clyde Wright's no-hitter, and Rod Carew's 3,000[th] hit.

He was also the voice of the Los Angeles Rams, tying him to Southern California sports fans in a way only Vin Scully has done, as well.

Enberg was thrown in feet first when hired by the club for the 1969 season. "My very first Angels play-by-play broadcast in 1969 was also my very first major league broadcast," Enberg said. "I was so nervous, thinking, 'This is it now. I'm a big-league announcer.'"

Whether or not he needed any advice, he got it anyway during that first broadcast. "Mr. Fred Haney, the general manager at the time, came into the booth and said, 'I just want to come in and wish you luck and give you one piece of advice: Report the ball. Don't tell me what you hope it does or what you think it's going to do. Just report the ball.'

"It was great advice because whenever I was in trouble and the ball was not doing anything, I would go back and say, 'The ball is in his hand. The pitcher is rubbing up the ball. He backs up. He hides the ball behind his back.' And that always got me back into the flow of the game."

Enberg went on to a successful career as a network broadcaster, and he even returned to Major League Baseball with the San Diego Padres. But he hasn't forgotten his roots with the Angels. Although it had been 17 years since he was the Angels broadcaster, when the team won the World Series in 2002, Enberg admitted it was an emotional experience.

"I was flying home during the seventh game of the World Series, and I asked the flight attendant if the pilot could find out the score, and if he did, would he please announce it," Enberg said. "A few minutes later, the pilot came on the PA and said, 'The Angels have won the World Series,' and I started to cry tears of joy.

"It was the culmination of all those years, and I was so happy for all the people who had lived through the growth and birth of this team, and now we had finally won."

Though Enberg did not get to feel the chills up his spine from being in the ballpark when the final out was recorded, he has fond memories of the Angels players he spoke about, particularly Ryan.

"Nolan Ryan always had the potential of throwing a no-hitter," Enberg said. "He did it enough times that fans started to look ahead and say, 'Ryan's pitching on Friday night, so let's get tickets for Friday because he could throw another no-hitter.'

"His curveball snapped so sharply, it was impossible to hit. Hitters had to be ready for his fastball, and then he would throw the curve and it buckled their knees. Of all the people that I've met in more than 50 years of sports broadcasting, Nolan Ryan is one of the top 10 greatest athletes—greatest people—that I've ever encountered."

89 1989—The Best Angels Team Nobody Remembers

The loss to the Boston Red Sox in the 1986 American League Championship Series didn't end with the final out of the series. There was a hangover effect that seemed to last a couple seasons. Manager Gene Mauch was replaced after the 1987 season by Cookie Rojas in 1988, but the results were no different. The '87 and '88 teams had an identical 75–87 record.

By 1989, the Angels' collective head seemed to be clear again—the '86 hangover had finally gone away. Or at least, it was now buried deep in their subconscious.

General manager Mike Port hired Doug Rader to manage the club, and Rader came with a reputation. He had worn out his welcome while managing the Rangers, and he was known as a crackpot during his playing days but more of a hothead as a manager.

But Rader came to the Angels saying he had learned from his past.

"I believe that the three years away from managing has enabled me to evaluate things objectively," said Rader, who had been fired by the Rangers during the 1985 season. "I'm an aggressive guy who wants to win, but I've learned that as a manager you need to temper your aggressiveness and intensity. I think the educational process I went through in Texas will allow me to be more effective at it. I have a better understanding of how to deal with the players on a one-on-one basis and a better feel for the context in which the writers ask their questions."

Port also made changes to the roster, trading for catcher Lance Parrish and pitcher Bert Blyleven, signing free agent outfielder Claudell Washington, and re-signing outfielder-turned-DH Chili Davis.

The club also had solid veterans returning in Wally Joyner, Brian Downing, Jack Howell, and Dick Schofield. Devon White had emerged as one of the best young outfielders in baseball, and Dante Bichette was just starting his career.

On the mound, the Angels had plenty of talent surrounding Blyleven. Chuck Finley, Kirk McCaskill, and Mike Witt were well-established, and they welcomed rookie Jim Abbott into the rotation. Bryan Harvey had become a dependable closer.

It was a team that had a good mix of veteran leadership and young talent, and it was Rader's job to put it together.

The Angels had a mediocre start, going 10–10 for the first few weeks of the season, but then they got hot. From April 26 to May 17 the Angels won 16-of-19 games, culminating with Abbott's four-hit shutout over Roger Clemens and the Red Sox in a 5–0 victory.

That moved the Angels into a first-place tie with the Oakland A's. The A's proved to be a formidable foe. Oakland was coming off a loss to the Dodgers in the 1988 World Series but was stacked with a talented pitching staff and the Bash Brothers led by Mark McGwire and Jose Canseco.

The rest of the summer was a dogfight with the Angels finishing the month of June a half-game out of first, but by the end of July they were a half-game up. The Angels and A's entered a three-game series in Anaheim in mid-August tied for first place, and the A's won the first two games of the series before the Angels closed out a win in the third game in front of more than 60,000 fans.

On August 20, the Angels extended their winning streak to five in a row on a four-hit shutout by McCaskill, who out-pitched Bud Black of the Indians in a 1–0 Angels victory. That left the Angels tied with the A's for first place at 74–48, but it would be the last the Angels would see of the top spot.

The Angels went 12–16 in September, and although they finished 91–71, their third-highest win total in franchise history at the time, they ended the season in third place, eight games behind Oakland and one game behind Kansas City.

Statistically, it was a good season for many Angels. Blyleven won 17 games, Finley 16, McCaskill 15, and Abbott 12. Offensively, White stole 44 bases and Davis hit 22 homers, one of eight players with homers in double-digits.

"The way we finished isn't something we're proud of, but 91 wins is," Rader said. "There was more good than bad." But that was as good as it got for the team under Rader, who was fired in August 1991 and replaced by Buck Rodgers.

Milestone Moments— 500, 3,000, and 300

There are certain statistical milestones that will almost certainly punch a player's ticket to the Hall of Fame—500 home runs or 3,000 hits for a batter and 300 wins for a pitcher.

The Angels have had three players reach those milestones, and all three took place at Anaheim Stadium within a two-year period. However, those players accumulated most of their numbers while wearing uniforms other than that of the Angels. And while all three eventually entered the Hall of Fame, none of the three entered wearing an Angels cap.

September 17, 1984—Reggie Jackson connected off Royals pitcher Bud Black for his 500th career home run, and it came on the 17th anniversary of Jackson's first home run.

"It was a fastball up, and the type of ball that Reggie would murder," Black recalled. "As he rounded third base, he kind of gave me a quick glance. It wasn't like he was saying, 'Thank you for giving me the 500th.' It was more an acknowledgment. Like, hey, I went after him and he got me."

There was a reason Black went after Jackson. Black and the Royals held a 7–0 lead in the seventh inning and were trying to win a game in a pennant race. The Royals won the game 10–1 and moved 1½ games ahead of the Angels in the AL West race. They eventually won the division by three games over the Angels.

Jackson entered the Hall of Fame in 1993 in a Yankees cap with 563 career home runs—123 with the Angels.

August 4, 1985—A curveball away, and Rod Carew did what he did so well—hit the ball where it's pitched. Carew slapped a single to left field off the Twins' lefty Frank Viola for his 3,000th career hit, on his way to 3,053 for his career. Ironically, it came against the Twins, the team whose hat he would wear when inducted into the Hall of Fame in 1991.

It was with the Twins that Carew won all seven of his American League batting titles and totaled 2,085 hits. He had 968 hits for the Angels.

"You don't start the game thinking you're going to get 3,000 hits, but when you're around long enough and get close, you can't help but get excited," Carew said. "I was joining a select group of players. You can imagine all the thousands of players that have played this game that didn't come close."

The 1985 season was Carew's last as a player as he gave way at first base to Wally Joyner starting in 1986.

June 18, 1986—Don Sutton got only 28 of his 324 victories with the Angels from 1985–87, but No. 300 came during a successful season for Sutton and the Angels, alike.

At age 41, Sutton went 15–11 with a 3.74 ERA in 34 starts, helping the Angels win the AL West for the third time in club history. He made one postseason start in '86, matching up with Roger Clemens in Game 4, a game the Angels won 4–3 to take a 3–1 Series lead.

Sutton's 300th win was no cheapie—he gave up one run and three hits in a complete-game victory over the Texas Rangers.

"I was always looking for a way to be better and a way to stay in shape," said Sutton, who pitched until he was 43 and entered the Hall of Fame in 1998 as a Dodger. "The best baseball advice I ever got in my life came from a man who never played a day in his life, and that man was my dad. The night I left for my first spring training, he said, 'Most of the people there are going to be better than you. But don't let anybody outwork you.' I like to think that I followed that advice."

91 Bleacher Bum—Charlie Sheen

Major League Baseball parks have that certain something, that ability to transform a hard-working, respected member of society into a child-like oaf, someone who will risk life and limb—and their dignity—all for the chance to snag a baseball worth $17.99.

There's something about catching a foul ball at a major league game that is so special it defies logic. But we've all been there. We've felt that rush of adrenaline when that ball has come close, maybe a few rows in front of you. And we've experienced the buzz in your section of the crowd after that mad scramble.

For those who've actually caught that foul ball—or even better, a home run ball—congrats, you're one of the lucky ones. That drive for cowhide can make you do crazy things, and if you have money to burn, you can take it even further. That's why actor Charlie Sheen—a big baseball fan and star of the movies *Major League* and *Major League II*—took it to another level on April 19, 1996, at Anaheim Stadium. That was before the stadium underwent the renovation that turned it into more of a baseball park than a football stadium. It was also a time when crowds were sparse because the Angels were not a good team—they finished 70–91 that year.

So Sheen probably could have had all those seats behind the left-field fence to himself anyway for that Friday night game against the Detroit Tigers. But just to be sure he would have no competition for a home run ball, he spent $6,537.50 to purchase 2,615 seats in left field.

He invited three friends, including Bret Michaels, lead singer of the rock group Poison, to patrol those seats and have unimpeded access to any and all home run balls.

"I didn't want to crawl over the paying public," Sheen explained. "I wanted to avoid the violence."

Sheen got the chance to interact with members of the Angels bullpen out in left field, exchanging autographed baseballs. Sheen signed his and added "#99" to reflect his character Ricky Vaughn's number in the *Major League* movies.

Angels starting pitcher Chuck Finley, always a quick wit, said, "He should have bought tickets when I was pitching. I could have served him up a couple."

As it turned out, the game pitted Angels starting pitcher Mark Langston against the Tigers' Scott Aldred. Langston pitched a complete game, earning the victory when Don Slaught's single to center field in the bottom of the ninth scored Dick Schofield for a 4–3 Angels victory.

As for Sheen, he went home empty-handed, except for those two thousand or so ticket stubs. There were two home runs in the game—one by the Angels' Tim Wallach, the other by the Tigers' Mark Parent—but both cleared the fence in right field, captured by fans the old-fashioned way.

Sheen's best bet for a home run ball was probably Tigers slugger Cecil Fielder. But Fielder, who wound up hitting 39 home runs that year, went 0-for-3 with a walk.

"It sounds like he has more money than sense," Finley said of Sheen. "But baseball needs 2 million fans just like him. Every game would be a sellout."

92 The Fungo Kid— Jimmie Reese

Jimmie Reese got a lot of mileage out of one quote, a short and sweet line to explain a brief time during a long baseball career when he was Babe Ruth's roommate while both were playing for the New York Yankees.

Reese was quick to point out, "I roomed with Babe's suitcase."

Reese was listed as the Angels' conditioning coach, but he was known more for his skills with the fungo bat. He'd work the pitchers in the outfield during batting practice, making them chase down the baseballs he'd hit with his customized fungo bat.

He coached with the team from 1972–94 and always had a smile for you whether he knew who you were or not. He called everybody "kid." He had great stories too, especially when asked about Ruth.

Reese liked to tell the story about when he was at Ruth's house shooting pool. He was beating Ruth when Ruth's wife called the two to the dinner table. As Reese began to move toward the dining room, Ruth stopped him in his tracks. Ruth wasn't done playing. As long as Reese was winning, the game went on. Reese said Ruth's competitive nature was as strong as any he'd ever seen. And so the two played on until Ruth had the upper hand. Only then did they come to dinner.

Reese began his career in baseball as a batboy with the Los Angeles Angels of the Pacific Coast League back in 1919. He made his professional debut in 1920 with the Angels and had his best season in the PCL in 1929 when he hit .337 for the Oakland Oaks.

That got him noticed by the Yankees, who brought him to New York to keep an eye on the Babe. Reese could also hit, batting .346 in 77 games with the Yankees in 1930.

He dipped to .241 in 1931, then he was traded by the Yankees to St. Paul of the American Association. The St. Louis Cardinals purchased Reese from St. Paul, and he hit .265 in 90 games for the Cardinals in 1932.

After the 1932 season, Reese was sold again as the Cardinals sent Reese right back to where he started—the Los Angeles Angels of the PCL. Reese remained in the PCL for the rest of his playing career and finished in 1940. But Reese wasn't done with baseball.

He served in the U.S. Army in 1942–43 during World War II, then he got right back into baseball, first as a scout with the Boston Braves and then as a coach with the San Diego Padres of the PCL.

In 1960, he was named the Padres' manager, but after starting the 1961 season as the club's manager, he stepped down. "I'm best suited as a liaison man, as a coach," he said. "I just am not suited to give a guy hell."

From there Reese continued as a vagabond coach with stops in Hawaii, Seattle, and Portland. He also served as a scout briefly for the Montreal Expos, and he was out of baseball in 1970.

A couple of years later, in 1972, Reese, who had never married, had no children, and was mostly estranged from his extended family, asked the Angels for a job at age 71. He got it. Reese's first year with the Angels was the same year that Nolan Ryan arrived, and the two formed a special bond. Ryan later named one of his sons Reese in honor of the coach.

Many years later, Reese struck up another tight relationship with an Angels pitcher, Jim Abbott, whose rookie year with the Angels came in 1989. "Jimmie Reese was the kindest man I ever met," Abbott said. "He just lit up whatever room, or dugout, or outfield he was in. Just his smile—it was infectious. It didn't matter who he was with or where he was at, he could charm anybody.

"He really took me under his wing, and I would sit and spend time with him, and he'd tell me stories of his playing days. I spent a lot of time in the outfield with Jimmie and that sawed-off fungo bat of his. He would hit balls at me, and I really think that helped me become a much better fielder at the major league level. I had to go through my motion with the glove and follow-through, and he had perfect timing like the timing on the field, which is very hard to replicate. We did that every day, and it really helped me."

Reese died in 1994 at age 92.

93 Buck Rodgers

Bob "Buck" Rodgers is one of only two people to both play for and manage the Angels—Jim Fregosi is the other—but Rodgers' long and varied baseball career almost never happened.

Rodgers was signed by the Detroit Tigers in 1956, but injuries and another year in the minors had him thinking baseball wasn't for him after the 1960 season. Then his dad had some news for him—the Angels called to say they had drafted Rodgers in the 1961 expansion draft.

"I was contemplating retirement when I heard the news," Rodgers said. "I did a double-take. I thought I was done. Instead I was a Los Angeles Angel playing for Bill Rigney at Wrigley Field [in Los Angeles]."

Rigney became a mentor of both Rodgers and Fregosi. Rodgers believed that Rigney saw something in his two young players. "I thought it was strange how he had the two of us at his side during the games," Rodgers said. "He told us, 'You two guys are going to manage one day.'"

At hand, however, was Rodgers' playing career. After getting a taste of the big leagues in 1961, Rodgers emerged as an impact player in 1962. He played in 155 games in '62—an unheard of total for a catcher today.

At age 23, Rodgers hit .258 with six homers and 61 RBIs and he handled the pitching staff. Rodgers finished second in the American League Rookie of the Year voting. He was the Angels' primary starting catcher through 1968 and played his last season in 1969.

But no season could match the 1962 season.

"We were a second-year expansion club with a bunch of rag-tag ballplayers who were either too young or flat-out discarded," he said. "But we had talent."

Though he was finished playing at age 30, he was far from finished with baseball. And all of that mentoring from Rigney began to pay off. Rigney, fired by the Angels in 1969, was hired to manage the Twins in 1970, and he hired Rodgers as his bullpen coach.

The Twins won the AL West in 1970, and though Rigney was fired in 1972, Rodgers remained on the Twins' coaching staff through 1974. He was the pitching coach of the Giants in 1976, then was the Brewers' third-base coach in 1978 and '79 before becoming the Brewers' manager in 1980.

He managed the Expos from 1985 until he was fired during the 1991 season. "Again, I was thinking I was done with baseball," Rodgers said. "But two days after I was let go, Gene [Autry] called."

Rodgers had been a favorite of Autry's original bunch, and Autry had followed Rodgers' career after he left the Angels way back in 1969. "He was our biggest fan," Rodgers said of Autry. "He would sit with us and talk for hours about the old days. He knew players, and he knew stats. He always made it a point to come into the clubhouse whether we won or lost. He would come down and sit with us, and we'd kid each other."

Rodgers' tenure as the club's manager, however, wasn't so carefree and easy. The club went 20–18 under Rodgers to close out the 1991 season, finishing 81–81 and in last place in the AL West.

The 1992 season nearly cost Rodgers his life—literally—when a team bus traveling from New York to Baltimore on May 21 veered off the highway and crashed into a wooded area off the New Jersey Turnpike. With multiple fractures, Rodgers was the most seriously injured and missed most of the season. In the meantime, the front office was an accident waiting to happen.

Autry had hired Richard Brown as team president in 1990, and he clashed with general manager Mike Port, eventually firing Port in 1991 and bringing in first Dan O'Brien and then Whitey Herzog. Herzog lasted only a few months and was replaced by Bill Bavasi before the start of the 1994 season.

During those four years of front-office turmoil, the Angels signed Gary Gaetti to a multi-million-dollar deal and let Chili Davis go. They traded Dante Bichette for a washed-up Dave Parker and traded Devon White for Junior Felix. They also traded for Von Hayes and Hubie Brooks, who were failures.

It was Bavasi who fired Rodgers early in the 1994 season, and there was no shortage of sniping afterwards. Rodgers first blamed Brown, but after Bavasi said it was his call, Rodgers figured the 36-year-old Bavasi was intimated by Rodgers' stature and experience in the game.

Ultimately, some people said it was Rodgers' outspoken nature and friendly relationship with the press that rubbed upper management the wrong way. Ironically, it was something Rodgers learned first-hand from his mentor Rigney some 30 years earlier.

94 Bavasi and Bavasi

No, it's not a law firm. Bavasi and Bavasi refer to Buzzie and Bill, the father-son combination in charge of running the Angels during long and varied baseball careers.

Buzzie was the Angels general manager from 1977–84, while Bill was GM from 1994–99. But it was Buzzie, the longtime general manager of the Dodgers, who enjoyed the most success between the two at the helm in Anaheim.

Buzzie was the GM for the Angels' first two division titles in 1979 and '82, and even though he was against the notion of free agency for players, he jumped in feet first. Buzzie put the Angels on the map as a destination for players, signing or trading for guys like Rod Carew, Reggie Jackson, Brian Downing, and Fred Lynn, among others. Buzzie also brought in—at the urging of owner Gene Autry—Jim Fregosi as the club's manager during the '78 season.

"He was a very good baseball man who thoroughly knew the game and contributed a great deal for the organizations he worked for, as well as the game itself," Carew said. "The organizations he worked for always came first in his mind, and he always tried to do the right thing for each of them."

Buzzie enjoyed the lion's share of his success, of course, with the Dodgers for whom he was the GM from 1951–68 and won eight National League pennants and four World Series titles.

"Buzzie was one of those rare baseball icons," Grich said. "His energy and enthusiasm were always contagious. It was a cherished opportunity to have been around him."

Buzzie was also old school—even though he spent money, he did so reluctantly, coming from an era in which players were told to shut up and play. It worked against him at times—like when he said he could replace Nolan Ryan, who went 16–14 in his final year with the Angels, simply by signing two 8–7 pitchers.

Even in retirement, Buzzie kept an eye on the economics of baseball and was quick with a verbal jab. When the Dodgers signed pitcher Darren Driefort for $55 million, Buzzie said, "To me, $55 million, you'd have to be a Koufax to get that kind of money." And when it came out that Chan Ho Park, then with the Dodgers, would be seeking a contract worth $20 million per year, Buzzie said, "What is he, 14–10? We used to release those kind of pitchers at least good clubs like the Dodgers and Yankees did."

Management Mobility

Stability was not their strong suit. Impatient in their quest to win a World Series for their popular owner, Gene Autry, Angels management wasn't exactly a study in stability. From 1961–2012, the Angels employed 11 general managers, none of them on the job more than the eight years put in by their first GM, Fred Haney (1960-68) or Bill Stoneman (1999–2007). Whitey Herzog's tenure was the shortest, lasting less than four months—September 18, 1993, to January 11, 1994.

Angels general managers: Fred Haney (1960–68), Dick Walsh (1968–71), Harry Dalton (1971–77), Buzzie Bavasi (1977–84), Mike Port (1984–91), Dan O'Brien (1991–93), Whitey Herzog (1993–94), Bill Bavasi (1994–99), Bill Stoneman (1999–2007), Tony Reagins (2007–11), Jerry Dipoto (2012–).

Before Stoneman hired Mike Scioscia as manager in 2000, the revolving door spun even more quickly for the managers. Through Scioscia's 13th season in 2012, the Angels used 17 managers, counting Gene Mauch twice but not counting those who served as interim managers.

Angels managers: Bill Rigney (1961–69), Lefty Phillips (1969–71), Del Rice (1972), Bob Winkles (1973–74), Dick Williams (1974–76), Norm Sherry (1976–77), Dave Garcia (1977–78), Jim Fregosi (1978–81), Gene Mauch (1981–82), John McNamara (1983–84), Gene Mauch (1985–87), Cookie Rojas (1988), Doug Rader (1989–91), Buck Rodgers (1991–94), Marcel Lachemann (1994–96), Terry Collins (1997–99), Mike Scioscia (2000–12).

Bill's tenure was more tumultuous, and it started that way by his own doing. Only a few months into his job as general manager, after working his way up through the minor league department, Bill fired manager Buck Rodgers, a favorite of Autry's.

Bill was in charge in 1995 when so many of the young and talented players he oversaw in the minors emerged as budding stars on the major league level. But that team proceeded to collapse like few other teams in major league history, then they followed it up with a losing season in '96.

Bill brought in Terry Collins to manage the team, which had winning seasons in 1997 and '98 only to fall short of a division title each year. Bill went out and signed Mo Vaughn to the richest contract in Angels history at the time—six years for $80 million—only to have it blow up in his face. Disney bought the team and took control after Autry's death in 1998, and Bill suddenly found himself having to answer to numerous upper management types. Bill's decision-making and direction were criticized, primarily by team president Tony Tavares, and Bill resigned at the end of the 1999 season amid chaos in the clubhouse and in the front office.

"We had every reason to believe that we had put together a club that would respond this year, but it didn't," Bill said of the '99 season after resigning. "If there were issues of composition and chemistry, and there were, I have to take responsibility for that. I put the club together."

95 Santana No-Hits the Tribe

Ervin Santana threw one of the nine complete-game no-hitters in Angels history on July 27, 2011, but the right-hander failed to do something that the others did in all eight—throw a shutout.

Santana's no-hitter at Jacobs Field was different than most no-hitters because he didn't blank the opponent. Instead, the Angels beat the Indians that day 3–1. It was just the 11th time in baseball history that a no-hitter was thrown but a shutout was not.

Who knows how many potential no-hitters are foiled because the pitcher succumbs to pressure as the game progresses. But with Santana, the opportunity for a shutout disappeared in the first

Ervin Santana pitches against the Cleveland Indians in the eighth inning of a game on Wednesday, July 27, 2011, in Cleveland. Santana pitched a no-hitter in the 3–1 win. (AP Photo/Mark Duncan)

inning, so it's possible the idea of a no-hitter didn't even enter his mind.

In the bottom of the first inning, the Indians' Ezequiel Carrera hit a slow roller to shortstop Erick Aybar, who booted it for an error. Carrera stole second and took third on a ground-out to second. With two outs and Travis Hafner at the plate, Santana threw a wild pitch and Carrera scored. The Indians led 1–0. That's when Santana went into lockdown mode.

The Indians went down 1-2-3 in the second, third, fourth, fifth, sixth, and seventh innings. By that time, the Angels had taken a 2–1 lead, scoring once each in the fifth and sixth innings.

With one out in the eighth inning, Santana cracked a little, walking Lonnie Chisenhall on a full-count pitch. But Santana quickly refocused and struck out both Matt LaPorta and Jason Kipnis to end the inning.

The Angels added a run in the top of the ninth to give Santana a little breathing room, and he responded by retiring the side in order in the bottom of the ninth inning. Santana got Michael Brantley on a fly ball to Peter Bourjos in center field to end it.

"Excitement," Santana said when asked how he felt when Bourjos squeezed the ball for the final out. "Lots of guys get to five, six innings. But that's when things get a little complicated. I'll just have to enjoy this."

It had been nearly 27 years since the Angels' previous complete-game no-hitter, which was also a perfect game. Mike Witt did it on the last day of the 1984 season against the Texas Rangers.

The Angels did have a combined no-hitter in between, as Mark Langston (seven innings) and Witt (two innings) combined to no-hit the Mariners on April 11, 1990.

For Santana, throwing the no-hitter in Cleveland had added significance. It was in Cleveland six years earlier that he made his major league debut. In the first inning alone, the Indians hit for the cycle, with Santana yielding a triple, double, single, and home run to the first four batters he faced. Now he was standing on the very same mound, mobbed by his teammates in celebration.

Asked by reporters about that inauspicious debut years earlier, Santana was rescued by his manager, Mike Scioscia. "Do we have to talk about that one?" Scioscia asked. "His command is like night and day," he said. "[In that first game], those guys were teeing off on him. He used that start as a stepping board."

96 Strike Three, Take Your Base

The Angels' 2002 World Series championship season was special because it was their first, but it was also the beginning of an era in which the Angels became perennial contenders.

It appeared the Angels might have what it takes to reach and win the World Series again in 2005, especially after winning the AL West and then knocking off the New York Yankees in the American League Division Series.

The Angels had beaten the Chicago White Sox in Game 1 of the American League Championship Series and were locked in a tight game in Game 2 at Comiskey Park. The score was tied 1–1 heading into the bottom of the ninth inning when Angels pitcher Kelvim Escobar quickly retired the first two White Sox hitters.

Escobar got ahead in the count with two strikes on White Sox catcher A.J. Pierzynski then threw a splitter that Pierzynski swung at and missed, striking out and ending the inning. At least, that's what Angels catcher Josh Paul thought.

Home plate umpire Doug Eddings clearly raised his right arm and clenched his fist. Paul rolled the ball back toward the mound, but Pierzynski, after first taking a couple steps toward the dugout, sprinted to first base.

Eddings explained he had signaled "strike three" but had not called Pierzynski out. Angels manager Mike Scioscia, a former major league catcher, wasn't buying Eddings' explanation.

"When he rings him up with his fist, he's out," Scioscia said.

Pablo Ozuna pinch ran for Pierzynski, stole second, and then scored the winning run on Joe Crede's double. The White Sox rode the momentum of the Game 2 victory and didn't lose again, beating the Angels in the next three games to close out the ALCS then sweeping the Houston Astros in the World Series.

The non-call on strike three was difficult to take for Paul and the Angels. "Customarily, if the ball is in the dirt, say if we block a ball for strike three, they usually say, 'No catch, no catch, no catch.' And I didn't hear any of that," Paul said. "That's why I was headed back to the dugout."

Replays appeared to show that Paul caught the ball cleanly without the ball hitting the dirt.

"I caught the ball so I thought the inning was over," Paul said.

Eddings disagreed but admitted he never said, "No catch."

"I did not say, 'No catch,'" Eddings said. "I'm watching Josh Paul, seeing what he's going to do."

After watching replays of the play, Eddings stood by his call.

"We saw it on a couple different angles, the ball changes directions," he said. "I had questions. I didn't have him catching the ball."

Pierzynski has been booed at Angel Stadium ever since, but he was simply taking advantage of Eddings' ruling.

"I thought for sure the ball hit the ground," Pierzynski said. "I watched the replay 50 times, and I still don't know. The third strike is in the dirt, you run. I didn't hear him say out, Josh didn't tag me."

97 Have Lunch with Mike Scioscia

Italians love their food. And Mike Scioscia, the winningest manager in Angels history, is as Italian as it gets. He is a second-generation Italian-American whose father's side of the family comes from the town of Naples and whose mother's side comes from the region of Abruzzo in central Italy.

Want to "bump into" Scioscia and join him for some bruschetta? Look on the schedule and watch for the next time the Angels play the Yankees in New York. Scioscia's favorite Italian restaurant is Cafe Fiorello in New York's Upper West Side. There isn't a trip to New York that goes by without Scioscia having a meal there, but his favorite Italian dish comes right from his own kitchen. "We make our own pizza," he said.

Spring training in Arizona is another opportunity to find Scioscia dining out. Angels beat writers have been able to observe Scioscia at his Italian best when invited by the club to have a meal with him.

It is pointless to order an appetizer—by the time all have placed their orders, if every appetizer on the menu has not been ordered already, Scioscia will make sure that is has. To be sure, once the food has been served, it becomes a family-style free-for-all.

Scioscia's love of food is well chronicled, and in fact, it was through Scioscia's stomach that Anne McIlquham became Anne Scioscia. She was 21 in 1982 when she went to a Dodgers game and noticed Scioscia, 23 at the time, and wanted to meet him. The next day was autograph day, so she decided to bake him some cookies.

Anne was disappointed to learn the next day that Scioscia's signing session had been canceled. But a security guard, upon seeing Anne with her cookies, told her he would introduce her to Scioscia after the game.

They met, Scioscia ate, and a relationship was born. Three weeks later, they had their first date—first it was tennis (Anne won), then they had dinner with Scioscia's teammate Ron Roenicke and his wife.

In recent years Scioscia has made an effort to watch his weight. Not necessarily lose weight, but, as Scioscia put it, "Anne didn't say I needed to lose weight, she said I need to get healthier. She kind of nudged me and said, 'I want you around.'"

98 Angels in the Outfield

When Mike Scioscia took over the reins as the Angels manager for the 2000 season, there were many things he needed to do in order to put the team on a winning track.

Finding enough talent in the outfield was not one of them.

One of his priorities in the spring of 2000 was to figure out a way to fit four outfielders into a lineup that only has room for three. Tim Salmon, Garret Anderson, Darin Erstad, and Jim Edmonds were all legitimate starters, but Scioscia had to balance putting one of them in the designated hitter spot or even on the bench from time to time without hurting any egos or causing any dissention.

Scioscia always insisted it was a "good problem to have," but the "problem" could be solved if the Angels traded one of them. Edmonds and Anderson were both entering the final season of their respective contracts, and one of them figured to go. The New York Yankees emerged as the team most interested in one of the Angels outfielders, but they targeted Erstad.

The Yankees learned quickly that Erstad wasn't for sale, so they turned their attention to Edmonds. Edmonds' career with the

Angels had been a mix of incredible displays of talent with maddening frustration from some people in the organization who believed Edmonds' easy-going nature meant he didn't care and possibly held him back from reaching his immense potential.

Anderson, meanwhile, was as soft-spoken and consistent as anyone in the league.

Eventually, Edmonds could not escape hearing the trade rumors, and it seemed to distract him. "Everyone says I'm going to be traded, but the front office says I'm not," Edmonds said. "Who do you believe?"

Angels general manager Bill Stoneman got wind that Edmonds was distracted and met with Edmonds to fill him in on the situation. Edmonds seemed to be satisfied with Stoneman's explanation, but Stoneman never guaranteed Edmonds that he wouldn't be traded.

Less than a week later Edmonds was traded, but not to the Yankees. Instead, it was the St. Louis Cardinals who made the deal, sending pitcher Kent Bottenfield and young second baseman Adam Kennedy to Anaheim. Bottenfield was the big piece of the deal, a starting pitcher who won 18 games in 1999 and was an All-Star. Kennedy found himself behind Fernando Vina with the Cardinals at second base and was expendable.

Bottenfield won only seven games with the Angels and was traded just a few months into the 2000 season, going to the Phillies in a deal for, ironically, another outfielder in Ron Gant.

Kennedy, though, turned out to be a mainstay with the Angels and was a key cog in the team's 2002 World Series championship season.

For Edmonds, the trade initially hit hard. A couple days after the trade, Edmonds returned to the Angels' spring training complex in Tempe, Arizona, to retrieve some belongings and say his goodbyes.

Edmonds walked into the clubhouse at 10:00 AM with the team already on the field for workouts. He peeked out the clubhouse door and looked at his former teammates before sitting down to talk to a reporter. A few players came in, one at a time, and wished Edmonds well. But when Anderson came in, the two hugged and Edmonds began to cry. "It's like moving away from your family," Edmonds said. "How do you react? It's hard to talk about."

When Edmonds was told that former teammates Gary DiSarcina and Tim Salmon had reminisced about playing with Edmonds in the minor leagues, Edmonds' eyes again welled up with tears.

Angels players were sad to see a talent like Edmonds go, but they also said the trade settled a possibly disruptive situation before the season even began.

"Now there's no rotation in the outfield," DiSarcina said. "Guys can come to the ballpark knowing where they're playing. Darin [Erstad] does not want to be a DH. He's 27 years old. It puts people in roles, and that's good for chemistry."

Edmonds turned out okay, too, hitting .295 with 42 homers and 108 RBIs with the Cardinals in 2000. He had even better numbers in 2004 (.301, 42, 111) when the Cardinals went to the World Series. He was also part of the Cardinals' World Series championship team in 2006.

99 Go See *Angels in the Outfield*

Shortly before Disney bought the Angels, the company made a movie about them. *Angels in the Outfield* was made in 1994 during a down time for the real Angels. They were smack dab in the middle of a 16-year playoff drought with no reason for optimism.

Angels in the Outfield was actually a remake of a 1954 movie of the same name. Only that movie was about the Pittsburgh Pirates. When Disney decided to remake the movie, using the real Angels made perfect sense. They had the right name and practically no hope for success.

The real Angels were a dismal 47–68 during the strike-shortened 1994 season. Only one pitcher won as many as 10 games for the club that year (Chuck Finley with 10). Chili Davis was the club's best hitter with 26 homers, 84 RBIs, and a .311 average.

The Angels also had Bo Jackson that season for 75 games, and he hit .279 with 13 homers and 43 RBIs. Certainly at that time the Angels' best hopes for a postseason appearance was in the theater in a fantasy movie made by a company that promises to make dreams come true.

Angels in the Outfield wasn't about Tim Salmon, Garret Anderson, and Jim Edmonds. It was about a young boy, Roger, who would sneak into the stadium with his friend to watch the dismal Angels. No stretch there.

The stadium shots, however, were filmed at the Oakland Coliseum because Anaheim Stadium was booked for other events when the filming was taking place.

The film also starred Christopher Lloyd, who played Jim in the television show *Taxi*. Only Lloyd wasn't driving a cab in this movie, he was an angel named Al, flying through the air and helping the Angels win games. Al showed up as an answer to prayers from Roger.

Roger was living in a foster home and had asked his widower father when they'd be a family again. His dad said sarcastically, "I'd say when the Angels win the pennant." So Al and other angels showed up during a game between the Angels and Blue Jays, but only Roger could see him. The Angels started to win games, and word of Roger's ability reached Angels manager George Knox, played by Danny Glover, who decided to keep Roger around as a good luck charm/consultant despite his skepticism.

Knox didn't believe it, but he couldn't argue with the results. The Angels made a second-half surge and were contending for a playoff spot. Meanwhile, Roger's father decided to give up all custody of Roger, devastating the boy.

To make matters worse, Roger's friend, J.P., accidentally revealed the reason for the winning to the club's annoying broadcaster, Ranch Wilder, who was no fan of Knox. Wilder told the press that the winning occurred on the advice of Roger, and Hank Murphy, the club's owner, threatened to fire Knox.

The Angels players, however, supported Knox and together with Roger, held a press conference to express that support. Murphy decided to let Knox stay on as the club's manager.

The Angels reached the final game of the regular season with the division title on the line against the White Sox. The Angels pitcher was Mel Clark, played by another former *Taxi* star—Tony Danza. Clark was a heavy smoker and apparently only had six months to live.

He got in trouble in the game and Knox paid him a visit on the mound. With everyone expecting Knox to take Clark out of the game after a remarkable 159 pitches, Knox instead left Clark in.

The Angels eventually won the game without any help from the angels—it's not allowed in a championship game according to Al—and won the pennant. And Roger, along with his friend J.P., were adopted by Knox, giving the Disney touch to a happy ending.

Eight years later in 2002, Disney owned the real-life Angels when they won the World Series.

100 Dick Williams' Undoing on the Bus

In the 1970s alone, the Angels had seven managers, eight if you include the one interim manager. It was a period in the organization's history during which patience was a four-letter word.

Quick fixes and reflex decisions dominated the decade, but that is not to say a few good baseball men didn't make their way into—and out of—the Angels organization. One such man was Dick Williams. Williams had managed the Oakland A's to World Series championships in 1972 and '73, and Angels owner Gene Autry wanted him.

Williams had been replaced in Oakland by Alvin Dark, but Williams was still under contract with the A's and Autry needed permission from A's owner Charles Finley to talk with Williams about the managerial job during the 1974 season.

Autry and general manager Harry Dalton had decided to fire manager Bobby Winkles, who had been hired only two years previously without any major league coaching experience. Winkles' previous managerial experience was at the college level with Arizona State, and his lack of experience in dealing with big-league players—with big-league attitudes—worked against him. Some said Winkles was undermined by Frank Robinson, who was at the tail end of his Hall of Fame career.

"I think everybody knew that I was uncomfortable with Frank Robinson around," Winkles said. "I admitted openly I couldn't handle him."

It caused a division in the clubhouse that ultimately resulted in Winkles' firing. Before they could let Winkles go, however, Dalton and Autry needed permission to talk to Williams about the job.

Finley agreed to meet with Dalton and Autry, and the three talked in an Oakland bar for more than six hours. The topic of Williams, though, did not come up until the very end of their conversation when Finley finally granted permission because he appreciated Autry's support when Finley moved the A's from Kansas City to Oakland.

Williams, eager to get away from the meddling Finley, agreed to a 3½-year contract—the remainder of the 1974 season and three years beyond that—for $100,000 a year.

Williams' first move was to appoint Robinson as team captain, the first captain in club history. But everything spiraled downward from there. The team lost its first 10 games under Williams, and Robinson didn't even make it to the end of the season in an Angels uniform—he was traded to the Indians in September.

The Angels went 36–48 under Williams in 1974 and got even worse in 1975 when they finished 72–89.

In '76, Dalton decided the organization had to change its philosophy—again. Pitching, speed, and defense were out; power hitting was in. Dalton traded pitcher Ed Figueroa and center fielder Mickey Rivers, two young, promising players, to the Yankees for Bobby Bonds.

Dalton also traded two other young players—first baseman Jim Spencer and outfielder Morris Nettles—for third baseman Bill Melton, who had won the American League home run title a few years earlier.

The experiment failed miserably as both Bonds and Melton were bothered by injuries and combined to hit just 16 home runs. Bonds actually led the team with 10 homers and 54 RBIs.

Williams wasn't around to see it, getting fired the day after an incident on the team bus that was taking the team from the airport in Los Angeles to Anaheim Stadium after a dreadful road trip.

Williams didn't like hearing all the laughter and jovial attitude during the ride and turned around from his seat in the front of the bus. "Quiet, all you winners," he said.

A response came from the back of the bus, "F--- you."

"Who said that?" Williams asked.

"I did, you [expletive]," said Melton as the two met in the aisle of the bus before being separated.

"You're suspended," Williams said.

"This is the happiest day of my life," Melton said.

The next day, Williams was fired and replaced by Norm Sherry. For Williams, his winning percentage of .431 (147–194) is the worst by any manager (not counting interim managers) in Angels history.

Bibliography

Books

Bisheff, Steve. *Tales from the Angels Dugout*. Champaign, IL: Sports Publishing L.L.C., 2003.

Donovan, Pete. *Under the Halo*. San Rafael, CA: Insight Editions 2011.

Goldman, Rob. *Once They Were Angels*. Champaign, IL: Sports Publishing L.L.C., 2006.

Loe, Kurt. *Angel Magazine*. New York: Professional Sports Publications, 2012.

Newhan, Ross. *The Anaheim Angels: A Complete History*. New York: Hyperion, 2000.

Salmon, Tim, with Rob Goldman. *Always an Angel: Playing the Game with Fire and Faith*. Chicago: Triumph Books, 2010.

Travers, Steve. *Angels Essential: Everything You Need to Know to Be a Real Fan!* Chicago: Triumph Books, 2007.

Magazines

Angel Magazine
GQ

Websites

angelswin.com
baseball-almanac.com
baseballlibrary.com
baseball-reference.com
bleacherreport.com
boston.com
espn.com
freep.com

justdisney.com
latimes.com
lucywho.com
mensjournal.com
muse.jhu.edu
ocregister.com
old.post-gazette.com
mlb.com
nytimes.com
sfgate.com
sportsillustrated.cnn.com
thegoal.com
wikipedia.org
yahoo.com
FoxSportsNet Television